BEYOND THE
BATTLE

A Man's Guide to His
IDENTITY IN CHRIST
IN AN OVERSEXUALIZED WORLD

NOAH FILIPIAK

ZONDERVAN
REFLECTIVE

ZONDERVAN REFLECTIVE

Beyond the Battle
Copyright © 2021 by Noah Filipiak

Requests for information should be addressed to:
Zondervan, *3900 Sparks Dr. SE, Grand Rapids, Michigan 49546*

Zondervan titles may be purchased in bulk for educational, business, fundraising, or sales promotional use. For information, please email SpecialMarkets@Zondervan.com.

ISBN 978-0-310-12014-8 (audio)

Library of Congress Cataloging-in-Publication Data

Names: Filipiak, Noah, author.

Title: Beyond the battle : a man's guide to his identity in Christ in an oversexualized world / Noah Filipiak.

Description: Grand Rapids : Zondervan, 2021.

Identifiers: LCCN 2021003555 (print) | LCCN 2021003556 (ebook) | ISBN 9780310120124 (paperback) | ISBN 9780310120131 (ebook)

Subjects: LCSH: Christian men--Religious life. | Men--Religious life. | Men--Sexual behavior. | Christian men--Sexual behavior. | Responsibility. | Sex in popular culture

Classification: LCC BV4528.2 .F55 2021 (print) | LCC BV4528.2 (ebook) | DDC 248.8/42--dc23

LC record available at https://lccn.loc.gov/2021003555

LC ebook record available at https://lccn.loc.gov/2021003556

Cover design: Tammy Johnson
Cover art: Flaticon
Interior design: Sara Colley

Printed in the United States of America

21 22 23 24 25 26 27 28 29 /LSC/ 13 12 11 10 9 8 7 6 5 4 3 2 1

To Pete, Chris, and Justin:
This second edition never would have been
published without your pushing me to it.

To all the beyondthebattle.net online alumni:
Your journeys have made this second edition stronger
than the first. Thank you for letting me walk with you.

To My Wife, Jen:
I'm sorry I didn't know what love was when we got
married. I'm sorry I thought love and marriage were
about my getting my desires met—that I thought love was
self-seeking. Because of this, I'm sorry for the impossible
expectations I put on you to fulfill. Impossible because you
aren't God and I was looking to you to give me what only
he can. In this book, I don't always talk about marriage
in the glowing Ken and Barbie fashion that Christians
are used to. Please know this is not a reflection on you
or even on us, but is a reflection on me. On my sinful,
insecure desires for my selfishness to be fulfilled. On my
utter need for the mercy of Jesus, which I starved myself
of for much of our marriage. I starved myself of Jesus as I
looked for this approval from you and from other women,
rather than from the only one who can truly satisfy. Thank
you for hanging in there with me through the ups and the
downs. You are a grace given to me by God for which I am
eternally grateful. Forgive me for when I haven't always
shown it. I will love, honor, and cherish you all the days
of my life.

CONTENTS

FOREWORD

Who am I? Who is Ron DeHaas in this vast universe or in this complicated culture or in his arena of relationships? Who is he supposed to be, in God's eyes?

In *Beyond the Battle*, Noah Filipiak engages men, both married and single, as we struggle with these deep questions about ourselves. From the beginning of the book, Noah recognizes God as sovereign in our lives; he is a loving God who forgives our sins, but to whom we have nothing to offer. Wretched men that we are, who will set us free from this body of death? Praise be to God through Jesus Christ our Lord that there are answers to these questions. Answers that lead us from disobedience to righteousness, from righteousness to sanctification, and from sanctification to eternal life.

Noah makes a convincing argument that our sense of entitlement lies at the root of many of our troubles. He depicts entitlement as our worst enemy. Entitlement is the sense that we deserve something. We have a right to it! And we do everything in our power to get it. But we deserve nothing other than an eternity separated from the goodness and grace of God. It is only through Christ's work on the cross—through his death and resurrection—that we receive mercy for what we have done and grace to become part of God's family. We must learn, as men, to move from our sense of entitlement to an attitude of deep appreciation. Realizing this need is the first step toward freedom from the false way we have looked at ourselves—and at women—to become the men God has made us to be.

So how does this book help us navigate from here to there—from entitlement to appreciation? Noah lays out a plan for this journey—a map that helps men embrace reality. One of the issues of entitlement we struggle with is our belief that we are entitled to our fantasies—fantasies that take us out of reality into a false world of death and destruction. Noah not only demonstrates the need for reality, he teaches us how to embrace it. This becomes the next step toward freedom.

But he doesn't stop there. He doesn't leave us stranded, as though partway on our journey from entitlement to appreciation we get dumped in the middle of a desert. Noah provides tools for the journey to wholeness. He likens them to the tools many of us use every day, such as hammers, saws, drills, and two-by-fours. Unlike other books that provide the tools without inviting God to change the heart of the man using them, Noah walks us first through the need for change, then provides us with the tools to build up our new understanding of ourselves. These tools, in chapter 11, take on a whole new power in light of the discussion in the earlier chapters. Each chapter is likely to spur you to push ahead to the toolbox and pull out one of the tools for the remodeling God is doing with you on your deepest self.

Your life, your relationships, your existence as a man in this oversexualized culture, your maneuvering through this vast universe may depend on your understanding of the truths in this book and the tools God gives you to use along the way. As you read, I hope you will commit to the path Noah offers to a healthier, more biblical view of women, sex, life, and especially yourself in Christ.

—RONALD DeHAAS, PRESIDENT, CEO, AND
FOUNDER OF COVENANT EYES

HOW TO GET THE MOST OUT OF THIS BOOK

Win Not the Battle but the War

The Lord of the Rings story comes to a climax in the final battle at Mordor as the forces of good square off against the insurmountable legions of evil. The king Aragorn, the dwarf Gimli, the elf Legolas, and the wizard Gandalf represent the best and strongest warriors for good in Middle Earth. These heroes huddle with their followers in the middle of a plain, while countless foes of darkness close in around them. For every one hero, there seem to be a million enemies.

This is the type of scene that comes to mind for Christian men seeking to fight off the temptations of an oversexualized world. Most men are taught simply to be better warriors—better Gandalfs, Aragorns, Legolases, and Gimlis. Well-meaning advisors and experts teach men how to try harder, think better, manage behavior through mental tricks, and even physically beat themselves into submission. The problem is, no matter how strong the hero in the middle, the enemy continues its barrage with no end in sight.

What Aragorn and his company knew is that no matter how strong they were as fighters, they were destined to lose. It is the same with men fighting against sin. When we adopt a symptoms-based or behavior-management approach to sin, we eventually wear down and lose. The key to victory in *The Lord of the Rings* story is found not in the mighty warriors' skill and tactics but in a small and meek hobbit named Frodo. Frodo isn't a mighty warrior but holds a different type of power. He has a subversive inner power because he knows that the way to defeat the enemy is not to attack his army but to go to the source of his strength. While Aragorn and his mighty company distract the enemy's eye, Frodo sneaks silently to the enemy's heart, the core of Mount Doom. This unanticipated move destroys the enemy once and for all—not with a sword but with a surrender of power.

The point to this metaphor is that while the short-term tactics of learning to be a better warrior play a necessary role in the war against sin and should not be dismissed, they must be undergirded with the power that kills the enemy once and for all. If this never happens, defeat is inevitable.

Beyond the Battle sets out to win not the battle but the war. Or rather, we will discover that the war has already been won in Jesus, and we will be guided through the process of learning to rely on and rest in his victory.

Getting Started

This book is written to married and single men. Most of it will apply equally to both, while some sections will feel heavily weighted to one or the other. I don't want you to be blindsided by this, and I ask that you glean what you can from these sections and stick with the book, knowing it will come back around soon enough.

You'll get the most transformation in your life if you read this book as a daily devotional. Stop after each section of reading when you see the day number cue and flip to that day's entry in the "Forty-Day Devotional Guide" in the back of the book for Scripture references, questions for reflection, and a prayer. These are often organized with unique content for married men and single men. You can use this devotional any way you want. You can keep this book next to your Bible and pull both out daily for the next forty days. Or if you'd rather read the book uninterrupted and in longer chunks, by all means do so. You can bypass the devotionals altogether and then do a second round of the book where you focus on the daily devotional exercises and revisit the chapters when needed.

The book is also best read with other men and we've made it as easy as possible for that to happen. Visit www.beyondthebattle.net/videos for free small group video curriculum that includes everything you need to run your own seven-week small group with your friends or men's group.

You can also visit www.beyondthebattle.net if you'd like to go through this curriculum with me and my Beyond the Battle team leading you. Alumni of the beyondthebattle.net online groups are invited into a free weekly video call with me and other alumni to review the truths of the book and for prayer, community, and accountability.

I'll describe Covenant Eyes software in chapter 11, but I encourage you to start your free thirty-day trial now so you have it operational while you are reading the book. This thirty-day trial is mandatory for Beyond the Battle small groups. You can download Covenant Eyes from your app store or at covenanteyes.com. Use promo code BEYOND to get your free thirty days.

THE CHURCH IS FOR SINGLES TOO

For some readers, this author note might be the most helpful part of the entire book, so I hope you read it. That said, it is written to singles, so if you're not single and would like to skip ahead to the first chapter, you are free to do so.

What's Wrong with You?

The Christian subculture has done an impressive job of glorifying marriage and stigmatizing singleness. Books and youth group sermons warn Christian teens against premarital sex and guide them toward marriage. As teens date, they are challenged to consider whether their fifteen-year-old girlfriend is someone who would make a good wife and, if not, whether they should be dating her. They are taught to direct their sexual urges toward marriage. Above all, marriage is presented as the reward for a disciplined pursuit of sexual purity.

This all sounds good, right?

Since Christian singles are to wait until marriage to have sex, they frequently get married at the young ages of twenty,

twenty-one, and twenty-two. Jokes are made about Christian women going to Christian colleges to get their "MRS degree." Wedding ceremonies cost tens of thousands of dollars, sparing no expense for the bride's special day as princess. The groom doesn't bat an eye at the price because he is finally getting his long-awaited prize of sex.

Christian singles are discipled to dream of idealized romance, utopian sex, and a "happily ever after" life if they do it God's way.

As the church teaches its promises about marriage, it churns out programs for married couples, families, and children. Many consultants who teach pastors how to grow their churches argue that attracting stable families through these programs is the key to leading a sustainable, growing church, and they are often right.

The church paves the road for youth to prepare for marriage, get married, and have children, counting on the church to be there for them all along the way with programs to encourage and strengthen their married lives. This becomes the focal effort of churches, leaving singles on the outside looking in.

But what are the implications of hyping marriage to fifteen-year-olds? And of so closely correlating dating with marriage and sex? And of treating wedding ceremonies like Ken-and-Barbie spectaculars? (On average, couples spend $30,000 on their weddings, and research shows that the more is spent on a wedding, the shorter the marriage often lasts.[1])

Doesn't it feel like marriage has become one of the Christian rites of passage? You go to church, you learn to read your Bible, you learn to pray, you get baptized, and you get married (and then have kids,[2] of course).

The truth is, the Bible doesn't mandate or focus on marriage

---

1. Meghan Walsh, "In Sickness and in Health . . . but Not in Debt," OZY, October 18, 2017, http://www.ozy.com/acumen/in-sickness-and-in-health-but-not-in-debt/38366?utm_source=NH&utm_medium=pp&utm_campaign=pp.

2. Yes, God commands Adam and Eve to be fruitful and multiply (Gen. 1:28). With a global population of more than 7 billion people, I think we've done a pretty good job of obeying this one. We need to stop teaching this as a mandate for individual Christians, especially since the Bible does not contain an individual command to have children. We see numerous examples of childless Christians, including Jesus and Paul. (If bearing children were a command to every individual, Jesus would have been in sin.)

and family the way the church does.[3] So much focus is given to marriage in the church that it can feel like if you're not married, there's something seriously wrong with you both personally and spiritually.[4] Cloaked beneath this is the message that if you aren't having sex, you're missing out. Secular culture already glorifies sex as the be-all and end-all of life. Christian culture adds a spiritual twist: sex *within marriage* is the be-all and end-all of life.

But what happens when we make anything other than Jesus the be-all and end-all of life? What happens is we develop an idol[5] that lets us down and leaves us disillusioned and disappointed.

Ironically, in its good intentions to teach teenagers about marriage and to support people who are married, the church has inadvertently turned marriage into a romanticized idol. We have become so accustomed to the idol that we don't even realize it's there.

Yet the impact of this idol lingers inside almost every Christian who is single.

Why do singles feel incomplete? Why do singles feel there's something wrong with them? Why do singles feel that they need to be married or they will never have their longings for intimacy

---

3. I recently attended a wedding in which the pastor used Ecclesiastes 4:9–12 as his text to describe marriage. "Two are better than one. . . . If either of them falls down, one can help the other up. But pity anyone who falls and has no one to help them up. Also, if two lie down together, they will keep warm. But how can one keep warm alone? Though one may be overpowered, two can defend themselves. A cord of three strands is not quickly broken." This text is not about marriage. The laying down together is not sexual; it was practical in an era when there was no indoor heating. And the third strand of the cord is not referring to God; it's referring to a third human. (The context of the list in these four verses is humans helping humans; when we read marriage into the text [as the pastor did], it not only shames and belittles singles ["Pity them!"], it also forces an unbiblical emphasis on marriage. While the text may hold tangential applications for marriage, it more accurately applies to friendship, Christian community, and the life of the church—areas singles are uniquely poised to excel and flourish in.)

4. A 2015 survey of 504 Christian singles revealed that 45 percent of singles surveyed felt they were devalued, were treated like outcasts, or were in a lesser life stage at church because they were single. View full survey results and analysis at www.noahfilipiak.com/singles.

5. See *Household Gods* by Ted and Kristin Kluck for a humble, transparent look at the many common things we have turned into idols: marriage, sex, and children included (Colorado Springs, CO: NavPress, 2014).

and companionship met? Because the church has taught them these things by putting marriage and childbearing on a pedestal—something the Bible doesn't do.[6]

The church has too often sent the message that marriage (and sex) will give you what only God can give, which is the very definition of an idol.

It's not that marriage is awful; of course it's not. Marriage was designed by God, and everything God institutes is good. An individual marriage can be great or horrible, with most landing somewhere in between. Regardless, the truth is that the realities of marriage mean that Christian marriages do not match the idealized version that the church markets and that many couples feel pressure to display in public. Why do nearly half of all marriages end in divorce?[7] Why do so many couples seek marriage counseling? And why do so many people who have had sexual relationships (whether inside or outside of marriage) still feel utterly disappointed with life?

The idea that marriage will fulfill you and solve all your problems is a lie that needs to be exposed. It's not that marriage is awful but that idolatry is. If we've created an idol, we need to be real about it. If someone thinks they can jump off a building and fly, don't we have a responsibility to convince them otherwise? Too many singles rush into marriage because they think they'll be able to fly when they take the leap. Perhaps if we didn't make marriage so enticing and made Jesus more enticing (which he is), fewer people would rush into bad marriages and singles would feel complete as they are.

I'm certainly not advocating for sex outside of marriage. I'm saying that once you can have sex, not all of your problems will be

---

6. There is, of course, the classic chapter on singleness, 1 Corinthians 7, and Paul's example of singleness therein, which we will delve into later. Read Mark 3:20–21 and Matthew 12:46–50 for some sobering passages on how marriage and the nuclear family are not to be the be-all and end-all for a Christian.

7. National Center for Health Statistics and the US Census Bureau information cited in Avvo Staff, "Marriage and Divorce Statistics," Avvo, April 12, 2010, updated 2015, http://www.avvo.com/legal-guides/ugc/marriage-divorce-statistics. According to the NHS and the Census Bureau, 48 percent of marriages end in divorce or legal separation within twenty years.

solved. Sex should not be your main motivation for getting married. We need to stop worshiping sex and marriage as idols. We need to understand that a life without marriage and without sex is a good life with nothing essential missing from it.[8]

If you are a single man reading this chapter, you need to know that you are already whole as a Christian who is single. There's nothing that marriage will add to you that will increase your spiritual significance or value or, honestly, that will automatically increase your satisfaction in life. While there are benefits to marriage, Scripture tells us it also adds considerable stress, pain, and problems to your life.[9]

There's nothing wrong with you if you aren't married. To think anything else is to buy into the lie that marriage is a god, and to miss out on the riches of who you already are in Christ.

The Gift No One Wants

If you've been around a Christian singles' ministry for any time at all, it's likely you've had 1 Corinthians 7 directed at you, specifically verse 7, where Paul speaks of singleness as a gift: "I wish that all of you were [single] as I am. But each of you has your own gift from God; one has this gift, another has that" (bracketed word added, from the context). And then you were likely told that you have the "gift of singleness." Upon which you wondered whether this gift came with a receipt so you could take it back.[10]

You're then told that God gave you the gift of singleness so that you can do more ministry for him.[11] And you're thinking, *Great, I get to clean the church and help with vacation Bible school while everyone else gets love, romance, and affection.* When the church paints being single as abnormal and defective and paints marriage as a dreamland of bliss, adoration, and acceptance, it's no wonder the gift of singleness comes across as lame.

---

8. Imagine someone telling Jesus he needed a girlfriend or wife in order to be complete!
9. Just as Paul says in 1 Corinthians 7:28b.
10. A joke you've probably already heard as well.
11. 1 Corinthians 7:32.

Marriage is not a dreamland of bliss, adoration, and acceptance. It is good, but it is also exceedingly difficult. For most men I know, marriage is the most difficult challenge they face. Marriage requires constant sacrifice. It takes away almost all your freedom to make choices without running them by someone else. It can have long seasons of little or no reward. It usually involves two very different people on very different orbits of personality, preferences, and convictions trying to live a unified life together. It is a lifetime commitment you make to someone not knowing how that person will change over the decades and how your feelings about them may correspondingly change. The self-sacrifice of a husband within marriage is described in the Bible as equivalent to Jesus' giving himself to be arrested, beaten, tortured, humiliated, and crucified for the sake of the church.[12]

The apostle Paul said you will face many troubles in life if you get married,[13] and that you are to sacrifice yourself for your wife as Christ did for the church. Anyone up for a sixty-year crucifixion?[14]

I'm really not trying to scare you away from marriage. But the problem is we've swung so far in the other direction that a sobering recalibration is desperately needed. The church feeds singles a utopian view of marriage to try to keep them on the straight and narrow, but this false view doesn't help anyone. In the long run, it can make singles feel worthless and cause them to jump into marriage with a host of unrealistic expectations.

The Marriage Santa Claus

Single men need to understand the realities of marriage for two reasons. The first is that if you plan to marry someday, you need to know what you are getting yourself into. You need to know that the mushy-gushy feelings of infatuation you feel toward your girlfriend or fiancee today will not last, nor will hers for you. Believing

---

12. Ephesians 5:25.
13. 1 Corinthians 7:28b.
14. Again, this is according to Ephesians 5:25, since a marriage may last up to sixty years or so.

otherwise is as naive as believing in Santa Claus. At the risk of being the Grinch of marriage here, I want to stop seeing grown men and women believing in Santa Claus.

Your wish list to Santa Claus is all about who? You. But marriage is not about you and making yourself feel good. The church tends to paint it this way because if the prize at the end of the race sounds as sweet as possible, it's more likely that you will stay strong and avoid premarital sex. The problem is that this approach equips singles to enter the lifelong commitment of marriage thinking it's going to be about getting their desires met, when in reality it is about meeting someone else's desires. Overhyping marriage, the church trains singles for the opposite of what they will face.

The second reason it's important to be aware of what marriage is really like is so you can enjoy the genuine gift of singleness and learn to utilize it.

There are reasons married people sometimes wish they were single, and not all of those reasons are sinful. The church and singles need to learn what is good about singleness. What are the things you lose in marriage that you can never get back?

Though Paul calls singleness a gift in 1 Corinthians 7, did you know that Jesus, after talking about how difficult marriage is, points out that some will *choose* to be single for the sake of the kingdom of heaven, and that the one who can accept this should accept it?[15] If Jesus speaks so highly of this calling (the calling he himself was living out), you would think the church would speak highly of it as well. But unfortunately this has not been the case, and that has caused cataclysmic damage to the Christian single's psyche and has greatly hamstrung the advancement of the kingdom of heaven on earth.

One of Satan's best tricks is to get married people to wish they were single and single people to wish they were married. In Christ, we have the power to be content, appreciative, and grateful for wherever we are.[16] Are there benefits to being married? Sure. But do they

---

15. Matthew 19:12.
16. Philippians 4:11–13.

outweigh the benefits of being single? No. It's not a competition between the two; it's a matter of living in your situation and maximizing the gifts God provides in that situation, rather than missing those gifts because you are longing for something else. Satan loves to steal life from us,[17] and discontentment is one of the most effective ways he does it.

Open the Gift

Because most churches focus on how to keep families in the church and don't do a great job of encouraging or supporting singleness, singles' ministries often are not places where authentic community develops. Many singles' ministries are not much more than pools of hopeful (sometimes desperate) people looking for a date (and, of course, marriage)—the opposite of what Christian singles actually need. The awkwardness, pressure, and fear of being hit on keeps many of the more spiritually mature singles away and perpetuates the isolation and rejection many singles face in the church.

The lack of quality resources in the church for singles does not negate your responsibility to develop those resources on your own. What happens too often is that singles complain, rightfully so, about how their church doesn't provide anything helpful for them. But rather than find or develop good resources, they wallow in self-pity and remain undeveloped as single Christians.

Another way churches fail to support singles is by a lack of representation among pastors, elders, and other leaders. (Which is so ironic, considering that Paul and Jesus were both single.) Single leaders can stand as models of the single life for the rest of the congregation, particularly to other singles who are struggling. Again, rather than viewing this leadership vacuum as a chance to gripe or wallow in self-pity, see it as your opportunity to step up. Perhaps God has called you to fill this leadership void in your church. Be the single Christian leader you're looking for and that your church needs.

One of the greatest advantages of being single is flexibility in

---

17. John 10:10.

one's schedule and freedom from responsibility for others. A man who is married understandably must focus considerable attention on his wife and children. This is exactly what Paul is talking about in 1 Corinthians 7:33–34; it's why, after your single friends get married, they can hardly ever hang out anymore. Marriage places restrictions on friendships. It's possible to maintain those friendships, but it takes a lot of intentionality, and frankly, it's never as organic and free as it was when a person was single.

Singleness allows you to engage more deeply in Christian community. So get heavily involved in Christian community, but don't do so as an attempt to quell your loneliness. Only Jesus can make you whole, not other people. If you get that backward, you'll end up disillusioned and disappointed. Once you're made whole in Christ, you will seek community no longer as a way of running from yourself or your loneliness but instead as a way of experiencing Jesus more deeply.[18]

If you're an introvert, diving headfirst into biblical community may sound like a nightmare. But being in community doesn't mean you have to develop lots of friends or be a social butterfly. It means that having friends and being a friend *is* ministry. What ministry boils down to is being a friend. Often, God will make you aware of a person who is desperately in need of a friend and has nowhere else to go for connection. Yes, we are to usher people into a friendship with Jesus, the ultimate healer of their wounds, but we are called as his followers to be his body,[19] his ambassadors.[20] We often throw the phrase "body of Christ" around without pausing to think what it means on the ground level. Jesus' body walked the earth for thirty-three years. Then it ascended into heaven. Next, we are told that we *are* his body. To paraphrase Neo from *The Matrix* movie: *Whoa.* We aren't just trying to get people to believe in Jesus. In a way, we *are* Jesus, or at least his representative and

---

18. For a great resource on Christian community, read *Life Together* by Dietrich Bonhoeffer (New York: Harper and Row, 1954).

19. 1 Corinthians 12:27.

20. 2 Corinthians 5:20.

a picture of his actual body at work. His face, his smile, his hugs, his listening ear, his hands, his feet.

We are to show people who Jesus is by the type of friend we are to them. Paul understood this when he penned 1 Corinthians 7. One has to wonder how many faithful friends in ministry Paul lost to marriage along the way. Enough that he could make the observation that marriage consumes a large portion of our time and energy that otherwise could be spent ministering to others.[21]

So if you are single, get out there and minister. Mostly this means simply redefining what we consider to be ministry. It's certainly not something you need a seminary degree for. Here are some ideas:

- Go to the same park regularly to play basketball and see what friendships develop there.
- Look up social events in your town, like board-game nights or groups that meet around an interest or a hobby you already enjoy.[22]
- Join a book club.
- Contribute to a community garden.
- Attend a variety of the small groups and Bible studies your church offers (even if they're lame).
- Have people over to your house.
- Invite other singles to hang out together. Initiate this rather than waiting to be invited.
- Live with Christian roommates.
- Join a small group at your church.
- Volunteer.
- Be a mentor.
- If you're longing for a family, adopt[23] or be a foster parent.

---

21. 1 Corinthians 7:32, 35.

22. Check out www.meetup.org.

23. Adoption does not have to be expensive, especially if you adopt children who are in the foster care system. Another option is to become a foster parent; in many states you receive a small stipend to help take care of the child, including tuition and health insurance

In the midst of doing these things, simply and intentionally show people the love of Jesus. The beauty of relational ministry is that you will be ministered to as well. As you become a friend, you will gain a friend.

For most of us, reading about these choices is not enough to push us to make them. Reach out to some trusted friends today and ask them to hold you accountable to taking one step toward community. Community is fertile soil for God's life-giving fruit, while isolation is a downward spiral of fantasy and despair.

Loneliness can be a major struggle for singles; their biggest fear is often that they will end up alone. But loneliness is not something only singles experience. Quite honestly, some married people long for the type of freedom single people have to develop deep friendships. Some married people feel lonely and trapped in their marriages, bound by obligations to the point that they no longer have meaningful friendships. Even those who count their spouses as great friends often long for the opportunity to cultivate deeper community outside of their families.

As a single person, you have the freedom and flexibility to cultivate meaningful friendships in your life, not just for your sake but for the sake of others and for the sake of the gospel. The worst thing you can do is know this and not do it. If you're going to be single, whether by choice or against your will, you might as well open the gift given to you and maximize it.

A Brief Word to My Brothers in Christ Who Struggle with Same Sex Attraction

If you struggle with same-sex attraction, it's important to me that I take a moment to say thank you for picking up this book. Thank you for walking with Jesus. Thank you for persevering through trials that I can't comprehend. I respect you. I look up to you. I love you.

This book was written to heterosexual guys and uses exclusive language. I ask for your grace with that and hope you are able to

---

benefits in many cases. Adopting or fostering a child is a demonstration of the gospel and a needed and wonderful calling.

translate accordingly for your life and context. After having several SSA[24] guys join my beyondthebattle.net online groups, I wanted to make sure I lay down a welcome mat for you in this updated edition of *Beyond the Battle*. Welcome, my brothers. I believe you will find hope and freedom in these pages. Not freedom from your attractions but freedom from porn and lust, and most important, freedom in Christ, who can satisfy you in a way only he can.

Those of you who are seeking to follow the Bible's design for a traditional view of sex and marriage are the most courageous men I know. Many of you are choosing to live single, celibate lives as a result. Others are attempting to walk the difficult terrain of being married to a woman you aren't naturally attracted to. You inspire me.

For those of you who aren't at that point of commitment, please know that you are still loved—by me and by our Father in heaven (whom you'll hear much more about in the pages to follow). I pray that his love does what only his love can, for all of us.[25]

In Your Small Group

Scan this QR code or go to www.beyond thebattle.net/videos to watch and discuss "Session 1: How to Start Your *Beyond the Battle* Small Group." (All small group resources are free.)

---

24. I also ask for your grace in using the label of SSA versus LGBTQ or gay. I know some of you strongly prefer one over the other and have a valid and often godly rationale for your preference. I hope not to widen any divides with how I've worded things here and ask for your grace in that.

25. If you haven't already read *Washed and Waiting: Reflections on Christian Faithfulness and Homosexuality* by Wesley Hill (Grand Rapids, MI: Zondervan, 2006), it is a must read. I highly recommend it to pastors and straight guys as well.

CHAPTER 1

ENTITLEMENT IS YOUR WORST ENEMY

The gospel says you are more sinful and
flawed than you ever dared believe, but more
accepted and loved than you ever dared hope.
—Tim Keller, *The Meaning of Marriage*

A Freeing Truth

If you took a survey to determine the worst enemy of men's marriages, what do you think some of the top answers would be? Maybe pornography, wandering eyes, lack of compatibility, and—don't forget the old classic—communication.

The truth is, it's none of the above. It is entitlement.

If you're married, it's likely you want to improve your marriage. There are a lot of books and seminars out there on how to do that, and some of them are quite good. And let me say I am very much in favor of marriage counseling, and my wife and I have gone several times in our marriage.

But often "working on your marriage" means "trying to get your spouse to change." There are many resources out there that give you tips and tricks on how to do this. But if any of them really worked for the long haul, we wouldn't need another one and another one and another one. The entire industry would go out of business.

So I propose the question: What if instead of improving your marriage, you renovated your heart?

My wife and I were virgins when we got married. My church upbringing and the sexual purity books I read in college told me that if I saved myself sexually until marriage, God would bless my marriage and, specifically, my sex life. (Another way of saying bless was "give you everything you desire.") I struck a deal with God: I do my part. You do yours.

This is entitlement. It's the feeling that I deserve something, that I've earned it. The irony is that the first step to receiving the gospel is to admit that I deserve nothing.

I don't deserve to be saved from hell.

I don't deserve to be forgiven by Jesus.

I don't deserve grace.

I don't deserve heaven.

I don't deserve life itself.

In Exodus 33:20, God tells Moses that no one can see God and live. Romans 3:23 tells us we've all fallen short of the glory of God. Romans 6:23 tells us that the wage we deserve because of our sin is eternal death. These biblical declarations on what we deserve are a far cry from the irreverent "buddy Jesus" mentality many Christians have.

Instead of living with humility as forgiven sinners before a holy God, we live as if we deserve every bit of comfort we desire, especially in our marriages. When we believe Jesus isn't all that holy and we aren't all that sinful, we think Jesus ought to hook us up. Not only should he slip us a free burger, like our high school buddy working the McDonald's drive-thru, but he must give us what we want because he *owes* it to us.

Realizing how far we really are from God's holy standard causes a drastic change in our posture toward him and toward our wives.

Thankfully, this is not our final identity before him, and I don't want you to get stuck here. But it must be where we start if we are ever to experience the depths of his grace. You can't experience the riches of grace if you think it's owed to you; it's not even grace at that point.

Knowing I don't deserve anything from God is a far cry from feeling like I deserve or am entitled to an easy and happy marriage because I was good enough to earn it. It's a far cry from setting expectations for my wife based on my perception of my meritorious behavior.

Unmet Expectations

At the root of almost all marriage problems are unmet expectations. I want my wife to do something or be a certain way, but she isn't doing or being it, so I get mad and start looking elsewhere.

Expectations and entitlement are two different things, though they typically work in tandem to wreak havoc on our marriages. An expectation is something we believe will happen. Expectations aren't necessarily bad. They come naturally in a marriage because they are based on the promises we make in our vows. But we get ourselves into hot water when our expectations are unrealistic (especially when we don't realize it) and then we respond with a sense of entitlement when they go unmet.

When our expectations (even realistic ones) aren't met, we have two options: One is to try to manipulate our wives into meeting them. The other is to accept that we have no right to expect anything from anybody, including our wives[1] and God himself.[2] With

---

1. It's not wrong to believe our wives will be good spouses, do kind things for us, want to have sex with us, and so on. What's wrong is believing we deserve these things, which changes our hearts' posture toward life and God.

2. This isn't to say we don't have value in God's eyes or that God didn't create us with innate dignity and worth, in his image. It's to say that we need to own up to the guilt of our sin and realize that because we are guilty, because we have committed crimes against God, we deserve punishment. We have no right to anything else. This is the only posture that allows us to receive and be transformed by God's mercy.

this understanding, we can receive anything that *is* given to us as an undeserved gift of mercy from God.

The first option leads to a lifetime of disappointment, disillusionment, and frustration. The second leads to freedom, peace, and gratitude.

In this book, we'll talk about posture and identity, which are two different things. Our posture before God must be one of humble brokenness, knowing we don't deserve anything from him. But that doesn't mean we beat ourselves up, get stuck in shame, or mope around like he doesn't love us. We'll later talk about our identity before God as his beloved sons, new creations resurrected to new life in Christ. But we can appreciate and unleash this identity only if we know by our posture that we never deserved it to begin with.

This humble posture can become an incredible weapon for you in your marriage and purity. The aim of this book is to dismantle the entitlement we've been taught to have in our marriages and replace it with the sound foundation of who we are in Christ. The truth is, we don't need to add anything to what he has already given us, because what he's already given us is the most incredible gift in the universe. Our lives will never be the same once we internalize this idea.

Entitlement for Singles

"God, I've done it your way. Now you owe me."

It's likely that entitlement is not foreign to you and your conversations with God, whether you are single or married. For singles, it's often our refrain to God when we are tired of singleness. There's a girl we are pursuing, or there's one who just left us, or we attended *another* wedding, or we're the third wheel again, and at the end of the day, we're just tired of being single. We've done it God's way. Other people got their prize. Now we want ours.

Entitlement does not discriminate. It plagues both the married and the single. If you are single and get married someday, learning to rid yourself of entitlement now will put you way ahead of the game later. And if you stay single, ridding yourself of entitlement and the aching disappointment in God that accompanies it will free you like only the mercy of Christ can.

> If you're using the Forty-Day Devotional Guide
> in the back of this book, turn now to **Day 1**.

Thousands of Mercies

> What does it matter if I suffer injustice? Would I not have deserved even worse punishment from God, if He had not dealt with me according to His mercy?
> —Dietrich Bonhoeffer, *Life Together*

Entitlement sneaks up on you like a carbon monoxide leak. You didn't cause it, you can't smell it or see it, but it's there and it's lethal. It's a slave master, working you so hard you break. Nothing can quench it. Nothing can satisfy it. The only way to be free of its enslavement is to receive the sobering truth of what you deserve and of what you have received from Jesus instead. This realization will free you from what burdens you in a way nothing else can.

Now get ready for some strong coffee. This isn't fun and happy news, but it is the death blow to entitlement, and that death blow opens the path of peace, lightness, and freedom. The truth is, apart from Jesus, we are sinners who deserve hell this very moment. We've earned it.

We don't deserve the soft couches we are sitting on. Or the shoes on our feet. Or the coffee in our hands. The food in our fridges. Our children. Our wives. Apart from Jesus, we don't deserve anything this moment except to be under a holy God's wrathful judgment.[3] This is what the word deserve means.

---

3. John 3:36; Romans 1:18–20, 32; 2:5; 3:23; 6:23; Hebrews 10:26–31; Revelation 20:11–15.

Take a moment to let that sink in.

To deny this truth is to deny that we are rebellious sinners who have separated ourselves from God with no way to repair this broken relationship using our own strength.

But when we let this truth sink in, we realize that everything we have—*everything* we have—is a gift of mercy from God. If in this moment I deserve eternal punishment but I get a cup of coffee instead, that coffee is the most incredible gift I've ever imagined. If in this moment I deserve eternal punishment but I get to be married to a woman, a life companion, instead, then that woman is an incredible gift. If in this moment I deserve eternal punishment, but instead I am single and free to explore my relationship with God in a way that many married people can't, this is an incredible gift.

When I think of life from this perspective, I realize there are thousands upon thousands of mercies that God has already shown me today, mercy upon mercy that I do not deserve.

Imagine someone is knocking on your door with an oversized check for five million bucks, balloons and news camera in tow. The feeling you get from this is a lot different from when your boss hands you your paycheck every other Friday, isn't it? Picture how you'd feel if payday came and your boss told you there would be no paycheck. How would you respond? You'd be irate! You'd file a lawsuit!

So why does the five-million-dollar check at your doorstep feel so different from the paycheck you collect on Friday? It's not only the dollar amount, it's that the check is undeserved, while your paycheck *is* deserved. Only after receiving one of the two will you be blown away with gratitude and joy.

When they knock on your door with the balloons and the huge check, can you imagine responding, "Only five million? Are you kidding me? I'm not letting you in this house unless you add at least another $500,000. How dare you insult me like this?"

Nobody would respond this way because the gift is already massive and because they never earned it in the first place. The only response is gratitude. Think again of the thousands of mercies Jesus has given you today. Mercies upon mercies that you don't deserve. Now how do you respond?

Entitlement goes out the window, and gratitude and appreciation reign. Instead of taking the couch I'm sitting on for granted or wishing I had a newer, nicer one, I wiggle back and forth and think, "Wow, a couch! I deserve hell, and I get a couch instead!" The joy this perspective can bring you over the course of a day will be more than the people around you can tolerate.

We are comfortable applying the appreciation of mercy to our salvation: we understand that we are rebellious sinners desperately in need of a merciful savior. So why do we forget it when it comes to the rest of our lives, and especially in our marriages or singleness? And how will embracing this truth transform us as husbands and men?

> If you're using the Forty-Day Devotional Guide
> in the back of this book, turn now to **Day 2**.

Kickback Love

Most people would define love as sacrificing yourself for another, putting someone else above yourself. The Bible tells us repeatedly to do this. It even tells us that the very definition of love is that it is not self-seeking.[4] We wax eloquent about this in our marriage vows, yet we are often taught the opposite when we look for help on having a happy and fulfilling marriage.

We give lip service to selflessness and sacrifice as the foundation of marriage, but in practice we try to coerce our spouses to do what we want. The premise of some of the popular marriage books, seminars, and counseling sessions available today is the idea of reciprocation. Your marriage doesn't feel good, and you want it to be better, so the way to make your marriage feel better is to get

---

4. 1 Corinthians 13:5.

your wife to do what you want. And the best way to get your wife to do what you want is to learn how to do what she wants.

It's rarely put this explicitly, but that's the message I embraced while working through the difficult years of my marriage. Sadly, it encouraged my selfish mindset instead of helping to reverse it.

One of the most popular marriage books available today is *The Five Love Languages* by Gary Chapman.[5] This book has helped many people over several decades. Chapman shares many solid principles in his book, but no book is perfect (including the one you are reading), and so I offer it as an illustration of why we need to be discerning, even with good books by Christian authors. (And I hope people will offer their own biblical critiques of my book to help future readers.)

The Five Love Languages can be an effective tool to learn how to sacrificially love your spouse. But its advice can also be easily hijacked by our sin nature. That's what happened to me. I'm easily motivated to have my desires met, and let's face it, marriage can be frustrating when your desires aren't met. We all act from mixed motives, and it is a relatively short step from showing your wife love for her own sake to manipulating her into doing what you want.

I'll Scratch Your Back If You Scratch Mine

Let's say you want your wife to show you affection. Your "love bank"[6] is empty, and that makes you feel lousy. Because your bank is empty, you want to cheat; you want to lust; you may even want a divorce. You want that bank full and you'll do whatever is necessary to make that happen. You believe that if your wife were a better wife and was doing her job, you wouldn't be feeling this way. You don't

---

5. Gary Chapman, *The Five Love Languages: The Secret to Love That Lasts* (Chicago: Northfield Publishing, 2010).

6. "Love bank" is the term used in *The Five Love Languages* to describe how loved a person feels. If your spouse has loved you in a way you connect with, your love bank balance goes up, making it possible for you now to give love to your spouse out of this bank. The book presents five ways of showing your spouse love (called "love languages") and presents an assessment to fill out to identify what each spouse prefers. The premise is that only love shown in the appropriate language will help fill the love bank.

want to feel this way, but you tell yourself it's her fault, not yours. But wait . . . there's a solution. Her account is empty too. All this time you thought you were being a great husband, but actually you were swinging and missing.

So you deduce that your wife isn't showing you the affection you want because you haven't cleaned the garage. You've drained her love account. Clean the garage, and *boom*, affection city. You've figured out the puzzle of what your wife wants, and so you give it to her—so that she will give you what you want.

Your back has been scratched, and now you are happy.

But this is still self-seeking. Another word for this is selfishness. This type of marriage counseling may be only an indirect route to selfishness, but the motive is selfish nonetheless. We see marriage as an agreement whose purpose is to get our desires met. And that's selfishness. What do you think will happen in a marriage that is rooted in selfish motives?

Experienced marriage counselors can pinpoint the factors that pushed their clients to have affairs. As they listen to couples over the years, they note the common themes and write books explaining what these factors are. You read the books and do the worksheets with your wife to make sure that each of you understands how the other wants to be shown love. If you do these things, not only will your wife be less likely to have an affair, she will be happy with you and reciprocate affection, making you less likely to be unfaithful as well. We love this because in the end we all get what we want.

This strategy of reciprocation does produce some good fruit in people's marriages, and those who came up with it genuinely desire to help. Maybe some of the marriage books that advocate it were very helpful to you and you're struggling with what I'm writing here. I want to reaffirm the good these books have done and can do, but I also want you to be aware of the danger. Can you see how easy it is for our sin natures to hijack this back-scratching strategy? All I ask is that you look beneath the surface, at the motives and appetites this strategy arouses, despite its good intentions or results. Like a dietary supplement that ends up causing cancer, if it does more harm than good, the benefit is not worth it. If a strategy creates or is fueled by entitlement, it's only going to set us up for failure. It's the wrong foundation.

Entitlement is a predator we cannot escape if we continue to feed it and negotiate with it. We must see the flaw in the reciprocation approach and fill in the gaps it leaves. For some, this approach can provide helpful tools for certain seasons of marriage if adopted with caution, but most of us should avoid it.[7]

While it's helpful to know how your spouse is wired and what factors cause unfaithfulness so you can guard against them, destructive and inevitable repercussions flow from the expectation of reciprocity. I say inevitable because your wife is going to continue to let you down. She is human and sinful (as are you) and will never be able to fully satisfy you. Can you continue to speak your wife's love language without feeling resentful if she doesn't speak yours? That is a path most of us simply can't handle.

What makes things worse is that this approach categorizes these factors as needs.[8] Needs are things like oxygen, food, water, and shelter. I am entitled to have my needs met. And when I approach my marriage with entitlement on my mind, it's bound to blow up in my face. You do not need your wife to show you affection. You don't. You aren't going to die without her affection. It's a wrong use of the word.

---

7. Gary Chapman has another book titled *The Five Love Languages of Children*. I have not read it, but I believe the love languages concept would work great to help parents learn how to love their children well. This is because a child *is* entitled to their parents' love and affection. The parent-child relationship is different from the husband-wife relationship. There is no scoreboard temptation in parent-child love. The parent loves the child and provides a secure, warm environment for them, but the child has no obligation to provide a secure, warm environment for the parent. The parent is already secure as a grown, mature adult. To approach the husband-wife relationship in the same way admits that a husband or wife is of the same maturity level as a child, with the same emotional vacancies. This is why the solution to marriage problems is not to get your spouse to fill that void, it's to get Jesus to fill that void. Two incomplete people will not make each other complete. Only Jesus can make a person complete. They can then take their complete, secure, whole self and offer it to their spouse as a gift, without needing their spouse to make them whole in return.

8. See, for example, Willard F. Harley Jr., *His Needs, Her Needs: Building an Affair-Proof Marriage* (Grand Rapids, MI: Revell, 2011).

The essential flaw of the reciprocation strategy is that it caters to our sinful, selfish nature instead of working against it. It starts with the premise, "I deserve to have my spouse love me in the way I desire." So every act of love I show her is not actually an act of love but an act of selfishness. Like depositing quarters into an arcade game or a vending machine, my love investments toward her are merely transactional means to an end: my satisfaction.

When we are counseled to show love to our wives in the hope that they will reciprocate, our sin nature immediately builds a scoreboard. And this scoreboard eventually spawns self-righteousness.

I've done my part, why isn't my wife doing hers? I'm filling her up, but I still feel empty. Why are my needs still unmet?

This self-righteousness promotes the mindset that I am the good spouse and my wife is the one slacking, making everything worse. Frustration reigns, and I feel I've earned the right to look elsewhere to fill up my love bank, because I've been told I need and deserve this. Heck, my wife has pushed me to look elsewhere. She read the same book I did, for crying out loud, and she's still not giving me what I deserve. It's her fault I have a wandering heart.

This attitude echoes what's been true of the human condition since the day Adam and Eve first sinned: We feel that we deserve to have our desires met and that the quality of our lives revolves around this. (And just as Adam did, we blame the woman rather than take responsibility when things go haywire.) We believe we deserve to feel good at any cost, and this becomes the primary motivation for everything we do.

Judging our marriages by the reciprocation scoreboard will leave us empty, frustrated, and wanting. It starts up a treadmill we can never climb off. By contrast, the gospel Jesus offers us turns this strategy upside down and reveals where we will find lasting freedom and joy.

If you're using the Forty-Day Devotional Guide
in the back of this book, turn now to **Day 3**.

CHAPTER 2

A WRETCH LIKE *WHO*?

Living Pardoned

You are a serial killer. The memories of your deeds haunt you when you try to sleep at night. You've been tried, convicted, and sentenced to death. You are spending the remaining months of your life in solitary confinement, living in a pitch-black cell the size of a small closet. A jailer tosses stale bread to you once a day as you await your day to die. You sleep on a cold cement floor and go to the bathroom in a hole.

You are getting what you deserve, and justice is being served.

After weeks without seeing another human face or even a beam of light, your prison door opens and light from the hallway's fluorescent bulbs blasts into your dungeon. Your eyes take a moment to adjust as you strain to make out the figure standing in your doorway. It's a familiar face. It's the judge from your trial.

This innocent, holy judge named Jesus Christ extends his hand to you. He tells you he will take your punishment. He is the judge, the only one in authority who can pull this off. He will die in your place. He will forgive all the crimes you've committed. You can walk away a free man.

You know you don't deserve this amazing offer, but you can't help but accept it.

Jesus dies.

You live.

The guards lead you to the prison entrance and release you.

You have been pardoned.

The sun shines down on you as you take your first breath of crisp air as a free man. A long, deep breath.

You ponder the depth of love Jesus showed you by paying for your freedom with his life. You can taste it. You didn't deserve freedom, and Jesus didn't deserve death.

Jesus rises from the dead and transforms your relationship with God from judge and guilty sinner to Father and beloved son. You are a new creation resurrected to new life in Christ.

How do you feel?

More important, how will you live?

What will you appreciate?

What will you feel entitled to?

The truth is, learning to live as pardoned rather than entitled revolutionizes our faith, our prayers, and our lives as married or single men. When you've been pardoned the way this hypothetical prisoner was from his dark cell into a new life of Christ-empowered freedom, you'll never feel entitled again. It will all be consumed by relief and gratitude.

The journey we are on in this book is not about how you can manipulate your wife to do what will make you happy. Nor is it about learning to perform the act of goodness that magically will make God transform your marriage into a utopia.

Have you ever thought any of the following things?

I married the wrong person.

I should have married _____.

I should have pursued _____.

Why isn't my wife more like _____?

My wife isn't as pretty as _____. Or my wife isn't as _____ as
_____. I bet I could have gotten or could get _____.

On a scale of 1 to 10, I'm a 7. My wife is a 7. That guy is a 5,
and he's with a 9. You're telling me I could've married
a 9?

I got married too young.

I got married for the wrong reasons.

My wife is a different person than the woman I dated.

My wife and I have nothing in common.

My wife won't speak my love language.

My wife won't meet my needs.

My wife won't fulfill me sexually.

My wife won't give me recreational companionship.

My wife isn't staying physically attractive for me.

My wife isn't providing domestic support for me.

My wife doesn't admire me.[1] (As other women do!)

Having ever indulged in any of these thoughts (and if you haven't, you're either lying or you've been married only a week) is an indication of entitlement.

This journey is about realizing we don't deserve anything. As we live pardoned, we quit seeing who our wives aren't and who some other woman is. Instead, we start seeing our wives as the complete women they are, the blessings they are, and the undeserved gifts of mercy they are.

Are you living entitled or pardoned?

> If you're using the Forty-Day Devotional Guide
> in the back of this book, turn now to **Day 4**.

---

1. This and the previous four in the list are a man's five needs, according to Willard Harley's *His Needs, Her Needs: Building an Affair-Proof Marriage* (Grand Rapids, MI: Revell, 2011).

From Entitlement to Appreciation

Your wife will never be able to compete with the women you compare her to.

No human could.

There is simply too much competition: throngs of real women looking for attention, and throngs of electronic female images vying for your mouse click.

Your wife is only human. Your fantasies are not. You know every flaw your wife has, whereas you see other women on a surface level. You see your wife on her worst days. You smell her breath when you wake up in the morning. (And she smells yours.) Your wife can't compare to the flirtatious snapshots that tempt you. You will always be able to find something your wife lacks that someone else seems to offer.

Instead of focusing on what we don't have (the premise of love-bank marriage strategies), living pardoned focuses on what we do have and celebrating that with gratitude.

Living pardoned makes me realize that when the classic hymn begins, "Amazing grace, how sweet the sound, that saved a wretch like _____," the name that goes in the blank is my own, not my wife's.

Living entitled means treating my wife as if she's the wretch in need of an overhaul.

Living pardoned realizes that without Christ *I* am the wretch, and no earthly overhaul can cure me. The only cure is Jesus' mercy. I am a shattered vessel that his grace has made whole. Such a thought makes me bury my face in my hands, while simultaneously lifting them in praise as far as they will reach.

In *The Way of the Heart*, Henri Nouwen quotes *The Sayings of the Desert Fathers:* "'It is folly for a man who has a dead person in his house to leave him there and go to weep over his neighbor's dead.'[2] Solitude leads to the awareness of the dead person in our own

---

2. Benedicta Ward, trans., *The Sayings of the Desert Fathers* (Oxford: Mowbray, 1975), 61.

houses and keeps us from making judgments about other people's sins. In this way real forgiveness becomes possible."[3]

Amazing grace, how sweet the sound, that saved a wretch like **me**.

The dead person in my house, my wretched sin, is plenty for me to concern myself with and to bring before the Lord. It makes no sense for me to cast judgment on others for their sins when I'm guilty of the same. We can't truly begin to forgive others until we realize that we're in the same boat.

My wife is no longer insufficient for "a stud like me." She is now a gift for a wretch like me. A gift I don't deserve. Even with all of her flaws and all I want to change, she is a gift I don't deserve.

You have been pardoned.

You are a new creation.

The sun shines down on you as you take your first breath of crisp air as a free man. A long, deep breath.

How do you feel?

More important, how will you live?

How will you live as a husband?

Stop paying attention to what your wife doesn't do. Stop keeping track of your love bank.

Apart from Christ, we are insecure, bankrupt, helpless sinners whose need for love will never be filled by another human being. To think our wives could do this for us is the definition of idolatry. It's the most unfair position we can put them in.

So it's time to stop keeping score.

One of the most dangerous prayers you can pray is, "God, give me what I deserve." Thank God that he doesn't keep score. We would all be in serious trouble if he did. Our side of the scoreboard would read negative infinity. But God doesn't keep score. You have no right to keep score either.

Pay attention to what your wife *does*. Pay attention to who she is. Appreciate her. At the very least, you can appreciate your wife for the "glue of grace" she is in your life, the glue God has given

---

3. Henri Nouwen, *The Way of the Heart* (New York: Seabury Press, 1981), 36. This is a fantastic book and a quick read.

you to keep together so much that you hold valuable. My marriage provides a stable, loving environment for my kids to thrive in. My marriage creates needed boundaries and accountability to keep me from being promiscuous, losing my ministry and testimony, and turning my heart into a black hole of self-consumption. This is the glue of grace I can be so grateful for every day, despite other circumstances.

Don't get me wrong: I'm not asking you to trick yourself. That misses the point of drawing on the power of the gospel to satisfy and fuel us. But appreciating your wife because of what Jesus has done for you is very different from appreciating your wife because of what she has done for you. The key to being grateful and living in the freedom Jesus offers is not to fool yourself into being thankful for qualities your wife doesn't have. While most husbands can think of at least a few reasons to be grateful for their wives, and that exercise is helpful to a degree, it is not the solution. It's not the solution because some men have been so burned, hurt, and rejected by their wives that they truly don't feel they have anything to be thankful for.[4]

To force ourselves to make a list of our wives' positive attributes and let those attributes carry us through our marriages' weak seasons is to fall into the kickback love mentality. That mentality is simply not strong enough to uphold us through the dry and difficult seasons. What we need to understand in the depths of our being, and what will truly transform us through the thick and thin of life and marriage, is that Jesus has done more than enough for us to be thankful for. Jesus fills our love tank to the brim, to overflowing, and nothing can change that. We have a choice: we can fuel ourselves with his love, or we can look for a cheap substitute elsewhere.

Your wife is not a gift because of who she is. (She's just as messed up as you are, after all.) She is a gift because of who Jesus is, because

---

4. This may not be your experience. Praise God for that. But don't judge the men who have this experience, or think that everyone has the potential to experience what you do in your marriage.

you deserve hell but Jesus has given you grace and life instead. He has made you a new creation, resurrected to new life in him.

Be grateful.

Show her your gratitude.

> If you're using the Forty-Day Devotional Guide
> in the back of this book, turn now to **Day 5**.

Forgive, or Else

I have read Jesus' parable of the unmerciful servant countless times.[5] In this story, Jesus tells of a servant who owes his king 200,000 years' worth of wages, a cartoonish amount the servant obviously never will be able to repay. The law dictates that the man and his entire family be sold as slaves to pay what he owes. The servant begs the king to forgive his astronomical debt, and the king mercifully agrees. The man is free to go. Pardoned.

On his way out, the man runs into a fellow servant who owes him around a hundred days' wages. While not a small amount, it is nowhere near the size of the debt he has just been forgiven.[6] Shockingly, the just-forgiven servant chokes his peer and demands that he repay him. When the second servant asks for patience and reassures him that he will pay his debt in time, the wicked servant refuses to show mercy. Instead, he has the man thrown into prison until he can pay him back.

When the king finds out what the unmerciful servant has done, he summons him and says, "Shouldn't you have had mercy on your fellow servant just as I had on you?" Angry, he hands the servant over to the jailers to be tortured until he can repay all he owes.

The conclusion of Jesus' parable recently hit me with sobering rawness: "This is how my heavenly Father will treat each of you unless you forgive your brother or sister from your heart."

---

5. Matthew 18:21–35.
6. The money owed him is .0005 percent of his own debt.

Over the countless times I have read this passage, I have found theological and contextual ways to soften Jesus' point. My motives were pure, of course: Taken on its own, this verse seems to indicate we can lose our salvation if we don't forgive others. It seems to say we must earn our salvation. It seems to suggest we have to walk around in fear of God's judgment, never knowing whether we have forgiven others enough. All of these things are contrary to what is taught in other parts of Scripture, so I would avoid Jesus' point when preaching the story.

It's true we shouldn't develop our theology around one verse when multitudes of other verses have contrasting emphases. It's true that because the Bible doesn't contradict itself, one verse doesn't negate a bunch of others. But it's also true we can't dismiss or dodge a verse because it jars us. We can't ignore the two points Jesus is making here: forgiving others is not optional for those whom God has forgiven, and a lack of forgiveness is punishable by eternity in hell.

As it turns out, my motive for dodging the punch of this passage wasn't so pure after all. The Holy Spirit hit me loud and clear: *The reason you don't want to believe verse 35 is because you don't want to forgive your wife.*

Ouch.

While I don't think it's possible to overemphasize God's grace toward us, I do think it's possible to cheapen it.[7] We cheapen his grace when we deemphasize his holiness and justice, when we tell ourselves we don't really need to fear God.

By fear, I don't mean be afraid of God. I mean the biblical fear of God referenced hundreds of times throughout Scripture. Fear is the natural feeling a sinful being has in the presence of a holy God. Fear is the understanding of who God is and who we are apart from him. It is knowing we have incurred an unpayable

---

7. The term cheap grace was first coined by Dietrich Bonhoeffer in his 1937 publication *The Cost of Discipleship* (New York: Simon and Schuster, 1995), 44–45. In this work, Bonhoeffer describes cheap grace as "the preaching of forgiveness without requiring repentance, baptism without church discipline, communion without confession. Cheap grace is grace without discipleship, grace without the cross, grace without Jesus Christ, living and incarnate."

debt that must be paid. It is awe, reverence, and humility taken to their utmost degree.

Modern Christians need major reposturing as sinners before a holy God. We've been conditioned to think that grace is cheap and that we aren't so bad on our own. We think that talking about hell or God's wrath is for radical kooks, not for cool and hip Christians like us. This mindset is as unbiblical[8] as it gets, and it has devastating effects on our ability to allow God's grace to transform us.

If we don't grasp God's justice and holiness and how far apart from him we truly are, we'll never be able to enjoy the depths of his grace.

If we think we've done only a nickel's worth of sin (or that God cares only a nickel's worth about our sin), it's no wonder the nickel's worth of grace we accept doesn't change the way we live. When we realize we've done 200,000 years of salary in sin, the equivalent amount of grace needed to compensate cannot help but reposture us. We are repostured from being arrogant, entitled self-gods who think we can look YHWH[9] in the eye, to being weak human beings overwhelmed by a tidal wave of grace, flattened like pancakes on our faces before an untouchable, holy God.[10] When this is our posture, God's grace and mercy frees and transforms us in miraculous ways.

Here's the point that will change your marriage forever, as it changed mine: God can send you to hell if you don't continually forgive your wife.

Does this scare you?

It probably does (and we need immediately to stop labeling that as a bad thing), but that's not the point. And it's essential we don't

---

8. Instead of trying to explain away the directness of God's wrath in the Old Testament, we need to realize that wrath is what sinners deserve before a holy God. Anything less, and God is no longer holy or just. How arrogant we are to think that we can stand before a holy God and not deserve his wrath, or that he is unjust in bringing it upon the earth.

9. YHWH are the Hebrew letters used for God's name in the original manuscripts of the Old Testament. God was so holy to the Jews, they would not even say his name! We can make only educated guesses as to how to pronounce YHWH, but some transliterate it to *Yahweh*.

10. I love Isaiah 6:1–8 on this subject.

miss the point here. Jesus' point isn't to scare you. His point is to get you to forgive.

Think a little about this parable: how in the world did this servant rack up 200,000 years' worth of debt? We all know people who are bad with money and who make foolish financial decisions, but 200,000 years' worth of salary in debt?[11] And he caused it himself. It's unimaginable what kind of wreck this person must be.

But that wreck is also you and me. We, of course, are the wicked servant in the parable. We caused our uncountable debt with our uncountable sins. And we struggle to forgive our wives because we forget what big wrecks we are before God and how ridiculous it is that he forgave our debts. To fail to forgive our wives continually, no matter what they do to us or deprive us of, is enough to punch our tickets straight to hell.[12]

If that doesn't motivate you to forgive, I'm not sure what will.

Don't focus on the hundred days of wages your wife owes you. Focus solely on the debt that you've been forgiven of. Never take your eyes off it, and you will be changed forever. Never stop being in wonder of God's forgiveness. Never stop being overwhelmed by it. Never stop it from making you jump and dance and sing and shout for joy. Never forget you don't deserve forgiveness and never will, but you have been forgiven and are now a new creation, resurrected to new life in Christ. Let this fact topple over any and every debt your wife—or anyone else—might ever owe you.

You may have heard the phrase "hurt people hurt people." This is true. People who have been hurt tend to hurt others. But the opposite statement is also true: loved people love people.[13] And oh, how you and I have been loved by Jesus.

How many times should you forgive your wife—seven times?

---

11. We're talking roughly 5 billion dollars in today's currency.

12. Please pay attention: I'm not saying you're going to hell if you don't forgive your wife. I'm saying that not forgiving your wife is enough sin for God to send you to hell. Arguing that "Jesus' grace covers me, so I'm good" dodges the point Jesus is making here about forgiveness and about God's holiness.

13. Thank you to my friend Andy Antcliff for this beautiful line.

No, Jesus says in Matthew 18:22, seventy-seven times (or seventy times seven, 490!)—a never-ending number of times, because the forgiveness shown to you is never ending.

You can either forgive your wife, or you can blatantly and aggressively rebel against our holy God by not forgiving her. The choice is yours.

Instead of making excuses for why you can't or don't have to forgive your wife, allow yourself to fear the Lord. Imagine what could happen if you don't.

Now feel the incredible freedom that comes when you do forgive. Feel what it means to quit holding someone's sins against them, to forgive them of the dead person in their house because you have one in your house too. Feel the freedom that comes when you love the other person unconditionally the way you have been loved and freed by a holy, wrathful, yet loving and merciful God. You'll never want to go back to unforgiveness again.

The Lower You Go, the Richer You Get

While Matthew 18 is only a parable, Jesus teaches the same principle in real life in Luke 7. A "sinful" woman has just washed his feet with her alabaster jar of perfume, and the religious leaders are aghast. Jesus uses yet another illustration both to show us our place and to show us the path of freedom, peace, and joy:

> "Two people owed money to a certain moneylender. One owed him five hundred denarii, and the other fifty. Neither of them had the money to pay him back, so he forgave the debts of both. Now which of them will love him more?"
>
> Simon replied, "I suppose the one who had the bigger debt forgiven."
>
> "You have judged correctly," Jesus said. . . .
>
> "Therefore, I tell you, her many sins have been forgiven—as her great love has shown. But whoever has been forgiven little loves little."
>
> —LUKE 7:41–43, 47

Sound familiar?

The lower you go, the richer you get; and the higher you go, the poorer you will be. When you don't think you need very much mercy because you're so righteous already, you will never get to enjoy mercy's abundant riches. Your feeling that you are already in such a high position will keep you impoverished. But the more you realize you need mercy because of your low position before God, the more of it you receive. The more of it you receive, the more you have to be grateful for. The more you have to be grateful for, the more freedom, peace, and joy you experience.

> If you're using the Forty-Day Devotional Guide
> in the back of this book, turn now to **Day 6**.

Christ's Example

The example Christ sets for husbands has been overused to the point that it has often lost its punch.

We often hear Ephesians 5:25: "Husbands, love your wives, just as Christ loved the church and gave himself up for her." This is followed by a message to picture Jesus hanging on the cross, the sacrifice he made, the pain he endured, and to love our wives in the same way.

A man may take this to heart and soon find himself feeling like a beaten down ox told to lower its head and keep plowing. When you're tired, keep plowing. When it hurts, keep plowing. The problem with this mentality is that it's not sustainable. It doesn't work because it's powered by our works and our strength, not by grace and God's strength. It doesn't work because it starts with an empty cup, whereas God has laid out a path where our cups are already full and keep being refilled by his faucet, which never turns off. The key is finding a practical way to access that faucet.

Because entitlement lies at the root of marital discontent, we must look to Jesus as the example of one who gave up what he actually was entitled to. Jesus wasn't just a guy like us who happened to do a really good job at loving sacrificially and whom we're now supposed to model ourselves after (the way Ephesians 5:25 is typically applied). The power of Jesus' example, and the irony of it, is that he is the only person who has ever walked the earth who actually did deserve abundant blessing. He was the only person who actually was entitled to have everything work out the way he wanted.

Philippians 2:6 clearly says that Jesus is "in very nature God," yet "did not consider equality with God something to be used to his own advantage." Jesus was God in the flesh, yet what did he do with everything God is entitled to? He gave it up for us, for our advantage, not his. "He made himself nothing by taking the very nature of a servant. . . . He humbled himself by becoming obedient to death—even death on a cross!" (vv. 7–8).

The person who was entitled to everything rejected what was rightfully his so that we, who are not entitled to anything, could gain what we have no right to.

Then we are told to love our wives like this, following Jesus' example. Good luck doing that in your own strength.

How full was Jesus' love tank or love bank while he was beaten to a pulp and hanging on the cross, rejected by the crowds and shouldering our sins?

Not full at all. Bone dry. According to some marriage experts' way of thinking, Jesus had every right to go off and have an affair, to ditch his loveless spouse (that's us) and find someone who loves him more.

We tell our wives, "I will love you if you live up to my standards. I will love you if you meet my needs. I will love you if you speak my love language and keep my love tank full." Yet this is not how Jesus loves us, and we'd be in serious trouble if he did.

Christians know why Jesus continued to hang on the cross, even though he could have snapped his fingers and been rescued by angels. He hung there because of his love for us. He hung there because it was the Father's will and the only way to fix our relationship with him.

But if we are to apply this to our marriages without feeling like we're plowing like an ox, we must ask *how* Jesus continued to hang on the cross. Jesus didn't use his "God card" to strengthen himself or make the pain go away. That would have nullified the point of coming to earth as 100 percent human, experiencing what we experience. He hung from the cross, 100 percent human, void of the love of the people he came to save, yet full of the love of his Father. His task would have been impossible without this love.

The only way to love our wives the way Jesus loves us is to be filled with our Father's love the way Jesus was full of our Father's love. We will explore this in chapter 3.

> If you're using the Forty-Day Devotional Guide
> in the back of this book, turn now to **Day 7**.

Conclusion: Charting the Course

I'm not trying to convince you to stop working on your marriage. I'm assuming that you've already tried reading marriage books, going in for counseling, and listening to marriage sermons and seminars in an attempt to improve it. I encourage you to continue doing these things. The problem is, as guys, we define *work on* the same way we define *fix*. We are men. We like to fix things. Give us some duct tape and the problem is solved. But you've probably come to a point where you realize that no matter how much duct tape you put on your marriage's leaky pipes, the pipes still leak.

No amount of counseling, advice, or methods you pour into your cup will do any good if your cup has holes in the bottom of it. The aim of this book is to repair the cup and get to God's faucet, not to add tips and tricks to improve your marriage.

I intend this chapter to unnerve you a little. You might feel a little defeated. Don't give up on this journey.

If we have a sense of entitlement, we will do what we feel we have the right to do: ditch our spouses and look elsewhere. Or at least disengage from them and seek relief.

But once you learn to appreciate your wife as a gift from God that you don't deserve, your stance toward her will change remarkably. You will be amazed by what appreciation does for your heart and for your marriage.

When it comes to entitlement, singles and married men are in the same boat, with the same invitation toward gratitude. Single men do differ from one another. Some feel entitled to get married someday, as if it were an inalienable right God is depriving them of. Some obsess over women and a future marriage like it is the one thing they can't live without. Others are fine with not being married but have other areas where they feel God is holding out on them. Some struggle with the burden of same-sex attraction, wondering why God isn't answering their prayers for this to change. Some struggle with comparing themselves to married men, wondering why the other guy got the perfect bride while he got nothing. At the end of the day, each of us needs to realize we have been given much more than nothing in the undeserved mercy of Jesus. This mercy is not a consolation prize, and we will find freedom and joy when we learn to live into it.

Singles also need to realize the grass isn't always greener on the other side of the fence. What might look like the perfect marriage or the perfect family likely isn't.

A common complaint and desire of Christian single guys is that it's not fair they don't get to have sex, so they despondently long for marriage or rebel against God's design and have sex outside of marriage. But which of these would you prefer: To be single and not have sex? Or to be married and not have sex—to want sex and be united to a wife you feel is supposed to have sex with you, but isn't, and to have to deal with that rejection? This is a reality more marriages deal with than you realize. (Like 15 to 20 percent of marriages.)[14]

---

14. It has been estimated that 15 to 20 percent of marriages are "sexless" or have had sex less than ten times in the last year. Tara Parker-Pope, "When Sex Leaves the Marriage," *New York Times*, June 3, 2009, https://well.blogs.nytimes.com/2009/06/03/when-sex-leaves-the-marriage. I borrowed this stat from Matt and Laurie Krieg's incredible book *An Impossible Marriage: What Our Mixed Orientation Marriage Has Taught Us about Love*

The ultimate point is, everyone has struggles, whether married or single. For some it's their marriage, for some it's their health, and others face a wide variety of other seen or unseen trials and stressors. No one has a perfect life. This fallen world will never be perfect. But we do have Jesus' perfect grace both to save us and sustain us, whether we are single or married.

In Your Small Group

Scan this QR code or go to www.beyond thebattle.net/videos and watch "Session 2 (Chapters 1–2): Entitlement Is Your Worst Enemy." (All small group resources are free.)

---

and the Gospel (Downers Grove, IL: InterVarsity, 2020), 67. If you want a fantastic follow-up to *Beyond the Battle*, read *An Impossible Marriage*.

CHAPTER 3

GOLDEN GODS WITH GOLDEN HAIR

*Lust is the craving for salt of a
person who is dying of thirst.*
—FREDERICK BUECHNER, *WISHFUL THINKING*

Our Power Source

Everything is fueled by something. We know this better in today's technological age than it has ever been known before. Whether it's your car, your smartphone, or your body, almost everything needs some kind of juice to function.

Our souls are no different.

The trick with technology is to follow the product manual, something that men aren't always the greatest at.

Have you ever taken a trip overseas only to discover the electric outlets differ from the plugs on the electronics you brought with you? Good luck with that.

We can make all kinds of mistakes with electricity. If you use the wrong AC adaptor for your fancy new gizmo, you can fry its circuits, ruining it and possibly burning the house down in the process.

Electricity and power are truly amazing, especially in the new wireless and lithium-ion-battery era we live in. But before wireless technology took the world by storm, the best thing since sliced bread was extension cords.

I've always been a big fan of extension cords. They are your best friend if you're trying to win the neighborhood Christmas-light contest or if you bought an electric weed whacker because you thought saving the money on gasoline would be worth it. (Bad idea, for the record.) You can have any technology anywhere you want if you have enough extension cords.

But what happens when you plug an extension cord into itself?

Well . . . nothing happens. You get a big circle of nothing.

No power. No fuel. No juice.

Now, what happens when you plug one end of an extension cord into an electrical outlet and the other end into an appliance?

You get toast!

You get television!

You get power.

The only way to get power is to use a power source. You can't plug a toaster into a TV and expect anything to happen. You can't connect two dead wires to one another and expect them to produce the living current of love: for better or for worse, for richer or for poorer, in sickness and in health.

Your love for your wife can't be rooted in her love for you.

You can't hold out on doing nice things for your wife until she does some nice things for you. You can't do nice things for your wife, expecting her to do nice things in return. And there is nothing you can do for your wife that will cause her, in response, to finally become the woman of your dreams.

This merry-go-round approach to marriage simply gets us nowhere. Because it's rooted in selfishness, it's not sustainable, and at the end of the day, it's not love.

Your love for your wife must be rooted in God's love for you.

This is the model of love Jesus showed to us, which Scripture tells us to show to our wives. It's the only model that's sustainable through the ups and downs of life, and it's the only one with power behind it.

Jesus' Power Source

One of the foundational doctrines to our faith is that Jesus is 100 percent God and 100 percent human. This statement is 100 percent true, though it carries mystery with it. When we read Jesus' biographies in Matthew, Mark, Luke, and John, it's important we don't lean too heavily on Jesus' humanity or on his divinity. For example, we know Jesus didn't use his "God card" to escape the physical pain and suffering of the cross. Conversely, he is always a fixture of the triune godhead, even when working on a carpentry project.

How does this relate to where we get our power to love from?

Whether he *needed* it or not in his full divinity, Jesus sets an example for us to follow by regularly "filling up" on the Father's love throughout his earthly ministry. The most foundational of these moments is at the very beginning of Jesus' public ministry, at the end of Matthew 3, when he is baptized by John the Baptist. And the timing can't be missed. The beginning of Matthew 4 has Jesus in the wilderness, being tempted by the devil. Satan does everything he can to get Jesus to doubt his identity as God's beloved Son and to turn to a cheap substitute to give him an identity fix.

It's no coincidence that in God's divine sovereignty, the event that took place immediately before this is Jesus' baptism, when he audibly heard the Father's voice saying to him, "This is my Son, whom I love; with him I am well pleased."[1] Jesus hadn't preached a sermon yet or done a single miracle. He hadn't done any earthly feats that the Father was congratulating him for. God the Father simply expressed his love to his Son because of his Son's identity as *son*. That identity is fixed, unmovable by anything, and tattooed on Jesus' heart, mind, and soul.

This immense love spoken to Jesus from the Father at his baptism powered him to resist Satan's temptation in the wilderness.

---

1. Matthew 3:17.

Satan was offering alternative paths to finding love and acceptance, which Jesus didn't need because he knew he was already loved and accepted by his Father.

We can't just look to Jesus hanging on the cross and say, "I need to love like that," as if Jesus loved by sheer human willpower and so can we. This is the "do better, try harder" approach we are all too familiar with, which fails every time. We need to look beneath the surface to discover the source of Jesus' love and intimacy. What fueled him to love like that? He *is* love,[2] and within the Trinity, he is always *being loved* by the Father and the Spirit, and so has an unlimited reservoir of love to show to humanity, even when hanging on a cross.

Loved people love people.

That same love is available to us to experience and to become our power source in loving others.

Jesus was able to show infinite love on the cross because he was experiencing infinite love from his Father. He was able to show infinite love as he walked around Palestine for three years being threatened, misunderstood, and rejected because he was filled to the brim with his Father's love.

You can love because you are loved by your Father. When you are filled to the brim with your Father's love, it will overflow to your wife and all those you come in contact with, regardless of the circumstances.

People constantly told Jesus who he was (and who he wasn't) and who they wanted him to be. This isn't much different from our experience today. Unlike Jesus, however, we end up basing our behaviors and choices on these messages because we forget who we are. We'll do whatever it takes to feel accepted, approved, and valued by those around us. The difference we see in Jesus, and the model we are to follow, is that he knew who he was, so he had no need to follow other voices.

Do you know who you are? And if not, where are you looking to

---

2. 1 John 4:8, 16.

find the answer? There's a good chance you are looking where most men look for their intimacy, approval, acceptance, and validation.

Women.

> If you're using the Forty-Day Devotional Guide
> in the back of this book, turn now to **Day 8**.

The Golden-Haired Woman

In his groundbreaking book on biblical masculinity, *Wild at Heart*, author John Eldredge talks about what he refers to as the Golden-Haired Woman.[3] The Golden-Haired Woman is the prettiest woman in the room. A man sees her and immediately falls for her. He wants to be with her. She fulfills his heart's desire.

The man drops his current relationship and pursues the Golden-Haired Woman. He succeeds in capturing her, which brings a wild rush of excitement, passion, and obsession. After a while, though, her golden sheen wears off and she becomes an ordinary woman. She becomes familiar, routine, and mundane.

The man walks into a new room and finds a new Golden-Haired Woman. She is the prettiest woman in the room. He sees her and immediately falls for her. He wants to be with her. She fulfills his heart's desire. He drops his current relationship and pursues the Golden-Haired Woman. He succeeds in capturing her, which brings a wild rush of excitement, passion, and obsession. After a while, though, her golden sheen wears off and she becomes an ordinary woman. She becomes familiar, routine, and mundane.

Until he walks into a new room and sees another Golden-Haired Woman. And the cycle continues.

Eldredge's point is that men look to women for mercy, comfort, beauty, and ecstasy, yet these are things which can be found only in

---

3. John Eldredge, *Wild at Heart* (Nashville: Thomas Nelson, 2001), 91. Eldredge attributes his idea to Robert Bly's *Iron John* (Boston: Da Capo Press, 2004).

God.[4] When I read this in the midst of my marriage struggles, all sorts of lightbulbs went off in my head.

Essentially I (and men everywhere) had taken women and put them in the place of God. Not unlike our spiritual ancestors, the ancient Israelites, who were constantly being drawn to worship the idol Baal, I was looking to women to provide for me what only God could.

The idea that women and sex have become idols in our culture should not be a difficult one to grasp. Our culture worships sex as its saving god and adores attractive women with the highest exaltation. If you want to sell a product, attach a sexy woman to the ad campaign. Turn on the radio to hear song after song glorifying sensual women, some explicitly. Listen to the way most radio and TV sports personalities talk about attractive women.[5] Realize pornography is a multi-billion-dollars-a-year industry. Look at the way the paparazzi stalk movie stars and how gossip magazines sell in droves. *Sports Illustrated*'s highest-selling issue by far is their swimsuit edition, which accounts for 11 percent of SI's annual revenue as a company[6] and in 2012 was the bestselling issue in Time Inc.'s magazine franchise.[7] The 2001 edition was aptly titled "Goddesses of the Mediterranean." We have turned attractive women into goddesses, and we worship them as such.

Once we know that attractive women aren't goddesses, we can see them for who they really are. We can learn to look past the goddess mask to see their souls. As we remove this goddess power, we give them the dignity and respect they deserve as daughters and as

---

4. Ibid., 115.

5. One example I remember is when I was watching *Pardon the Interruption* on ESPN. After going on for some time about Victoria's Secret's beautiful women, host Michael Wilbon said to the viewers, "If you don't watch the Victoria's Secret fashion show tonight, you aren't a man!" Pretty lofty definition of manhood there. Thanks for that, Mike.

6. Catey Hill, "For Sports Illustrated, Breasts 5x More Profitable Than Sports?" *New York Daily News*, February 10, 2009, https://www.nydailynews.com/news/money/sports-illustrated-breasts-5x-profitable-sports-article-1.391635.

7. Dina Spector, "How the Sports Illustrated Swimsuit Issue Became Bigger Than the Magazine Itself," Briefing, *Business Insider*, February 14, 2012, https://www.business insider.com.au.

complex, whole human beings. This is a crucial step in our journey to freedom that we'll talk about in chapters 5 and 6.[8]

Today's culture of goddess sexuality is not much different from in Paul's era when he penned God's commands for sexual purity in 1 Corinthians 6:12–20.[9] The Corinthians' carnal attitude toward sex is reflected in the common cultural phrases of the day. Paul quotes a couple of them in verses 12 and 13: "I have the right to do anything," and, "Food for the stomach and the stomach for food."

I can do anything I want sexually, so don't try to stop me.

The stomach is for food, so eat up. The body is for sex, so sex it up.

The people of Corinth were also known for the Temple of Aphrodite, where goddess worship was highlighted by the shrine prostitutes who served there, offering sex to worshipers.

They turned sex into a god.

You can imagine a man waking up on a Sunday morning and having to decide whether he will go to worship God at church or go to the Temple of Aphrodite to worship women and sex.

Who created the world, God or women?

Who can save us from our sins, God or women?

Who will never leave us or forsake us, God or women?

Who can satisfy our deepest longings, God or women?

We ought to realize the obvious answer to these questions. And this realization ought to shine the light of truth on the absurdity of our fantasies. There is no way attractive women can compare with God. To think any of these women, whether in our minds or in our beds, could satisfy us more than God is preposterous. So why do we keep falling into the trap of seeking from women what only God can give us? Why does our culture continue to be so obsessed with

---

8. A friend of mine shared with me a transformative experience he had at the #WeToo Conference. Women came to the front to receive prayers of healing from being objects of lust and objectification. He describes hearing them wail and cry out their pain, pain that he had caused by thinking of them, looking at them, and otherwise treating them as sub-human, whose purpose was to satisfy his desires for love, intimacy, affection, and sex. This is seeing beyond the goddess mask in a deep and sobering way.

9. This passage is explored in more detail on Days 24 and 25.

exalting women and sex when human experience tells us they never fulfill their promises?

The answer is because we are so hungry for intimacy, comfort, acceptance, approval, and validation that we will seek out anything that gives us a whiff of these things. Both married and single men need to grab hold of this concept or we will never find the lasting rest Jesus offers. Jesus' need for intimacy, comfort, affection, approval, and validation are already filled by the Father. This powers his engine, an engine that will never fail. He needs no other alternative, and neither do we.

It's fine to have a secondary engine of intimacy with our wives, but they can never become the primary. They are only human, with limited love and intimacy to supply. That engine is bound to sputter out. If they're all we have, what happens then? We're stuck in the desert with no way out.

It's the same for single guys. A fleeting satisfaction is too easily found in a woman's touch or in the allure of a future marriage. It's too easy to believe the fantasy that the secondary engine of a woman's intimacy can be your primary means of propulsion. It's too easy to convince yourself you need it. But when the Father's affection given to you through Jesus is your primary engine, the secondary one can come and go without stalling your life, joy, and peace.

We have believed the myth that "two halves make a whole" for far too long. *Jerry Maguire* made the line "you complete me" famous, and way too many of us live as if it's true. A woman will never complete you. And your love will never complete a woman. Let the Father's love complete you. It's the only way to wholeness. Whether you are married or single, you can take this to the bank. It has nothing to do with your circumstances. Your wholeness will remain—for better or for worse, for richer or for poorer, in sickness and in health.

Whether you're married or single, if you're plugged in to the primary engine of the Father's affection for you, you won't end up stalled on the side of the road, desperate, longing for something or someone to pick you up.

> If you're using the Forty-Day Devotional Guide
> in the back of this book, turn now to **Day 9**.

When Even Burger King Looks Appetizing

Do you ever go grocery shopping when you're hungry? You get to the checkout aisle and wonder how so many chips, Oreos, and donuts ended up in your cart. Then the cashier asks if he can scan the wrapper of the Snickers bar you've already torn open and chomped into.

It is usually a bad idea to go shopping on an empty stomach because everything looks appetizing when you're hungry. The same is true when watching television commercials for food. I hate to admit it, but when I'm really hungry, even Burger King commercials look appetizing. It's as if my stomach takes over my brain and all of a sudden dinosaur-shaped chicken nuggets sound delicious.[10] When I'm hungry, it doesn't really matter what it is—if it looks or smells halfway decent and will fill my empty stomach, it will do.

The same is true of our drive for intimacy, validation, approval, and acceptance. If we are running on empty and don't already know who we are, we are bound to be drawn to sources of affection which are temporarily satisfying, yet ultimately toxic.

Pornography.

Wandering eyes.

Lust.

Fantasy.

Affairs.

In all of these, I find the Golden-Haired Woman, the "10 out of 10," and I create a situation in which she accepts me. She is attracted to me. She tells me I'm valuable.

The reason the Golden-Haired Woman is so appealing is because of how she makes me feel about *me*. She adores me. She worships me.

---

10. Admit it, you have eaten these. And you still haven't digested them.

If we are being honest, we'll admit that much of our lust and longing comes from wanting to be gods ourselves.[11] We'd never think of it this directly, but what else is at the root of the desire to be adored? We want to have sex with the pretty girl in the room because it would mean she adores us. (We aren't planning to care for her as long as we both shall live. We are planning to use her, then discard her.) We want her to desire us. And if we can't get the girl to have sex with us, or if we don't want to risk the consequences of having sex with her, we can at least flirt with her or fantasize about her, simulating the rush of being desired by such a prize.

If I feel like a loser but the most desirable girl around wants me, then everything changes. I'm not a loser anymore, because this bastion of beauty has said otherwise. My self-perceived value skyrockets.

The allure of being made into a god is extremely powerful. It's the same snare Satan used to get Adam and Eve to rebel against God in the first place: "'You will not certainly die,' the serpent said to the woman. 'For God knows that when you eat from it your eyes will be opened, and you will be like God.'"[12]

Becoming "like God" snared Adam and Eve, it has snared world leaders throughout history, and it snares us when we long for women to worship us.

What better place to find this worship than pornography?[13] The "10 out of 10" women simply line up, all posing passionately for me, all of them wanting me, and I can fantasize about their worshiping me in every way, shape, and form I desire.

The more I look at pornography, the more I get hooked on this craving. The more I get hooked on this craving, the more I see women in real life as an outlet to get my fix. My lustful glances

---

11. We long for this, yet Paul and Barnabas tear their clothes in terror and immediately give God glory when it happens to them (Acts 14:8–18).

12. Genesis 3:4–5.

13. The *Journal of Adolescent Research* reports that 87 percent of men ages eighteen to twenty-six are using pornography. Jason S. Carroll et al., "Generation XXX: Pornography Acceptance and Use among Emerging Adults," *Journal of Adolescent Research* 23, no. 1 (January 2008): 6–30.

at waitresses and receptionists are fueled by this same longing: *Worship me. Please. Tell me I'm desirable. Tell me I have value.*

Saying "I want you" is inaccurate. I care nothing for them. I want what they can offer me, but I don't want them as human beings. "I want you to worship me" hits it spot on. It's not much different from when Caesar demanded that his subjects worship him. The prospect of receiving this type of adoration is tantalizing.

Some will push back here and say that their lust or looking at porn is only about the naked body parts and not about this acceptance and validation stuff. I want you to consider something: Have you ever had a sexual fantasy—in your head, on the porn screen, in real life—in which the woman rejected you, in which she called you ugly, disgusting, and spit in your face? I would wager any amount of money that you never have.

Our sexual fantasies (and the vast majority of porn and sexy advertisements) revolve around seduction. The woman has a look in her eyes and in the shape of her lips that says *I want you, I desire you*. It's not the body parts we are after, it's being wanted. If it were about the body parts, we'd be satisfied with the nude bodies even if we were being rejected. Hear me out, I'm not saying you don't desire the body parts. I'm saying there is a desire deeper than the physical, whether you recognize it or not. You desire physical sex, yes. But what makes the physical sex captivating is the welcome that comes with it. The welcome that says, "I will do this with you. I want you." Do you see the difference?

So if it's not the body parts we are after, what is it?

Acceptance. Value. Approval.

Faux intimacy is better than no intimacy, right?

Even Burger King tastes good when you're starving.

But have you ever watched TV commercials for food on a full stomach? You've just had Thanksgiving dinner and you are stuffed to the gills with your fourth helping of turkey and gravy. You of course have a second stomach for dessert, and the homemade pecan pie was out of this world. So you had three pieces, which you washed down with a big glass of apple cider. Wiping your face with a napkin, you call it a day and somehow roll yourself onto the sofa to turn on the Lions game (which they lose; the Lions always lose).

The first commercial you see is for Burger King. Is it more likely to make you head to the drive-thru or to the puke bucket?

Food looks different when we are stuffed than when we are hungry. The key to avoiding junk food isn't to tell yourself not to eat it; it's to stay full on the right foods. If you're used to eating the good stuff and you're full, the junk is naturally going to lose its appeal.

Temptation looks different when we are filled to the brim with the love, intimacy, and affection of our Father. Whether it's the seductive eyes of pornography, the flirtations of a cute acquaintance, or the temptation to withdraw our affection from our wives, we respond differently if we have experienced wholeness in Jesus.

Jesus was tempted beyond what we can imagine, yet was without sin. He did this by being filled to the brim with his Father's love and living in the truth of his identity as a beloved Son.

Being filled with this moment-by-moment wholeness of who you are in Christ doesn't happen because you make a microwaved acknowledgment of this truth. Jesus fasted for *forty days* meditating on the truth that he was the Father's Son, whom the Father was well pleased with.[14] He had forty days of spiritual meals reminding himself of the truth of who he was. When the lies came, they didn't stand a chance. You have to carve out a daily rhythm in which you too meditate on the truth of your being a beloved son of the Father. (If you're skipping the devotional readings as you read this book, that would be a good place to start.)

Whether it's real life or porn, when we feel our eyes being drawn to a woman, we need to identify what's really going on. We aren't attracted to her just because she's pretty, we are attracted to her because we want her to worship us. We want her to want us.

Name this when it happens.

God comparisons don't typically end well in Scripture. Read 1 Kings 18 if you don't believe me. Putting yourself on the same level

---

14. Matthew 3:16–17.

as the holy God who made Mount Sinai violently shake with fire, smoke, thunder, and lightning (and who struck dead anyone who touched the mountain)[15] is a pretty sobering turn-off to fantasies of being worshiped.

Our natural longing for love, intimacy, and approval doesn't need to be fulfilled romantically or sexually. This is one of the biggest misnomers in our culture today.

Henri Nouwen, who lived a single, celibate life, articulates this struggle and his moment of freedom so well in *The Return of the Prodigal Son*:

> I had to choose between destroying myself or trusting that the love I was looking for did, in fact, exist . . . back home [with God the Father in the parable of the prodigal son]! . . . A voice, weak as it seemed, whispered that no human being would ever be able to give me the love I craved, that no friendship, no intimate relationship, no community would ever be able to satisfy the deepest needs of my wayward heart. . . . [God's voice] called me "son." . . . I started to walk home [to the Father's house] slowly and hesitantly, hearing ever more clearly the voice that says: "You are my Beloved, on you my favor rests."[16]

We find freedom when we realize we don't need someone to validate us because we already are filled up with the validation of Romans 8:4 and Colossians 1:22:

- "In order that the righteous requirement of the law might be *fully met in us*, who do not live according to the flesh but according to the Spirit" (Rom. 8:4, emphasis added).
- "But now he has reconciled you by Christ's physical body through death to present you holy in his sight, without blemish and free from accusation" (Col. 1:22).

---

15. Exodus 19:9–25; 20:18–21.
16. Henri Nouwen, *The Return of the Prodigal Son* (New York: Doubleday, 1992), 50.

We already are filled with Jesus' approval of us, which satisfies our appetite so we don't have to look elsewhere.

So the question is how did our appetite for the affection of a woman and the temporary feeling of wholeness it brings get so disproportionately large? And more important, how do we grow our appetite for God's love and affection so it can replace the unnatural and unhealthy appetite?[17]

Growing this appetite requires training and new rhythms—training to call out the lies, to deeply root ourselves in our adoption as sons, and to hang on to the truths of Scripture and consume them like a buffet over and over again. It requires time with Jesus, the lover of our souls. As you experience the freedom this relational time with Jesus brings, you will long for it more and more.

> If you're using the Forty-Day Devotional Guide in
> the back of this book, turn now to **Day 10**.

---

17. Desiring affection is natural for many, but our culture's appetite for it (and thus our appetite for it) has grown grossly out of control and become distorted.

CHAPTER 4

A FULL JESUS IN AN EMPTY WORLD

Stop Living like They Were Right about You

Too many sermons assume that significant spiritual transformation can happen by acknowledging truths alone. Look back on all of the sermons you've ever heard and nodded your head thinking, "I agree," but then put those truths on the shelf to collect dust for the rest of your life. It's one thing to identify and even confess how we've turned women into gods and sought from them what only God can give us. It is another thing to replace their approval with the approval we already have in Jesus.

When I first read *Wild at Heart*, I thought I was cured. I figured, "How could I possibly continue these fantasies about the Golden-Haired Woman when I know they're idol worship? How could I do that to my God, whom I revere and love?"

Yet it continued.

The answer to why is that we are conditioned to be addicts of approval and acceptance. For most of us, this conditioning began at a very young age. Most of our modern social constructs revolve around it. If we perform well, we are given approval and acceptance.

We are told we are valuable. If we don't perform well, we receive dishonor and punishment. We are told we aren't valuable. This idea of "perform or you are nothing" is as foundational to American culture as apple pie.

If you can hit a curveball, you're praised as valuable and you make the Little League all-star team. If you can't chew gum and walk at the same time, you're picked last in gym class and no one likes you.

If you perform well on a test, you get a good grade and are praised by teachers and parents. If you don't perform well, you fail and no one praises you.

If you accomplish something positive as a child, your parents approve and accept you. If you do something wrong, you are punished and sometimes treated as if you aren't valuable.

If you dress, look, and act a certain way, the popular crowd will accept you. If you don't, they reject you.

Performance-based conditioning comes in all shapes and sizes, most of them unhealthy. They communicate a subtle but potent message: there is something severely inadequate about you.

This message is identical to what Satan told Jesus in the wilderness. And how did Jesus respond? He knew there was nothing inadequate about him because of his identity as the Father's beloved Son. He knew he had nothing to prove. He knew that Satan was wrong and that Satan's judgment of him had no authority.

Most of us can identify key people in our past who have branded us with the message that we are worthless. It may have been a harsh, abusive, or neglectful parent, a reckless coach or teacher, the popular guy or girl who shunned us, a bully. Even if we can't pinpoint a person or a situation, we are bombarded, just living in our culture, with daily messages that we aren't good enough, that we don't fit in, and that we need to do more.

These messages create a void inside that cries out, "Am I lovable? Am I important? Am I acceptable? Am I valuable?" In adult life, if we've been rejected by women (including our wives), that rejection only compounds the voices and doubts from childhood.

We often subconsciously take the faces of these voices and plaster them over the face of God. We now hear God telling us we don't measure up. We hear him telling us we need to do more to earn his love. When we see his face, we don't see love and joy, we see shame and disappointment.

To compensate for this void inside of us, we seek affirmative answers to our questions. The classic case is the teenage girl who doesn't have a loving father in her life. She seeks the love she should have received from her dad from young men who don't really care about her. They make her feel beautiful, important, and powerful during the sexual encounters she has with them, then ditch her once they're done with her. Or she ditches them after getting her fix.

Why does she continue to do this? Her dad told her she was worthless, so she seeks acceptance and approval wherever she can find them.

But here is the key question: is her dad correct?

We'd all answer no. Of course she isn't worthless. Her dad is a jerk and he is wrong.

And this needs to be a turning point for you.

The people in your past who have branded you with the message that you are worthless and need to prove your value are wrong. You need to name these people, acknowledge that their judgment of you has no authority to dictate your value, and then stop living as if they are right. I recommend doing this exercise with a licensed Christian counselor who has a good handle on the gospel.

You are valued, accepted, and approved. This is much more than a feel-good message or pop psychology. This is the foundation of what we receive from the gospel and is backed by the truth of the authoritative Word of God.

Colossians 1:22 and many other passages of Scripture make it clear we are accepted by God because of what Jesus did for us, not because of what we can do for ourselves. This unconditional acceptance is the epitome of love.

We have to relearn to see the biblical face of our Father when he looks down on us. The priestly blessing of Israel gives us this beautiful picture of God's face:

> "'The Lord bless you
>   and keep you;
> the Lord make his face shine on you
>   and be gracious to you;
> the Lord turn his face toward you
>   and give you peace.'"
>
> —Numbers 6:24–26

God's face is shining upon you! He is turning his face toward you![1] When he sees you, he is pleased with you. You can close your eyes and picture this love, joy, and acceptance shining from God's face when he looks at you. *This* is God's face, not the face of your dad or Little League baseball coach. We have to let this truth wash over us again and again.

The gospel tells us that, in Christ, God can't love us any more or less than he already does. The problem is we protect ourselves by building a false self that doesn't allow us to receive this unconditional love and acceptance.[2] The false self is our performance self, our image self, the self we portray to everyone so they'll think we're okay. We strive for goals and achievements, many times in the name of God, to show the world and those who most harmed us in our past that we are valuable. We try to show God and everyone else that we can earn our right standing. We feel too unworthy just to receive it from him, so we try jumping through hoops to feel we can really claim it as ours.

---

1. For more on God's face shining upon you, which authors Jim Wilder and Michael Hendricks describe as the definition of joy, I highly recommend their book, *The Other Half of Church: Christian Community, Brain Science, and Overcoming Spiritual Stagnation* (Chicago: Moody, 2020). The book uses brain science to show how this joy sensation is crucial for our emotional and relational development (pp. 54–56).

2. To read more about your false self and true self, read *Strengthening the Soul of Your Leadership* by Ruth Haley Barton (Downers Grove, IL: InterVarsity, 2008), a book that God used to transform my life as I entered the freedom of his love and grace.

The truth is, we are too ashamed of our true selves to receive God's unconditional love on his terms—that we get to receive it in spite of our limitations, shortcomings, and sinfulness. We know it's not fair (not just) to be loved unconditionally, and we've always been told we don't deserve to be loved like this, aren't worthy of love like this, and need to prove ourselves to be lovable.

Admittedly, this love that gives us our identity as sons can feel contradictory when coupled with living as pardoned sinners before a holy God. Which is it? Are we supposed to live groveling before a holy God, knowing we're not worthy of his love? Or are we supposed to live jumping and dancing with the joy of being new creations[3] who are whole, loved, and accepted as sons of God? The answer is both: a posture of humility plus an identity as beloved. To be more specific, our posture of humility and awe before a holy God (living pardoned) is what allows us to experience with gratitude the full riches of our identity as unconditionally loved sons of the Father. The first truth puts us in the position to experience and be elated by the second. The fantastic news is we get to live in that elation as new creations, not in the despondency of what we used to be before we knew Jesus. But if our gratitude meter ever lags, we only need to go back to the holy mountain of Exodus 19:9–25 to remember how little we deserve the love that's been lavished on us. When the gift begins to feel inconsequential, we allow God to remind us how huge and consequential it is, and then we are able to enjoy it for all it's worth.

Without Christ, we don't measure up. But he makes us new creations. We live in his resurrected power as beloved sons of the Father with a new identity of wholeness, righteousness, and belovedness. This is the oversized five-million-dollar check presented to us on our doorstep. When we become entitled and take the gift of his mercy for granted, it's a healthy reset to remind ourselves that it's a gift we don't deserve, but only so that we can fully live into the riches of the gift once again.

---

3. 2 Corinthians 5:17.

The difficulty is in believing it truly is unmerited. When we believe the lies embedded in us in our childhood and by our culture, we miss the freeing and transforming truth that in Christ, God does indeed unconditionally love us as we are. He's already done all the proving needed for this love to be ours. When we strive to earn this love, we cancel our ability to receive it.

How can someone receive a love they can't earn?

How can a person who believes love is conditional receive unconditional love? They can't.[4]

To receive this kind of love, we have to put our guard down, a guard made of the lies we've been coerced into believing about what we must do to be loved. We have to stop protecting ourselves and lean into Jesus to protect us.

You can't do anything to achieve being lovable, so stop trying.

But Jesus did do something for you because he loved you and found you lovable, which means you *are* lovable. This love didn't grow from your effort. It was proven by his. Understand that this doesn't make his unconditional love any less true. It makes it more true, because if we could gain this love by our merit, we certainly would be able to lose it by our lack of merit. But since Jesus gained it for us by *his* merit, the merit and righteous standing he gave us aren't going anywhere, ever. We will always be loved by God, and we will always be found righteous in Christ.

So now you need to connect the dots.[5] What were the wrong messages people gave you about your worth? In what ways have you attempted to live out these messages, especially in the area of sexual sin? How are your urges for sexual sin fueled by your desire to feel valuable?

Take extended time in solitude with God to allow his unconditional love to melt away the false self that has served you for so many years.

---

4. They certainly are still unconditionally loved by God (that's the beauty of unconditional love!), they just can't embrace it and enjoy it like God intends.

5. Again, I recommend doing this with a licensed Christian counselor. Or better yet, check out PureDesire.org and connect with a counselor who specializes in this.

Develop a daily rhythm with God that prayerfully reminds you of these truths.

Stop living as though hitting a curveball or attaining the perfect woman will make you more valuable as a person.

Know at your core that God didn't make you worthless and that in Jesus' redemption, you are a holy and righteous, approved, accepted new creation.

This is the antidote to shame. Guilt is what we feel when we *do* something bad; shame is what we feel when we think we *are* bad. There's a huge difference. Most of us live mired in shame, and sexual sin only compounds these feelings. There is no more shame once we are in Jesus. Nothing you do can make the Father love you more or less than he already does right now in this moment. I know this because Jesus didn't fail when he died on the cross. His death didn't make you just partially righteous, leaving you to do the rest. He didn't do a B+ job. He did a perfect job.

We are made whole, righteous, and perfect in him. We can live into these truths by being vulnerable to ourselves, God, and others. We already are accepted by the one who matters the most, so we no longer have to hunger for this acceptance from others. We can bring our true, vulnerable selves to the table, and in the right context of other believers, we will be received with the embodiment of our Father's love, being loved as the Father's sons, in whom he is so pleased.

Society says you are what you produce. The gospel says you are what Jesus produced. Your Little League baseball coach was wrong. God is right.[6]

It's time to start living that way.

> If you're using the Forty-Day Devotional Guide in
> the back of this book, turn now to **Day 11**.

---

6. If it's hard to internalize this truth, read *Choose and Choose Again* by Kevin Butcher (Colorado Springs, CO: NavPress, 2016).

Adopted

Do you believe you are God's son, whom he loves and in whom he is well pleased? These are the words God spoke to Jesus, so you might feel like they don't apply to you in the same way.

But consider:

> For those who are led by the Spirit of God are the *children* of God. The Spirit you received does not make you slaves, so that you live in fear again; rather, the Spirit you received brought about your *adoption* to *sonship*. And by him we cry, "Abba, Father." The Spirit himself testifies with our spirit that *we are God's children.* Now if we are children, then we are *heirs*—heirs of God and *co-heirs with Christ*, if indeed we share in his sufferings in order that we may also share in his glory.
>
> —Romans 8:14–17, emphases added

> Therefore, there is now *no condemnation* for those who are in Christ Jesus, because through Christ Jesus the law of the Spirit who gives life has set you free from the law of sin and death. For what the law was powerless to do because it was weakened by the flesh, God did by sending his own Son in the likeness of sinful flesh to be a sin offering. And so he condemned sin in the flesh, in order that *the righteous requirement of the law* might be *fully met in us,* who do not live according to the flesh but according to the Spirit.
>
> —Romans 8:1–4, emphases added

> But now he [God] has reconciled you by Christ's physical body through death *to present you holy* in his sight, *without blemish* and *free from accusation.*
>
> —Colossians 1:22, emphases added

> *Both* the one who makes people holy [Jesus] and those who are made *holy* [us] are of the *same family.* So Jesus is not ashamed to call them *brothers and sisters.*
>
> —Hebrews 2:11, emphases added

What is a co-heir? A co-heir is someone who receives the same inheritance from the king as someone else. So a co-heir with Christ receives what Christ receives. If you are a co-heir with Christ, adopted as God's son, you receive the word, "This is my [s]on, whom I love; with him I am well pleased."

But how can God be well pleased with a sinner like me? Won't my identity always be one who deserves death by a wrathful God on thundering Mount Sinai?

It's all laid out in God's Word.

The "righteous requirement of the law" is "fully met" in us.[7] This means that when Jesus' blood covers us, his perfection is bestowed on us. Like a big blanket placed over us,[8] his perfect blood covers us so that when God looks at us, he sees Jesus' righteousness. Jesus' righteousness becomes our righteousness. Jesus makes us holy. We are without blemish and free from accusation just as Jesus is.[9] This is unconditional love from God. This is salvation. We get 100 percent on the final exam, compliments of Jesus.

God is well pleased with you and approves of you.

So who does God say you are? He says you are his son. He has adopted you.[10]

What happens to someone's last name when they are adopted? It changes. Their identity changes. Their identity is secured. The old has gone, the new has come.[11] They now have the right to their new Father's inheritance, just like the other children in the family. You are not an orphan, so don't live as one. God paid way too much for you.

Not only are you an adopted son of God's, you are also Jesus' bride, whom he is madly in love with.[12] It might feel strange, as a

---

7. Romans 8:4.

8. Galatians 3:27 says we have clothed ourselves with Christ. Romans 13:14 tells us to put on the Lord Jesus Christ.

9. Colossians 1:22.

10. Romans 8:14–17.

11. 2 Corinthians 5:17.

12. Bible verses about God's people being his bride: Isaiah 54:5; 62:5; Jeremiah 2:1–2; Ezekiel 16:8; Hosea 2:16–20; Matthew 25:1–13; Mark 2:19–20; John 3:29; 2 Corinthians 11:2; Ephesians 5:31–32; Revelation 19:7–11; 21:2, 9.

man, to think of yourself as a bride. The point is not to be taken in the physical or literal sense but is a metaphor to communicate the spiritual reality of God's love as more intimate, intense, and powerful than we typically envision it to be. It's essential we comprehend this, because if we don't, it can feel like God's mercy toward us is only a begrudging acceptance of us, rather than the passionate love and desire our hearts thirst for. We can view our atonement as if it were a transaction God made for us just because he's God. We know we'll be in heaven, but we miss out on the romantic love and passion Jesus feels toward us. Ephesians 5:31–32 makes sure we don't miss this: "'For this reason a man will leave his father and mother and be united to his wife, and the two will become one flesh.' This is a profound mystery—but I am talking about Christ and the church."

We'll thoroughly unpack the "one flesh" concept in chapter 8, but in a nutshell, it is referring to sex within marriage. What Scripture is telling us here is that Jesus' relationship to us, the church, is that of a husband's desire for his wife, which is best demonstrated through the act of sex. If you've ever wanted someone to desire you, you have it here with Jesus. God uses the most vivid metaphor in human experience to communicate his love, goodness, approval, embrace, desire, attraction, validation, and acceptance of you. This goes well past a simple acknowledgement that your sins are forgiven. It's a living, breathing longing of God.

This is not the faux intimacy of porn or fantasy. This is intimacy in its purest and most substantive form.

Many of us have been burned by intimacy, rejected by women or rejected by our parents as children. These traumatic and formative experiences have messed with the wiring of our brains in such a way that the idea of intimacy with God is undesirable to us.[13] Meanwhile, here is Jesus saying he is our husband and we are his

---

13. See Curt Thompson, MD, *Anatomy of the Soul: Surprising Connections between Neuroscience and Spiritual Practices That Can Transform Your Life and Relationships* (Wheaton, IL: Tyndale, 2010), for more on how our brain chemistry is changed by childhood trauma and how it can be renewed with spiritual formation in Christ.

wife. Like a battered woman who refuses to trust a man again or an abused foster child who won't receive his adoptive parents' love, we protect ourselves rather than letting our husband, Jesus, protect us.

Are these deep waters? Sure. But you wouldn't be reading this book if you hadn't already tried all of the surface-level stuff.

In the first century, a woman was vulnerable in society if she didn't have a husband. Only men were educated, and only men learned trades, so they were the sole source of economic provision. It was up to fathers to protect and provide for their daughters until the time of each daughter's marriage. At this point, the daughter's husband formally took on the responsibility of providing for and protecting her. For women in the first century, marriage wasn't a matter of convenience or even romance. It was a matter of survival. There were even laws which dictated that if a woman's husband died, his brother had to marry her to ensure her provision and protection.[14] If a woman had no husband or father, she might be forced to turn to prostitution just to survive.

So when you hear that Jesus is the groom and you are the bride, you need to think about the relationship in that context. Can you imagine being a woman all alone in the dark, barbaric first-century world? Can you imagine the fear, the pain, and the longing? Can you imagine how many men you'd chase after, like the Samaritan woman at the well,[15] to attempt to protect yourself and fill your insecurities? This is our state today when we don't find our primary intimacy, affection, and approval in Jesus, our groom.

Ask Jesus if he'll protect you and see what he says.

Ask Jesus if he's like those other voices from your past (or present) who told you you're not valuable and need to earn approval, and see what he says.

In your daily quiet time with the Lord, these are the things to soak in. Throughout your day, these are the things you are to pray without ceasing. This transformation doesn't come through

---

14. Called Levirate marriage. See Deuteronomy 25:5–6.
15. John 4:1–42.

cognitive recognition or through reading this book. It comes through repeated, rhythmic, relational times of prayer with Jesus. If you don't know where to start, prayerfully hear the Father's words to you over and over again: "You are my son, whom I love, and in whom I am well pleased."

Transformation lies in creating new rhythms that allow you to spend daily and weekly times alone with Jesus so he can embed these truths deep into your soul. In an earthly marriage, knowing *about* your spouse is not intimacy; being intimate with her is. The same goes for the spiritual marriage of Christ and his church. If you know this truth in your head but it still feels like you're white-knuckling it in your fight against temptation, chances are you need to spend more of this intimate, relational time with Jesus, your groom. You need to listen more intently to his voice. This goes beyond Bible reading. It is setting the Bible before Jesus and asking him to fill you with its truths, to fill you with the sobering knowledge of the mercy you don't deserve, but that he has lavishly given you. It's asking him to help you believe the Bible's truths in the core of your being, believe to the point where you're not afraid anymore. It's asking him if he is trustworthy and listening to his response. Every step you take in trusting Jesus more securely is one step farther away from thinking that women will fulfill you.

Let him love you.

What separates Jesus and his Word from all other suitors is his authority. Jesus isn't some namby-pamby husband hoping he can protect his bride when the bad guys come knocking. He is a fierce warrior with the ability and authority to protect his wife from anything this dark and barbaric world throws at her. Jesus rested in this authority when Satan tempted him to seek fulfillment elsewhere, and it's the same authority available for you to rely on.

In Matthew 4:1–11, Satan essentially tells Jesus over and over, "You ain't much. Nobody is going to believe you are the Messiah. No one will accept you. Do something impressive! Protect your image! Prove yourself!"

And Jesus replies with truths from his Father, knowing that what

Satan claims as truth is irrelevant, but what God says stands. Satan has no authority as a judge, only God does. So if God, the judge, says you have incredible value as his son, you do. It doesn't matter what Satan says or what your coworkers say or what Hollywood says or what women say about you (and this includes your wife).

If you already know who you are, you don't need to go looking elsewhere in the hope of finding out.

Jesus knew who he was. So whether he was starving in the desert[16] or being abandoned by throngs of followers[17] or hanging from the cross,[18] he didn't need to seek something out to make himself feel whole.

And neither do you.

> If you're using the Forty-Day Devotional Guide in
> the back of this book, turn now to **Day 12**.

My Wife Is Not God Either

My wife is not God.

And neither is yours. Quite a revelation, I know. But you'd be amazed at the change believing this will make in a marriage.

While we view the women we lust over as gods—looking for the things only God can truly provide us with—we do the same thing with our wives, in subtler ways. The marriage school of "you scratch my back and I'll scratch yours" teaches this directly.

When I'm looking to my wife to fill up my love bank, I'm putting expectations on her that should be placed only on God. She becomes my fuel source rather than God. If we ever look to any human, our wives included, as the source of our acceptance and fulfillment, we will be sorely disappointed as well as guilty of idolatry.

---

16. Matthew 4:1–11.
17. John 6:25–71.
18. Luke 23:34, 46. Notice how Jesus continues to go directly to the Father for his strength, even on the cross.

When we realize we've made women into false gods, we are freed from looking to our wives to satisfy our deepest longings. Many of us look to our wives to be perfect and to give us the unending approval we crave. When they're not able to live up to these expectations, our hearts long for them elsewhere.

Sometimes the switch from entitlement to gratitude can be as simple as realizing we've been expecting the wrong things from our wives. I've had three ACL surgeries (do the math: I only have two knees) and as a result have really bad tendinitis in my knees that hinders my playing sports. This can bring on some serious pain if I'm not careful. At this phase of my life, this is probably my biggest health complaint.

If I'm convinced that my morning cup of coffee is going to cure my tendinitis, what is bound to happen? I'm bound to be super disappointed and discontented with that cup of coffee. And if for some reason I'm convinced that coffee is supposed to cure tendinitis, I'll ditch that brand in a hurry (and write a scathing letter to the owner of that coffee company) and then try brand after brand until I find the cure that I'm sure is out there. This analogy is, of course, ridiculous, but isn't this exactly what we do when we expect our wives to fulfill us in the way only Jesus can? On the flip side, if I know that a cup of coffee will never cure my knees, I can instead enjoy it for what it is and be deeply grateful for it. I can let it be coffee. I can savor its aroma, its warmth, and its taste as I savor my morning, thankful to have another day in front of me to live.

Wives are wonderful allies God has given us, but they are not God. They cannot fulfill our every need and deepest longings or satisfy our needs for acceptance and validation. Only God can do that. When we realize this, it brings incredible freedom to our marriages. This freedom allows us to accept our wives' imperfections because we no longer expect that they will give us what only God can. We can simply love them as the broken and imperfect humans they are, who are still very much gifts of mercy from God.

It should not come as breaking news to us that our wives are broken, incomplete sinners. If it does, we need to take a long look at the sinner in the mirror and realize how far from being perfect or godlike we are. Many times, our condemnation of our wives' inadequacies is simply a reflection of our own self-righteousness. We are the good spouses doing what the marriage books tell us to do, and they are the negligent spouses not holding up their end of the deal.

They're not being God for us, and we are not happy about it.

Women are not God, period. If your wife has let you down and you think finding another woman will solve your dilemma, you are simply trading one idol for another, moving from one Golden-Haired Woman to the next.

Men will trade in everything for a divorce or an affair: their relationships with their children, the stability of a two-parent home for their children, their testimonies, their reputations, their ministries, their communion with God, sometimes even their professions—all in the name of plucking out the thorn of their marriages and exchanging them for perceived relief. As if their only meaning in life is found in who they are sleeping with. The irony is, if you ask a man to trade in his divorce or affair for God's will, he won't. One trade-in is worth it to him, but the other somehow isn't.

The Bible is clear about what we undertake when we follow Jesus. We agree to a trade-in: our will for his. Contrary to the instruction of Hollywood's romantic comedies, we are to find our purpose in something much greater than who we go to bed with, something that a man living in a fantasyland fails to grasp.

In Luke 9:23, Jesus tells us, "Whoever wants to be my disciple must deny themselves and take up their cross daily and follow me." Taking up our crosses, like Jesus took up his for us, is the definition of love. We are to love our wives this way, but this is also how we show love to God himself.

There are plenty of days when we won't feel like loving our wives. On these days especially, we need to reorient ourselves to what Scripture tells us worship is and, thus, what our purpose is.

Our purpose is not to be loved by humans. It is to love.[19] Our purpose is not to be worshiped. It is to worship God.[20]

Some husbands endure trials when it comes to sex. Perhaps a wife is going through an illness and is unable to have sex or no longer desires it. Or a wife may no longer desire sex after having a child. Maybe there is hidden trauma that has suffocated a wife's sex drive. These sexless seasons can go on for a long time, sometimes even indefinitely.

As difficult as these trials are, what if you embraced them as opportunities to pick up your cross, worshiping God in the way you show love to your wife, rather than caving to the flesh and its selfish desires? Rather than worry about your needs, what better time to entrench the Father's love for you as your source of fulfillment, filling you up so you can overflow with love to your wife?

I am overwhelmed by how often Jesus showed compassion instead of resentfulness toward people in the pages of the Gospels.[21] He calls us to show the same compassion to our wives.

We don't love our wives for what they can give us. We love our wives because it glorifies God. We love our wives as an act of worship to God. Romans 12:1 tells us true and proper worship is to offer our bodies as living sacrifices to God. Worship is way more than singing songs at church. It is doing God's will daily. The best way we can worship God is to sacrifice ourselves for our wives, to show our wives the love and compassion of God.

Colossians 3:23–24 continues to pile on this truth about worship. It tells us that whatever we do, we should do it with all our hearts, not as if we are doing it for the human in front of us but as if we are doing it for God. There will be days, sometimes many, when your love bank is bone dry and there is no kickback in sight. The natural human

---

19. Matthew 22:36–40.
20. Romans 12:1.
21. Matthew 9:36; 14:14; 15:32; 20:34. And most powerfully, the Father showing compassion to the prodigal son in Luke 15:20.

response is to be resentful. If you can't muster the desire to show her love for her sake, do it for God's. Give him this great gift.

Rather than love your wife in order to be loved in return, love your wife as an act of worship to our merciful God.

> If you're using the Forty-Day Devotional Guide in
> the back of this book, turn now to **Day 13**.

Water Boys for Jesus

You may have heard the chair metaphor for trusting God. It's one thing to look at a chair and believe it will hold you up if you sit on it. It's an entirely different thing to actually sit in the chair. Learning to trust God is one of the hardest things there is.

The Bible verses don't always help.

- "Ask and it will be given to you; seek and you will find; knock and the door will be opened to you. For everyone who asks receives; the one who seeks finds; and to the one who knocks, the door will be opened. Which of you, if your son asks for bread, will give him a stone? Or if he asks for a fish, will give him a snake? If you, then, though you are evil, know how to give good gifts to your children, how much more will your Father in heaven give good gifts to those who ask him!" (Matt. 7:7–11).
- "You do not have because you do not ask God" (James 4:2).
- "You may ask me for anything in my name, and I will do it" (John 14:14).
- "And we know that in all things God works for the good of those who love him" (Rom. 8:28).

It's easy to read verses like these and wonder why God is holding out on us when we ask him for help in our marriages or dating lives.

Why wouldn't God want us to be happy? Why would God want us to suffer?

The reason we get confused is because God answers prayer in accordance with his will, his name, his plan, and his glory—not ours. For the glory and goodness of his kingdom,[22] not our kingdom (you know, that little plot of land you have in your head where you sit on a tiny throne with a tiny crown on your head).

Which is the greater good, God's good or your good?

The answer is obvious. So the next question must be, What is God's good?[23] And to be honest, we aren't always going to like the answer.

You often hear sermons about the powerful metaphors Scripture uses to describe our relationship to God, several of which we've already gone over in this chapter: we are his sons,[24] his friends,[25] his co-heirs,[26] his bride,[27] and his image bearers.[28] But how many sermons do you hear about how we are God's slaves? Romans 6:16–22 clearly calls us slaves to God and slaves to righteousness.

Thankfully, we live in a country where slavery isn't legal anymore. The existence of slavery in today's world ought to make us bristle. But what is slavery? It is one human owning another. The slave who is owned has no rights. No entitlements. The slave is controlled by the master.

Being God's slave is not our only scriptural identity, but it is an important identity we can't ignore. It puts us in our place before a holy God, before the King of Kings.

---

22. Jesus' model prayer, the Lord's Prayer, says this clearly: our Father, hallowed be *your* name. *Your* kingdom come. *Your* will be done (see Matt. 6:9–13). This is the foundation of every prayer we utter.

23. What's ironic about Romans 8:28 is that verses 29–30 tell us what "good" verse 28 is referring to: our justification and glorification. Yet we take verse 28 out of context and take it to mean whatever we want it to mean.

24. Romans 8:15–17; Galatians 3:26–4:7.

25. John 15:15.

26. Romans 8:17.

27. Revelation 19:7–9; 21:2; Ephesians 5:21–33.

28. Genesis 1:27.

Our slavery to God is also unique in that it's a relationship we chose to enter when we received Christ's forgiveness and were freed from being slaves to sin, which is our only other option. Jesus bought us[29] from the captivity of our sins, making the payment through his perfect sacrifice on the cross.

Sin was once our master. Jesus is now our master.

So how does being a slave tie in to trusting God?

Using the same Greek word for slave, Jesus gives a helpful teaching about this in Luke 17:7–10. It's likely not a familiar passage to you, since I doubt it's on many preachers' lists of top ten texts they love to preach: "Suppose one of you has a servant plowing or looking after the sheep. Will he say to the servant when he comes in from the field, 'Come along now and sit down to eat'? Won't he rather say, 'Prepare my supper, get yourself ready and wait on me while I eat and drink; after that you may eat and drink'? Will he thank the servant because he did what he was told to do? So you also, when you have done everything you were told to do, should say, 'We are unworthy servants; we have only done our duty.'"

While these verses are unlikely to appear as framed cross-stitch art hanging in our living rooms, they are helpful when it comes to trusting God in our marriages and dating lives. They are helpful because they put us in our proper place before our master.

If I'm the water boy on the baseball team (which I was in ninth grade[30]), I'm going to have a frustrating season if I keep wondering why the coach doesn't put me in the game. If I eagerly expect to play third base or to pinch-hit, it's only a matter of time before I grow resentful toward the coach and attack his character.

Have you ever been here with God?

This is why Luke 17:7–10 is so helpful. We are water boys in the kingdom of God. We are servants. Apart from Christ, we are *unworthy* servants. We shouldn't even get to be in the dugout or

---

29. 1 Corinthians 6:20; 7:23.

30. Because I didn't make the squad as a player. They called it equipment manager, but we all know a water boy when we see one. I was good at it too.

wear the team hat. Our role is not to play third base. It is to serve the coach, who is guiding the team, and to do whatever he tells us. When we know this, we can thoroughly enjoy the growing relationship we have with our coach and be grateful he lets us be on his team at all.

So what has God, our master, told us to do? What does it look like to serve him and his kingdom? And going into this role, do we fully understand our service is for his glory and his kingdom, not our glory or our kingdom? Do we understand that the good we pray for is his kingdom's good, not our personal good, and that only he knows what this looks like, how to get there, and how to use us as a part of that process? (A process which is spread out over millennia within a fallen world, not just in our lifetimes.)

Do you realize the suffering you experience is maturing you into the man God wants you to be?[31] The overarching good of this maturation is enough that we are to rejoice in the midst of our suffering.[32]

I'm reminded of fasting. I hate fasting. I hate it because I love to eat. But whenever I fast, I always look back on how great an experience it was spiritually, how it kept Jesus on my mind and forced me to draw closer to him to sustain and strengthen me.

The dry seasons in our marriages function the same way. When we hunger for affection in our marriages, we are forced to press into Jesus' affection, just as when we're hungry for food during a fast. We never would be stretched and strengthened if it weren't for the season of scarcity we are going through—and yes, sometimes this is a long season, possibly even an unending one. But if the answer to our prayers is that we become more intimately connected with Jesus and thus become more like him, learning how to love like him, there is truly no better answer in the entire world.

Did you grow up in church singing the song, "I'd rather have

---

31. Hebrews 12:3–16 explains that God will use suffering as a discipline to mature us and refine us.

32. Romans 5:3–5; 1 Peter 1:6–9.

Jesus than silver or gold. I'd rather be his than have riches untold. . . . I'd rather have Jesus than anything"?[33]

I did.

This is your chance to put that song into action.

Would you truly rather have Jesus than anything? If so, pray these prayers the next time you are struggling:

Jesus, I want you more than women.
Jesus, I want you more than sex.
Jesus, I want you more than marriage.
Jesus, I want you more than a _____ wife.
Jesus, I want you more than anything.
And I have you.

Can you feel that?

He truly is the best thing in the entire universe, and you have him.[34]

Have this conversation with Jesus often, especially when you're struggling.

The truth of the gospel is that we need nothing in addition to what Jesus provides us.[35] He is all sufficient.[36]

Do you realize God sovereignly and specifically chose you to show his unchanging, unconditional love to your wife, that you are *the* agent and witness of this love to her?

The point is that marriage is not for our comfort, so why should we be surprised when God doesn't answer our prayers for relational comfort in the way we expect?

---

33. Rhea F. Miller, "I'd Rather Have Jesus," 1922.

34. For more on this, see Noah Filipiak, "House Money: Releasing God from 'Your Best Life Now' and the Freedom This Brings," blog post, January 28, 2019, https://www.noahfilipiak.com/house-money-releasing-god-from-your-best-life-now-and-the-freedom-this-brings, and Noah Filipiak, "When Your Hope Is in the Best Thing" (sermon), The Flip Side with Noah Filipiak, August 14, 2019, https://www.noahfilipiak.com/ep-14-noahs-sermon-when-your-hope-is-in-the-best-thing.

35. For a life-changing book on this, read *Jesus + Nothing = Everything* by Tullian Tchividjian (Wheaton, IL: Crossway, 2011).

36. 2 Corinthians 12:7–10.

Marriage isn't designed to fulfill our selfish desires or to make us happy.[37] It's designed to make us holy. In the long run, holiness produces lasting peace and joy as God uses it to craft us into the persons we were always meant to be.[38]

First Peter 2:18–25 goes so far as to say that suffering is a way of following in Jesus' footsteps. We are to respond to it the way Jesus did. Jesus chose to trust the Father to take care of his needs rather than to take things into his own hands.

This setup isn't unique to you. The Bible is full of stories describing times when God's servants suffered greatly for the good of God's glory and kingdom. It's pretty hard to find people in the Bible who didn't suffer for God's kingdom.

Look at Jesus, praying in great anguish in the garden of Gethsemane, "Father, if you are willing, take this cup from me; yet not my will, but yours be done."[39] Of course, the cup he is referring to is the death he is about to endure on the cross. Jesus asks the Father to spare him of this, a prayer we know isn't answered the way Jesus wants. Not only does the Father not spare him, physical torture soon accompanies the emotional anguish Jesus is praying through.

And we can't forget our buddy Hosea. I say "our buddy" because if there's anyone who can teach us about serving God through our marriages, it's Hosea. God told Hosea to love and marry the prostitute Gomer as an example to the Israelites of their unfaithfulness to God. Talk about suffering as a husband. Yet Hosea trusted God and remained faithful to Gomer and to God because he was a servant of God, just as you and I are. He surrendered his will and rested in God's.

We don't always see the big picture, but we know God, and we know God is faithful, good, sovereign, and trustworthy. And we also

---

37. It's not a sin to be happy or to want to be happy. But we need to find our happiness in Christ and not approach marriage as if that were its purpose.

38. Tim Keller, *The Meaning of Marriage: Facing the Complexities of Commitment with the Wisdom of God* (New York: Dutton, 2011), 132–33.

39. Luke 22:42.

know Jesus has already won the victory and there will be a day when we are with him and suffering is no more. Finally, we know God has given us a job to do today: to love our wives the way Jesus loves us. In so doing, we advance God's kingdom on earth and become more and more conformed to the image of his Son.[40]

> If you're using the Forty-Day Devotional Guide in
> the back of this book, turn now to **Day 14**.

The Replacement Program

I'll end this chapter with a disclaimer, as I did in chapter 2. I'm not advocating that you turn a blind eye to the problems in your marriage or to the areas your wife needs to grow in. I'm saying there are two ways to approach these issues: one is with God calling the shots, and the other is with you calling the shots.

You must put God on the throne and no one else—not supermodels, not your wife, and not you. You must make God your power source, the engine that propels your fulfillment, the food that fills your stomach, and the groom who protects and provides for you. Let God quench your thirst for validation, which he promises to do, so you don't have to go looking for it elsewhere.

We have to develop an appetite for God's truth that replaces our unhealthy, overdeveloped appetites for sex and for being worshiped via sex. A biological drive for sex is natural and created by God, but our contemporary appetite for it is out of control.

Coffee, sushi, and beer are all considered to be acquired tastes. Many people don't like them at first but by incremental exposure develop an appetite for them. Something similar happens with sex. At no time in history has there ever been as much exposure to sex as in our culture today—whether it's images of scantily clad women on social media, barely-dressed NFL cheerleaders,

---

40. Romans 8:29.

streaming TV's sex and nudity norms, or the *Sports Illustrated* swimsuit edition in the checkout aisle.

Yet any man born after 1980 has been raised on them.[41]

To curb this appetite for sex, we have to do more than shut it off: we also must replace it with something that is even better in the long run. In the same way our voracious appetite for sex was acquired by exposure, we must raise our appetite for God's truths.

At first taste, sitting down to open the Bible as a daily practice or taking an extended time in solitude with the Lord might feel mundane and difficult, like trying to stomach your first-ever cup of black coffee. But when the solution for our sexual immorality is to realize that we are approved and whole in Christ and that we don't need to look for approval and wholeness in lust or in our marriages, we are compelled to sit in the stream of God's healing presence, to soak in it daily, just as Jesus did in his forty days in the wilderness. I encourage you to set up a covenant with some other men to do this daily. What I love is that when we commit to this, eventually what once felt like an obligation becomes our life-giving fuel station. When we experience the change in perspective we get from this time with the Lord and the feeling of freedom it brings, obligation soon turns to desperation and anticipation.

What's exciting about all of this is that it is possible.

Write down the truths of who you are in Christ and allow the Holy Spirit to remind you of them day after day after day.

Don't spend time with God out of discipline. Do so out of desperation.[42] It will soon become a delight you can't live without.

Spending this time with Jesus and knowing that your value and identity are in him will relieve your impulse to turn women into objects, which we'll turn to next.

---

41. Estimating roughly when the internet became commonplace during a boy's adolescent years.

42. This is a quote from a talk I heard by Gary Haugen of the International Justice Mission at the 2013 Justice Conference in Philadelphia. Gary was referring to the two fifteen-minute breaks IJM's entire office takes during each workday to pray. IJM is a leading Christian antitrafficking agency composed mostly of lawyers.

In Your Small Group

Scan this QR code or go to www.beyond thebattle.net/videos and watch "Session 3 (Chapters 3–4): Golden Gods with Golden Hair." (All small group resources are free.)

CHAPTER 5

OBJECTIFICATION

The Loss of Humanity

Strings Attached

The reason the Golden-Haired Woman seems so irresistible is because we place godlike expectations on her. This is why she loses her sheen. We see the woman and become infatuated with her as if she were divine, only to be sobered later when we discover she is a limited human being. She didn't just appear gorgeously out of nowhere, no strings attached, only to return to the fantasy sky.

There are always strings attached, strings that only a husband can tend within the one-flesh union of marriage. This is what it means to be a human being.

She's not madly in love with us the way it seems in the photo or in our imagination, and her hair and makeup don't always look perfect in real life. The Golden-Haired Woman has needs. She has hopes, dreams, and ambitions. She has a personality, flaws, quirks, strengths, and weaknesses. She has secrets, vulnerabilities, and hurts. She has insecurities, boundaries, and limitations. She has a soul.

She has strings attached.

We may think it's a compliment to give a woman godlike status. But what are gods and goddesses? What are idols? Idols are objects. They are lumps of gold or bronze or stone, molded or chiseled into figurines. They are statues, they are legends, but they are not real. They are figments of our imagination.

A woman is a *her*; a goddess is a *that*.

And a *that* can be easily consumed and discarded.

We dehumanize a woman when we ignore or deny the limitations, flaws, and vulnerabilities that make her human.

Meanwhile, these limitations, flaws, and vulnerabilities are some of our greatest weapons to destroy lust's tractor beam. When we see a woman as a human being, we realize the inappropriateness of seeing her any other way.

Do you want to be attracted to a *her* or to a *that*? Which do you think we were created for?

One of the biggest things the pornography age has done is separate sexual intimacy from human intimacy, body parts from human beings. This separation goes against what makes us human. It has been forced on us and has forced its way into our interactions with women and our desire for sex.

The root of lust is this dehumanization, whether in pornography, in an indulgent gaze on the street, or in the fantasy of running off with a flirtatious friend. Every time we lust over a person, we dehumanize that person. We see and covet body parts while ignoring what makes that person human.

We turn into soul-devouring, soul-crushing, soul-discarding, selfish beasts.

Can you think of other sins that take away someone's humanity? Murder, rape, slavery, abuse, and exploitation all come to mind. Not a pleasant grouping. But why are these things wrong? Why do they go against God's perfect and loving design for his creation? The answer may seem obvious: We are created in God's image[1] with dignity, depth, wholeness, and value. It's who we are. When we murder, rape, abuse, enslave, and exploit, we discard the innate

---

1. Genesis 1:27.

dignity, depth, wholeness, and value God has given a person. We use someone else for selfish gain.

The dehumanization in lust follows the same pattern of selfishness, exploitation, and entitlement that those more gruesome acts do.

Every time we lust, we condition ourselves to see all women this way. Our neural pathways have been patterned by the porn we grew up on, the cleavage of NFL cheerleaders, the Victoria's Secret fashion show, the promiscuity of pop culture, and the myriad other lustful stimuli that we've taken in. Our brains operate the way they have been trained to operate.[2]

These stimuli teach us to see women as some*thing* to consume, rather than as some*one* God has made. There is no on-off switch for this pattern of thinking, as if we can compartmentalize our porn thinking and keep it from invading our real-world thinking.

This is a huge problem even if you're single and never plan to be married. You will never be able to be in healthy community with women if your mind is stuck in this pattern. And I wouldn't want my wife or daughters to be in your line of sight.

We cannot merely treat the symptoms of lust and expect to be victorious. We can't put filters on our computers, meet weekly for accountability, and whip our physical selves into submission to "bounce our eyes"[3] and expect change to follow. These things have their place, but none provide lasting solutions as primary strategies.

When lust has infected our hearts, we no longer see women

---

2. Luke Gilkerson, *Your Brain on Porn: Five Proven Ways Pornography Warps Your Mind and Three Biblical Ways to Renew It*, Covenant Eyes ebook, https://learn.covenant-eyes.com/your-brain-on-porn-1/.

3. Stephen Arterburn and Fred Stoeker, with Mike Yorkey, *Every Man's Battle: Winning the War on Sexual Temptation One Victory at a Time* (Colorado Springs, CO: Waterbrook, 2000), 125–39. To "bounce your eyes" is to train yourself to immediately look away from women and lustful images so that your attraction to your wife will increase and be more fulfilling. I found this strategy to be too symptoms-based, not addressing why I was looking in the first place. This approach also leads to disillusionment and frustration if the "sexual payoff" promised in *Every Man's Battle* (138–39) never happens for you. Trying to bounce your eyes to get a sexual payoff trains us to continue to live in entitlement.

the way God created us to see them. We are crippled in our following Jesus' path of lovingly bringing dignity to others. Let's call this infection out for what it is and get to work on curing it.

The next time an attractive woman crosses your path and lust starts to numb your mind, snap out of it by seeing the strings attached. Declare "daughter, mother, wife, sister" over and over again. See her soul. It sounds clumsy, but in the heat of the moment, it will sober your mind and allow you to see who this woman really is and what your relationship to her should be.

> If you're using the Forty-Day Devotional Guide in
> the back of this book, turn now to **Day 15**.

Daughters

Like many couples, my wife and I have had up-and-down seasons in our marriage. There have been times (more often than I'd like to admit) when I've fantasized about getting a divorce, especially in the early years of our marriage. I even seriously considered it once. (See chap. 9.) One common denominator in our marital struggles has been my idolatrously large—and thus unmet—desire for human affection, fueled by my insecurity. Most of the things I've written about so far are things I've been guilty of: feeling entitled to my unrealistic, godlike expectations of my wife, operating with a kickback mentality when I show her love, and fantasizing about some other woman being the god my wife can't be for me.

Selfishness.

Our first child was born in 2011, a girl. As soon as she was born, I was in love with her. Loving her through her toddler years was a breeze. We were (and still are) best buddies, always laughing, playing games, and cuddling.

I pray a lot for my daughter. I pray for her to fall in love with Jesus and put her faith in him. I also can't help but think about the man she may marry someday, the man who will hold her hand at the altar, look into her eyes, and before God, friends, and family (including me) vow to love her, protect her, and cherish her forever.

For better or for worse.

Through thick and thin.

Through gaining weight.

Through illness.

Through flaws.

Through mood swings.

Through needs.

I then think about what I would want to do to this man if he were to break this vow he made to my precious daughter. If he were to put his selfishness in front of his faithfulness to her. If he were to chase after some other woman or some other dream because it was easier for him or made him feel better.

Let's just say Galatians 5:12 comes to mind.[4]

My daughter isn't going to be a perfect wife. She's human. But she is my precious and beautiful daughter. And she will always be precious and beautiful to me. If she opens herself up to a man, putting herself in the most vulnerable position possible, marrying him and trusting him with all of her heart, and he leaves her in the dust because something better comes along—I will lose every ounce of respect for that man.

I then look at photos of my wife when she was my daughter's age. Playing with her dad. Cuddling with him. Laughing with him. She looks strikingly similar to our daughter: blond hair, pale skin, huge smile.

And I think about her dad.

And how her dad must have cherished her, the very same way I cherish my daughter. And how her dad still cherishes her, the very same way I will cherish my daughter when she's an adult. And how if I had left my wife for any of the selfish reasons I've listed, he would

---

4. Galatians 5:12: "As for those agitators, I wish they would go the whole way and emasculate themselves!"

have had every right to pummel me into the ground (and God forbid, go Galatians 5:12 on me).

Why this sharp contrast in perspective?

Because a dad doesn't objectify his own daughter.[5]

A dad doesn't see his daughter as a means to his pleasure or as someone who always has to be perfect. He doesn't see her as body parts, as a potential conquest, or as the one responsible for showering him with adoration and making him whole.

He sees her as a soul.

He sees her as a human being.

It's ironic that I expect my wife to be perfect, but with my daughters I go out of my way to reassure them that it's okay not to be perfect, that my love is most tender and expressive toward them when they are imperfect.

Every woman on this earth is a daughter. Because my wife is a daughter, I am called to honor and cherish her with the dignity she deserves.

The women I'm tempted to lust over are daughters as well. Daughters of their earthly dads, but also daughters of God, the Father of all. How does *he* feel when I look at his uniquely created daughter with lust in my heart?

When you see a woman, imagine her in her childhood. See her soul beam forth. See her soul as it was before the universe ever existed.

Every woman has the same dignity and value my daughters do, and I need to view them that way. One of the most helpful tools for me when I'm tempted to check a woman out is to pretend she is one of my young daughters all grown up. I feel anger and disgust against lust when I frame it this way, seeing and feeling my response the

---

5. I wish this were true 100 percent of the time. I know of several sex-offense cases where a father has molested his daughter. I lament this and pray for the men who struggle with this. If this is you, dig deep into the truth of the gospel in these pages and get help before you act out. But I don't believe this is the norm, and thus a valid point remains that will help many men. For the men who can't fathom sexualizing their daughters, this point of relation to all the women they see carries immense power. We all know why the dad in the doorway is holding the shotgun when the boyfriend pulls up to pick her up. Because this is *his* daughter and you'd better treat her as such.

way God does. When my flesh wants to consume her, I can remind myself of the truth that she is worth so much more than that. When my flesh wants to turn her into an object, a slave, my heart jumps in and says, "How can you do that to someone's daughter?"

If I wouldn't want someone looking at my daughter this way, I'd better not look at this woman this way.

> If you're using the Forty-Day Devotional Guide in
> the back of this book, turn now to **Day 16**.

Objectification All Grown Up

"Porn will lead you places you never thought you'd go," says Craig Gross and the XXXchurch team as they discuss their experience of helping people out of porn and sex addiction.[6] Gross recalls a time when they were ministering in Amsterdam's red-light district (where women are legally sold in storefront windows for sex) and their cab driver told them that what they were seeing was nothing. If they wanted to see the real place to get extreme sex for sale, he could drive them twenty miles outside of the city.

At 2:00 a.m. and in subzero cold, Gross and his XXXchurch team observed rows of cars on a dead-end street a mile off the freeway. A car would pull up and a male, female, or transvestite prostitute would go into the car to have sex with the tourist. These prostitutes didn't have legal papers, so they would sell themselves for half of what it cost in the red-light district. There were about twenty carports, like those you'd find at an apartment complex, where drivers would park for their paid sex. Gross describes feeling like he was at the gates of hell, with condom wrappers littering the ground and the empty faces of the prostitutes of all ages staring out through the freezing air.

The drivers weren't there because they lacked money. Many of the vehicles bore Mercedes-Benz or Jaguar logos. These drivers were

---

6. See www.XXXchurch.com.

coming twenty miles outside of town because there were fewer regulations, and they could do whatever they wanted to the prostitutes because they were undocumented and couldn't seek help.[7]

Porn will lead you places you never thought you'd go. Why is this?

People sometimes use the candy store analogy to justify their porn usage. It's okay to look, as long as you don't touch. Or it's okay to have a little, as long as you don't get carried away. If this theory were true, then how did the tourists in luxury cars end up where they did? Their journey into the extremes of paid sex certainly didn't start in Amsterdam.

Where do rapists get their start?

Where do most child molesters and the people on the sex-offender registry get their start?

Where does the mindset that women can be bought and sold as sex slaves come from?

It all starts with pornography.

Think about it: If people are trained to turn women into objects, why is it so surprising when someone acts on that training? If porn has trained your mind to see women as objects, isn't the next step to act as if they are objects?

It's like training a soldier to kill. Sure, soldiers train with dummies and rubber bullets, but the purpose of the training is to get their bodies and minds ready for war. We aren't shocked when they kill enemy soldiers. It's what they've been trained to do.

Porn trains the brain in the same way. It's naive to think that a person won't eventually touch the candy, then eat the candy, and then want more of the candy.

When you realize how much our culture celebrates pornography (including Victoria's Secret fashion shows and *Sports Illustrated* swimsuit editions), the shock we express at sex crimes is the ultimate cultural hypocrisy. The greatest shame in our culture is to be a child molester; in prison, even other inmates will beat you up for this. Yet we pump softcore pornography into every checkout aisle

---

7. Craig Gross, *The Dirty Little Secret* (Grand Rapids, MI: Zondervan, 2006), 122–23.

and every TV channel and think of consuming hardcore porn as a rite of passage into adulthood.

The truth is, many times the girls you see loaded onto your computer screen are the same girls who are pimped as sex slaves in an East Asian brothel. They are property. And as with any commodity, their owners want to squeeze the maximum profit out of them. When they aren't selling them to tourists to be raped, they'll put them in front of a camera, forcing them to smile at you as if they are loving the attention you're giving them and the time you're spending on their sites.

You are also enriching their pimps and casting your vote for more sex slavery by financing it. Even if the porn site is free, your clicks bring in revenue from advertisers.

Sobering, isn't it?

Did you know there are more than 4.8 million sex slaves in the world today, more than 1 million of which are children?[8]

Did you know the average age of a girl taken into sex slavery *in the United States* is thirteen years old?[9]

Did you know human trafficking is the fastest growing and second largest criminal industry in the world, behind drug trafficking?[10]

Did you know sex slavery rakes in billions of dollars each year, with a pimp able to make $150,000 to $200,000 per child they "own"?[11]

Did you know the average victim of human trafficking is raped

8. *Global Estimates of Modern Slavery: Forced Labour and Forced Marriage* (Geneva: International Labour Organization, 2017), 39–40, https://www.ilo.org/wcmsp5/groups/public/---dgreports/---dcomm/documents/publication/wcms_575479.pdf.

9. Development Services Group, Inc., "Commercial Sexual Exploitation of Children Sex Trafficking: Literature Review," Office of Juvenile Justice and Delinquency Prevention (2014), 2, https://ojjdp.ojp.gov/mpg/literature-review/csec-sex-trafficking.pdf.

10. United States Department of Health and Human Services, "Human Trafficking Fact Sheet" (2004), https://www.hsdl.org/?view&did=23329.

11. United States Department of Justice, National Center for Missing and Exploited Children, Demi and Ashton Foundation, cited in web page sidebar for Youth Radio, "Trafficked Teen Girls Describe Life in 'The Game,'" *All Things Considered*, December 6, 2010, https://www.npr.org/2010/12/06/131757019/youth-radio-trafficked-teen-girls-describe-life-in-the-game.

six thousand times and the life expectancy for sex trafficking victims is seven years?[12]

Did you know you support this industry, either directly or indirectly, every time you look at porn?

Did you know no industry can survive without a demand for it?[13]

Even if you could guarantee your porn activity isn't with any girls posing against their will (which would be nearly impossible), you're still creating demand for the product. You're still keeping the business booming. You're still allowing your mind to be contorted to the thinking that it's okay to buy girls for sex, that it's okay to consume women, a mindset that will inevitably lead you places you never thought you'd go.[14]

> If you're using the Forty-Day Devotional Guide in
> the back of this book, turn now to **Day 17**.

When Women Want to Be Objectified

Defining lust as the dehumanization of a human being can be a pretty convincing argument to avoid it. This objectification could be labeled mental rape, something none of us would want to be associated with and which Jesus condemned.[15]

But what about the women who want to be objectified? What about when they go along with it?[16]

---

12. Into Freedom, http://www.intofreedom.org/issues.

13. Visit http://sharedhope.org/become-a-defender/ and become a Defender (it's free), committing to end the demand for sex slavery.

14. Even if you never end up parking your Mercedes in a sex carport in the Netherlands at 2:00 a.m., porn and the mindset of objectifying women will still plague your life and your relationships in a multitude of ways.

15. Matthew 5:27–28.

16. It's important that I define what I mean by objectification here. I do not mean the physical abuse that many women have to endure at the hands of men, which is the lowest form of being treated as an object. This type of abuse is also seen in strip clubs where women are treated like absolute trash by men's words, even when physical abuse isn't occurring. No woman wants this type of objectification, and to ever think they do is how rape culture is created. The way I'm using *objectification* here is consistent with how I've

Surely not every woman in pornography is doing it against her will. Not all of them are involved in sex trafficking or owned by a pimp. Many elect to go into the sex industry of their own volition. They want you to buy their magazines or visit their strip clubs. Some crave the attention, others need the money, and for others it's just a necessary part of their gig. Many of these women, especially sensual pop stars and swimsuit models, are A-list Hollywood celebrities.

Isn't it okay to objectify someone who is longing for it? Both sides are getting what they want, aren't they?

Or what about the girl who is hoping a guy brings her home from the bar?

Or your girlfriend who knows she's just the flavor of the month but is okay with that?

Or the flirtatious young lady you work with who wears the tight tops and short skirts? She must know what she's doing, right? Guys are bound to gaze at her, which is what she has in mind when she meticulously fashions her hair, makeup, and outfit in the morning.

The lies of Satan cut both ways. While Satan lies to men by telling us it's okay to devour women for our enjoyment, he lies to women by telling them that exploiting their bodies is a valid way to find value, approval, significance, or even a lucrative career.

Whether they know it or not, women who exploit their bodies have bought Satan's lie that they are worth nothing more than their body parts.

The tragedy is that body parts age and their beauty fades. Why do you think so many "age-defying" products are sold to women of all ages so they can try to look twenty-three again? This lie is why—the lie that value and identity are found only in physical appearance.

But physical appearance has nothing to do with our souls. Women are told they are nobodies, with nothing of substance to offer the world besides their bodies, and many have bought this

---

been using it in this book: that sex is only about body parts. When a man looks at a woman as only body parts and is attracted to that, he is objectifying her. So in the following paragraphs, I'm referring to the women who seek out and enjoy this type of visual attention or enjoy this type of casual sex and seek it out.

lie. Many would ardently disagree with me for even claiming this. Some will argue that porn and promiscuity empower women, that they give them power over men or power over their own finances. But being empowered by a lie is not the kind of power we should be seeking, nor is domineering the opposite sex, a sword which cuts both ways. Endorsing this sort of empowerment is like praising drug dealing because it earns income for dealers and gives them power over addicted users.

Sexual empowerment through objectification tells women that they are unworthy to be accepted as fully human. It tells them that instead they need to exploit their bodies, the outer shell of who they really are, in order to get ahead and receive the attention and acceptance already due them as dignified image bearers of God. In Christ, there's no need to wield this sort of power. There's no need to snatch at this type of validation because Jesus has already paid for us at great price and given us true validation.

So even if a woman begs you to objectify her, don't cave in to her confused demand. Do not reinforce the lie she is projecting about herself. Instead, pray for her. Share Christ with her. Do anything but make matters worse by feeding the fiery lie the enemy has convinced her of. When you reject the empty lie she's been deceived into believing about herself, you are instead showing her that she does have value.

Picture a child who was born into labor slavery. He has no memories outside of being owned, beaten, and forced to do manual labor. Every message ever given to him is that he is property and that outside of this, he is worthless.

The slave master dies, and you happen to meet this child, now a teenager. "Put me to work," he says. "Beat me. It's who I am and all I know." How do you respond?

While this example is a little far-fetched, I hope you understand the point. There is no way you would beat that poor child just because he told you to. You would be aghast and drop the whip immediately. You would plead with him, trying to communicate to him that he is so much more than property. He is so much more than an object to be used for someone else's gain and pleasure. You would tell him about how much Jesus loves him and longs to adopt him and give him a new identity, about how God created him with dignity and purpose in God's own image. You would pray for him. You would do everything in your power to convince him that what he's been taught about himself his entire life is not the way it was meant to be.

And if all else failed and the child persisted in believing a lie about who he is, you still would not cave. You would be sad, and you would leave, but you wouldn't strike him or force him to work. You wouldn't reinforce the lie that he already believed about himself, the lie Satan deceived him into believing.

Mouse clicks are like votes of support—the porn companies know this. When you click the mouse for more porn, you are telling those women, "Satan was right about where your value comes from." None of us wants that.

What if the child in the metaphor never found another person willing to take up the whip? What would this eventually force the child to understand?

What if the demand for pornography and strip clubs suddenly dried up? What if the clicks stopped? What if nobody bought the *Sports Illustrated* swimsuit edition anymore? What if skin stopped being the top-selling global commodity because consumers finally stopped reinforcing the lies that models and actresses have been deceived into believing about themselves? What if we treated every girl and woman with dignity and respect for her character, personality, and accomplishments, rather than rewarding her for showing off her skin? How would this change the way women think about and advertise themselves? How would it change what they think a man is looking for? How would it change how they dress? How would it change the way they act? How would it change their sense of self-worth?

Exactly.

We'll never be able to make wholesale change in the lost and fallen world that we live in, but we can dream about what this could look like in the church. What if women were treated the way Jesus treated Mary Magdalene, the sinful woman who washed his feet with her hair,[17] or the Samaritan woman at the well, who had been through five husbands and was now testing out a sixth?[18] Why did all of these women turn to Jesus? What if he had objectified them, flirted with them, and lusted over them instead of honoring their personhood as daughters?

Treating women the way God designed, rather than the way culture screams for them to be treated, creates such a beautiful picture of the Father's love. It carves a clear path to the gospel and to authentic Christian community for the church and a watching world.

We must create this picture in our marriages as well, though. Otherwise we will have only traded one form of objectification for another.

> If you're using the Forty-Day Devotional Guide in
> the back of this book, turn now to **Day 18**.

---

17. Luke 7:36–50.
18. John 4:1–42.

CHAPTER 6

MARRIED TO OBJECTIFICATION

Turning Your Wife into Porn

The sexual purity advice given to me during my single years was to "starve your eyes" from attractive women by "bouncing your eyes" away from them.[1] When you see an attractive woman or an arousing advertisement, you are to bounce your eyes away and look at something else. Friends have told me they were advised to wear rubber bands on their wrists so they could snap themselves every time they had to bounce their eyes.

The idea behind this type of eye-aversion training is if you starve your eyes of sexual stimuli, you will increase your hunger for your wife. If you are constantly looking at sexual stimuli, your wife can't compete and she will become less attractive to you. The theory is that your body has a quota of "sexual bowls" it desires to eat each day. If you fill those bowls with lust, your body won't be hungry for your wife. But if you starve yourself and save the bowls for your

---

1. Stephen Arterburn and Fred Stoeker, with Mike Yorkey, *Every Man's Battle: Winning the War on Sexual Temptation One Victory at a Time* (Colorado Springs, CO: Waterbrook, 2000), 125–39.

wife, you will see her as attractive and desire her. This methodology supposedly ensures that if you do this well, you will receive a "sexual payoff"[2] in return.

While it is necessary to abstain from lust to have a healthy sex life in your marriage, this approach is fundamentally flawed. While training yourself to bounce your eyes is a good discipline, the way the payoff is described still defines sex on Satan's terms. It might work in the short term, but in the long run, it leads to frustration and disillusionment. This discipline simply trains us to view our wives as our porn. It still defines sex as being about body parts, not about a person. It still defines sex as an act of consuming. Instead of objectifying unknown women for our pleasure, we objectify our wives for our pleasure. Sex is not about one person eating "bowls."

This strategy is like saying, "We know what you really want is to go to the all-you-can-eat buffet rather than eat the bread and water at your house, but if you stop yourself from walking into the buffet, if you starve yourself from it, eventually your body will become hungry enough that the bread and water will actually taste good to you." This is not God's intention for our marriages, nor is it a sustainable solution.

This strategy enlists our wives in an unwinnable competition that still degrades them as pieces of meat. While they aren't the grade-A we desire, their lower-grade bodies will carry us through our body-parts fix if we are able to block everything else out. Like being stranded on a deserted island with only one picture of a naked woman, it's better than nothing.

This obviously is not God's design for the way we view our wives. He want us to see them not as consumable objects but as whole and unique persons within a one-flesh[3] relationship. The "starve your eyes" method still defines our wives as a set of body parts we are in love with, not as whole persons we are in love with. In God's design for intimacy, we don't fall in love with a human body; we fall in love with a human person. There is a huge difference.

---

2. Ibid., 138–39.
3. Genesis 2:24.

This strategy is also not sustainable. Pitting your wife as an object versus the buffet of objects available in an oversexualized world makes the latter even more desirable when you get a whiff of it as it passes by, reminding you of what you're missing out on. It's only a matter of time before the lure of this aroma becomes too strong and you stumble through the buffet doors to satisfy your watering mouth.

We cannot fight fire with fire, because in doing so, we concede to Satan that sex within marriage is of the same substance as sexual immorality. We accept his definition of sexual attraction: that it's all about body parts and objectification.

The Bible calls us out on this when it tells us sex isn't like simply filling up the stomach with food (a carnal act of consumption); it is the act of bringing two people together as one flesh—one complete, deep, complex being.[4] Bouncing your eyes so you can reluctantly consume less-appetizing sexual bowls from your wife only reinforces the "sex as food" mentality. Instead, you need God to rewire your mind to embrace his design for sex, marriage, and ultimately people.

> If you're using the Forty-Day Devotional Guide in
> the back of this book, turn now to **Day 19**.

Turning Your Wife into an Object

When you're first married, bouncing your eyes is fairly easy because your wife has an attractive body that is youthful and new to you. Her body serves as an adequate substitute for what you'd find in porn or other lustful avenues. But what happens a few years into marriage when she becomes familiar and routine or begins to put on weight? What do you do? You're now up a creek if your love for her has always been predicated on her appearance and her appearance isn't what it used to be. Even if she has kept herself in tip-top shape,

---

4. 1 Corinthians 6:13–16.

her appearance still becomes familiar and routine, the opposite of what the world of sexual temptation offers you.

Once you're up this creek, the amount of gratification you came to expect from your wife in your early years of marriage becomes just that: an expectation. An unmet expectation you feel entitled to. And we know where entitlement leads.

If your wife has put on weight and it bothers you, there's a good chance you are objectifying her and you're more in love with her body parts than with her as a person. Think about it: If you love your wife less because her stomach or legs got bigger, then what is determining your love for your wife? Her body parts. And if her body parts are the predicating factor for your love, she is now an object. She's no longer a person with a million other attributes of greater importance than her body.

Objectification begins with the body. If the body is good, the rest of the person is attractive or acceptable as well. You see this all the time: If a girl is hot, a guy isn't going to care if she's also materialistic or insecure or shallow. The infatuation begins at first sight. A-list celebrity women never have problems finding boyfriends, regardless of how unattractive their personalities might be. Hotness covers a multitude of sins. The guy gets his trophy and consumes it for his pleasure.

Now turn the tables. Yes, God created the woman's body to be attractive to a man. But he did not intend it to be the totality of attractiveness. When you marry a woman, are you marrying her or her body? If you were marrying only her body, then when that body shape changes, you'd be free to leave the marriage. But obviously you are marrying *her*, all of her. This view of marriage means you are committing to love, cherish, protect, uphold, and be attracted to all of her. So your wife gains some pounds. So what? If you married her and not her weight, then this shouldn't rock your attractiveness meter. She is still your wife to cherish, protect, honor, and support. This is what draws you to her, and the extra weight she carries or the wrinkles that have set in just become part of the background. They aren't make-or-break factors. They provide you with an opportunity to cherish, protect, honor, and support her because she knows she's put on weight and is self-conscious about it. She knows the size she used to be and the clothes that she'll never fit into again. When you marry a whole woman and not a set of body parts, you are drawn to her sexually because of what you share together in vulnerability, trust, and commitment, not because of the shape she is in.

This view of marriage requires us to redefine the purpose of sex. It's pretty obvious that our culture believes the purpose of sex is pleasure, and thus body shape and appearance are of the utmost importance. Author Todd Wilson argues that in the biblical vision of sex, sex is a blessing not because of the pleasure it brings but because of the purpose it serves: to unite lives and to create life.[5]

Thinking of sex as the way to unite two lives is a game changer. For one, it makes you look at a person's *life*, their personhood. It makes you appreciate the sacredness and responsibility of being united to someone else, of your carrying them and their carrying you. You aren't in this relationship to use this person. You are in it to hold them, support them, and share everything with them. You don't resent them and wish they'd do better when they stumble. You comfort them and console them. You put your arm around them and hold them close, assuring them that things will be okay as long as you're near.

This is light years away from seeing your wife as the bowl to gratify your sexual appetite with.

Seeing sex as the way of creating life is equally profound, and this might be especially helpful to single guys struggling with lust. Before birth control was invented, sex would have always been connected with the responsibility of having children. Whatever your view on birth control, no one can argue that it hasn't made sex much more accessible, casual, and commonplace. But when God designed sex, he tied it directly to the huge responsibility of parenthood: a permanent, committed, cooperative partnership of trust

---

5. Todd A. Wilson, *Mere Sexuality* (Grand Rapids, MI: Zondervan, 2017), 97.

and fidelity. If you wanted to have sex with a person, you had better have really wanted it, because you most likely would have been raising a kid with them for the rest of your life. Sex and the permanent uniting of two lives would have always been tied together by this likelihood of creating new life.

For married and single guys today, when the tractor beam of lust starts to pull you in, ask yourself if you could realistically raise children with this woman. If not (probably 99 percent of the time), allow this redefinition of sex's purpose to break the power of lust's magnetic pull, showing it for the fraud it is.

The purpose we give to sex matters. It makes a huge difference in our marriages. It puts a ridiculous amount of pressure on our wives—an unfair, unloving, not-of-Christ type of pressure—if we opt for the bowls mentality of consumption rather than the one-flesh mindset of uniting our lives. If your wife feels she has to keep up with the Joneses, she knows you are comparing her to other women on a regular basis. Is that what you vowed to her on your wedding day? That she'd have to worry the rest of her life about getting a higher grade than all of the other women in your life? No, you vowed you would love her through sickness and health, ups and downs, thick or thin, happiness or sadness—the same way Jesus loves us.

I'm not saying the human body is bad. That's wrong theologically. God made the human body and he created it good. Good theology tells us that body + spirit = whole person. Since the beginning of Christianity, many heretics have lived on either side of this balance, downplaying either the body or the spirit. That's not what we're doing here. If anything, we are correcting the scale. While our culture has taught us that a woman's value comes only from her body, we declare that a woman's body does not predicate her personhood. We are on a journey to see women as whole persons, which includes their bodies but takes in all of who they are.

I'm also not saying you shouldn't be sexually attracted to and aroused by your wife's body parts. Proverbs 5:19 makes this crystal clear:

A loving doe, a graceful deer—
  may her breasts satisfy you always,
  may you ever be intoxicated with her love.

What's even more relevant about this passage, though, is the verse right before it. I've heard verse 19 used as justification *to* objectify your wife, or as biblical justification to be fixated on her body parts. But verse 18 says, "May you rejoice in the wife of your youth," just before calling her the loving doe and graceful deer. If you say "the wife of your youth" to someone, how old is the person you are talking to? They aren't young anymore. You'd never say "rejoice in the wife of your youth" to a twenty-two-year-old who just got married. You'd just say, "Rejoice in your wife." This passage is being spoken to an older man about his older wife.

The proverb is saying, "Do you remember how you were intoxicated with your wife's breasts when her body was young? Be equally intoxicated with her breasts today in her later years." (Even though they don't have quite the same appearance.) It's not the appearance that matters. It's that they are hers. What makes sex and body parts so intimate and pleasurable is that your lives are united. So enjoy her breasts. Not because they match an idealized objectification of what you want a breast to look like but because they are hers and she is yours and you are hers. Because she's the same person today as she was when you first got married, and the appearance of her body won't ever affect that.

Your life has been united to your wife's. Take joy in that and celebrate it with her. Protect her and cherish her. Release her from the prison of having to keep up with the standards of objectification. Release her from the soul-crushing burden of measuring her self-worth by what the mirror reflects. Every product, TV channel, and media personality under the sun already feeds her this malicious lie. Her husband shouldn't as well.

If you're using the Forty-Day Devotional Guide in
the back of this book, turn now to **Day 20**.

Loving Sex or Loving Your Wife

Ask yourself this challenging question: do you love your wife because she's the one you get to have sex with, or do you love having sex with her because you love your wife?

A simpler and blunter way to ask this is: which do you love more, sex or your wife?

Of course, the Sunday school answer is "I love my wife." And your first reaction might be to argue that you can love both simultaneously.

Nine years into my marriage, through some marital counseling my wife and I sought, I realized I loved having sex, and that my wife was the one I got to have sex with. That's painful for me to write. It was never intentional. It was simply the outflow of being taught that if I saved sex for marriage, then my sex life would be great. It was the outflow of being told that bouncing my eyes from sexual stimuli and focusing my eyes on my wife would result in a happy and God-honoring sex life. It was the outflow of being taught, at least implicitly, that the purpose of marriage is so that we could finally have sex.

All of these strategies essentially say, "You love sex? Well, let's harness that love for sex exclusively toward one person. Technically speaking, you'll be obeying God's commands for sex—and he'll surely bless you sexually for that."

Meanwhile, sex is still displayed and promoted all around us, and we still feel entitled to it. Any attempt to make it about our wives becomes an effort to make them more receptive to giving us all the sex we want—which, again, is about us.

This is a major problem because porn, lust, and objectification are all about us too, so marital sex conveniently fits into this selfish, well-worn groove we've carved out over the years.

The whiplash effect is caused by the fact that the biblical definition of love says it isn't about us.[6] So we stand at a wedding altar and vow to our wives that we love them, but we subconsciously see our vow of love as a convoluted way to serve ourselves. Sounds like Satan at his best: undetected, deceptive, and deadly. It's no wonder it

---

6. 1 Corinthians 13:5 says that love is not self-seeking.

feels as if the entire world is crashing in when sex is not as frequent or as fulfilling as we expected.

Is it a sin to want to have sex with our wives? Of course not. The point is that we need to place everything in the proper order. Sex is meant to be a gift we share, not something we take. The way it becomes a gift is when I love my wife as a whole person, when I devote myself to her and treasure her, appreciating her as a gift of mercy I don't deserve. Sex becomes a gift when I pledge myself to her for better or for worse, in sickness and in health, whether rich or poor. I can then say that because I love my wife, I desire sex with her, rather than that because I desire sex, I love my wife. And that is a huge difference.

Sex becomes a small piece of the puzzle, not the entire picture.

My wife becomes someone I serve, not someone I use.

I'm not loving a body; I'm loving a person.

And *then* there's a big kickback, right?

Wrong. Wrong idea. Wrong intention. Wrong motivation. Wrong foundation.

For us to truly learn what love is, we have to eliminate the kickback notion altogether. You can use sugarcoated Christianese and call it "receiving a blessing,"[7] but in our hearts, where it counts, it's the same old selfishness. This kickback motivation doesn't lead us to love; it merely disguises the way we get our next hit as a self addict.

We need to stop telling God what we deserve or how things should be. God is the sovereign one, not you or me. The book of Job, the Psalms, and the Prophets are full of accounts of people waiting for what they thought were well-deserved kickbacks for their faithfulness.[8] The cycle is the same: I've obeyed God; I think God should reward me. He isn't rewarding me, but he does seem to be rewarding everyone else (especially the wicked). So now I am struggling with depression and frustration.

God isn't in the kickback business. But he is in the loving Father business, he is in the sovereignty business, and he is in the

---

7. Do we receive blessings for obeying God in our marriages? Yes, of course. But the only blessing we are promised is the spiritual blessing of closer intimacy with him.

8. 1 Kings 19; Job 21; Jeremiah 12:1–4; Psalm 73.

sanctification business. And I know of nothing on planet earth that will thoroughly sanctify a man's heart more than marriage.

Bounce with Me

I'm certainly not arguing against bouncing our eyes away from temptation. But this action should be a byproduct of our strategy, not the strategy itself. This discipline is a good tool but the wrong foundation for solving our lust problem. If we adopt it as our primary strategy, it conditions us to continue viewing sex in fleshly terms rather than in God's terms. We never deal with the root issue and find freedom.

The solution must be to reprogram our minds to reflect God's view of sex. When this is our primary goal, everything else takes care of itself. Yes, we still bounce our eyes, but it's because we no longer desire to turn women into objects, not because we've mechanically whipped our eyes into submission. If we think bouncing our eyes from temptation and fixing them on our wives is the way to find sexual purity,[9] we only end up turning our wives into objects, which is the opposite of what we're trying to accomplish.

If you're using the Forty-Day Devotional Guide in
the back of this book, turn now to **Day 21**.

In Your Small Group

Scan this QR code or go to www.beyond thebattle.net/videos and watch "Session 4 (Chapters 5–6): Objectification: The Dehumanization of Women." (All small group resources are free.)

---

9. And of course, bouncing our eyes gives no solution at all for single guys.

CHAPTER 7

THE COMPARISON GAME

Who Made Sex?

Every summer, our church has a weekly youth ministry at two inner-city parks in town. Most of the kids and teens who come aren't Christians and have had very little exposure to biblical concepts. We were teaching the teens about sex one week and showed them in Scripture how God created sex. I remember a fifteen-year-old who flat out didn't believe us. He was convinced the devil had made sex.

He associated the devil with sex because it feels good and he knew it was "against the rules." The thing he couldn't get his mind wrapped around was that (in his view) a stuffy, rules-making, dull God would have anything to do with something that felt so good.

It is important for us to understand that sex is God's invention, not Satan's. We need to understand that our sexual urges are, on some level, God's handiwork. Satan wants us to think the entire conversation about sex is on his home turf. He wants us to think it's all about body parts and impulses.

We can end up feeling like God simply wants us to behave and follow his rules, that he wants us to live out mundane sex lives with our one spouse. Meanwhile, we look across the lawn at Satan's playground and wish we could have some of the fun our lucky non-Christian friends are having.

Is my own lawn really all there is?

We will always be trapped and frustrated when we approach sex on Satan's terms. When our efforts for purity are on his turf, we are trying to take something broken and morph it into something that follows God's design. We find freedom only when we start at the source and build from there.

How do you know to put gas and oil in your car to make it go? The creator of your car wrote a manual to tell you how to operate the vehicle. The manual tells you exactly the type of gas and oil to put in, as well as where and how often. When you follow the creator's design, the car runs well.

But what happens if you decide to take matters into your own hands? What if you decide to ignore the creator and put some other substance into your car's engine? How about lemonade? Or coffee? Or kerosene?

Men love to be successful. Why would you continue doing something (like putting lemonade in your gas tank) that always fails? Lust has never led to success, only disaster.

As more and more people look at their sex lives and see disaster, one must wonder whether the creator of sex can finally get an audience so we can learn what the design for sex is.

Genesis tells us that God, on each of the six days of creation, looked at what he had made that day and called it good.[1] Yet Genesis 1:31 tells us that after God finished his final day of creation, he pronounced what he had made *very* good. What caused God to change his rating from good to very good?

Genesis 1:27–28 tells us, "So God created mankind in his own image, in the image of God he created them; male and female he created them. God blessed them and said to them, 'Be fruitful and increase in number.'"

---

1. Genesis 1:4, 10, 12, 18, 21, 25.

"Be fruitful and increase in number" is a reference to sex and all that goes with it.

Creation was good. Then God created man and woman, and sex, and creation became very good.

God created sex and wrote the recipe for it. Just as you can use or ignore your car's manual, you have the choice of listening to the designer or doing it your own way.

If you're using the Forty-Day Devotional Guide in
the back of this book, turn now to **Day 22.**

Apples and Oranges

Before we look at God's recipe for sex, it's important we understand that we are not comparing God's way to have an orgasm to Satan's, as if we are rating which is better. I say this because that's often how sexual purity strategies are taught to Christians: "Save yourself until marriage because then you'll have no regrets and the sex will be better." You should view skeptically any Christian command that concludes "and then the sex will be better."

The problem we typically run into when talking about God's design versus the world's is that we try to compare apples with apples, as if God's design for sex and Satan's were two versions of the same substance, as if God's sex apple tastes one way and Satan's tastes a different way. As if we can analyze the two tastes and go with the one that tastes best.

At the end of the day, though, you're still eating an apple. You're still viewing sex the way Satan wants you to.

In chapter 6 we saw how this apples-to-apples game plays out when we shift our appetite from objectifying all women to objectifying only our wives. In both situations, we are still consuming. We are still looking at women as food for our gratification, which is Satan's design through and through.

When we look at God's recipe for sex, we see that his design and Satan's are completely different. If Satan's design for sex is like taking a bite from an apple, God's design is more like owning the entire apple orchard. Taking a bite from a single apple and operating an entire orchard are completely different experiences.

Which physical experience is more of a rush: the one with the blazing hot woman from the bar who's all over you, or the one with your wife of twenty years? It's really no contest. Telling ourselves (or being taught) that married sex is more of a rush is a charade that eventually caves in on itself.

When we compare the two experiences this way, we end up feeling like the person stuck in their room doing math homework, longing for the playground across the street. We begrudgingly obey God's commands to be faithful to our mundane wives, all the while yearning to have what our non-Christian friends are enjoying. When we think sex is about eating apples, about objectifying and consuming, it's only natural we'd feel this way.

We slave away in our apple orchards, tilling the soil, organizing rows, planting seeds, fertilizing, watering, weeding, straining, and sweating. We figure out how to organize the harvest in a sustainable and profitable way, efficiently market and distribute the apples, eradicate the disease that affected a quarter of the crop, and prepare for the next season—and labor all over again. Meanwhile, our non-Christian friends are just running around the orchard like children, randomly picking apples from trees, taking gleeful bites out of them, then tossing them aside to grab another apple from another tree. No work. No hassle. All fun.

We can feel like we made the wrong choice when we compare the immediate benefits of Satan's way with the immediate benefits of God's way. With this formula, Satan's way is going to win out nearly every time. But when we reflect on the big picture, it doesn't take long to realize where wisdom lies.

Whether we're considering Proverbs 5 or Aesop's classic fable "The Ant and the Grasshopper," we can see that instant gratification has major shortcomings and that investing in the big picture is where major benefit is found. But if we look only at the immediate benefits of Satan's way with the immediate benefits of God's way, Satan's way will almost always look better.

The way we teach teenagers to save sex for marriage is comical at times. We tell them they can get STDs or get pregnant, though they know if they use condoms this is unlikely to happen. Their hormones are raging and we tell them, "The feeling of sex will be better when you and your spouse are virgins on your honeymoon night." The reason I find this comical is because these types of statements all compare God's sex to Satan's, using Satan's metric of sensual gratification. "God's sex feels better, believe us!" we say. No kid, or adult, is going to believe that because in the short term, it is seldom true. Any man would love to be worshiped by a pretty new thing. While, for good reason, no wife of twenty years is going to worship her husband.

We neglect to acknowledge what Proverbs 5 isn't bashful about: that extramarital sex feels really good. Proverbs 5:3 describes this well: "For the lips of the adulterous woman drip honey, and her speech is smoother than oil." The author of this proverb points out there is intense pleasure to be had with an adulterous woman. Honey was *the* delicacy of the ancient world. Before there were fudge brownies or ice cream, there was honey, and it was a much sought-after delight. The author's vivid depiction of a woman's lips dripping with such a delicacy was meant to make the reader's heart race. We miss this truth when trying to teach others (or convince ourselves) that sexual purity is even better, and our words fall on deaf ears.

While Satan wants the discussion to end with the delicious honey, the proverb continues in verse 4, "but in the end she is bitter as gall, sharp as a double-edged sword." How quickly the imagery changes! One minute you are savoring the sweet taste of honey and the smooth feeling of oil, the next you are puking up bile and a double-edged sword is ripping through your body.

The writer of the proverb concludes the thought in verse 5: "Her feet go down to death; her steps lead straight to the grave." Not only has the adulterous woman left you in intense pain, she is slowly dragging you to your death, a concept the rest of Proverbs 5 describes with incredible clarity. This path to the grave is well worn to addicts, to whom it feels the only thing that will heal the wound of the sword is more honey and oil.

The pain that comes when we fall is a much higher intensity than the feeling of peace when we are living in obedience. Think of the last time you had the flu. You're shivering. Your body is racked with aches and pains. Head spinning. What was the one thing you were wishing? That you didn't have the flu anymore. You were miserable. This is the addict after another bout of pornography-fueled masturbation. After his wife is finally fed up and files the divorce papers. All he wants is the pain to go away. To be able to push the reset button, wishing he'd never infected himself with this disease. Wishing that with a snap of the fingers, the flu would be gone. We've all been there.

But what happened to you when your flu gradually went away? It got a little better one day, then a little better the next. You gradually restarted your normal life's activities bit by bit as you regained your strength. Did you jump for joy that you were healthy again? Did you appreciate your health with the same intensity you lamented the misery of your illness? Were you bursting at the seams with gratitude? No, you weren't. You just went on with your normal day, doing normal tasks, hardly even thinking about it. Just like you aren't thinking about it now.

Things are pretty dull and ordinary most days when you're walking in obedience. Not a great sales pitch, I know. It's not meant to be. You won't convince a cocaine addict that he'll feel a higher high when sober than he does while using. You try to convince him to appreciate his ordinary life, to be grateful for all he has and all he has to lose if he continues in his addiction. You try to convince him he's worth more than this and has a greater purpose.

Freedom from sexual sin is no different.

This is orchard life. You're working the orchard every day. You're digging holes in the ground to plant new seeds. You're pulling weeds. You're trying to keep invasive species away. There's no glamour in these things. But there is so much to be celebrated.

We need to embrace the ordinary and find gratitude in it. You're not in a mangled car wreck on the side of the road. You're not stuck in a pit of excrement with no way out. You don't have the flu. You don't have a broken leg.[2] Take a deep breath. Kick those legs. Take a long, full breath. Rejoice! There's so much to celebrate when everything isn't broken and is working toward the purpose it was designed for. We just forget because we get used to it. It's like living in paradise every day, forgetting what the alternative is.[3]

The conversation about sex must zoom out to a view that encompasses much more than just the act itself. It must because the repercussions are bigger than the act, and because God's design is greater.

Sex was never meant to be an isolated experience, something God's recipe will make clear as we lay out its ingredients.

If you're using the Forty-Day Devotional Guide in the back of this book, turn now to **Day 23**.

Food for the Stomach and the Stomach for Food

Our culture tells us sex is purely for pleasure, with no strings attached. You can have a one-night stand with a stranger or date someone simply for the pleasure you gain from it. You can turn on the television to find plot after plot centered on casual sex, or you can watch the most recent action or comedy movie and be flooded by sexualized bodies, eye candy that viewers have come to demand. With these trends, it shouldn't be surprising that one in three singles say they have had sex with another person before they have had a first date with that person, which is now called a "sex interview."[4]

---

2. Apologies to those reading this who do. Hang in there. You'll be better soon!

3. People living in Southern California have no idea what they're missing. When it's 72 and sunny every day, you just yawn. For those of us living in Michigan, we fully appreciate and celebrate the two weeks of nice weather we have all year.

4. "Singles in America: Match Releases Largest Study on U.S. Single Population," Match.com press release, February 26, 2017, https://match.mediaroom.com/2017-02-06-Singles-in-America-Match-Releases-Largest-Study-on-U-S-Single-Population.

Or that 62 percent of heterosexual singles say they would be open to a threesome.[5]

A college student from my church was a resident assistant in a freshman dorm at Michigan State University. When he showed me his dorm room, I was startled to see a sizable box of condoms attached to the outside of his door with a note on it that said, "When these are gone, you can get more at the nurse's office." He said all RAs were supplied with these and required to display them outside their doors. This was a far cry from what I was accustomed to at Cornerstone University, the Christian college I attended! What does this box of condoms communicate to a bunch of hormone-crazed eighteen-year-olds away from home for the first time? The same thing TV shows and movies communicate, a message most people now have embedded deep into their worldview: Sex is like food. When you're hungry, eat. And when you're in the mood for sex, have sex. The body is meant for pleasure.

It feels good, so do it. There are no strings attached.

Take a bite from an apple. Throw it to the side. Grab another apple.

Objectify.

Consume.

It's all about you.

This worldview is identical to the culture Paul addressed nearly two thousand years ago when he penned a book of the Bible to believers living in Corinth, Greece. In the context of sex, the saying of the day was, "Everything is permissible for me."[6] Essentially, "I'm a free adult, and I can do whatever I want sexually," the same message communicated to those Michigan State freshmen.

Some things just haven't changed.

Another Corinthian saying in regard to sex was, "Food for the stomach and the stomach for food."[7] God created the stomach for

5. "Singles in America: Match Releases Largest Study on U.S. Single Population for Eighth Year," Match.com press release, February 1 2018, https://www.multivu.com/players/English/8264851-match-singles-in-america-study/.

6. 1 Corinthians 6:12.

7. 1 Corinthians 6:13.

what? Food. So take in food because it feels good. Then move on, no strings attached. God created the sexual organs for what? Sex. So use them for sex because it feels good. Then move on, no strings attached. Bite the apple, then throw it aside, having no regard for the orchard.

We are meant to be orchard people, not apple people.

The Bible's teachings on sex are just as relevant today as they were the day they were written. Our creator's design for sex is not about consuming someone else for pleasure. It never has been, and it never will be.

Todd Wilson's reminder that one of the biblical purposes of sex is to unite lives is once again helpful here. Uniting two lives is orchard work. It's slow and hard and all encompassing, but it produces lasting fruit.

Seeing sex as a way of uniting two lives is so different from seeing it as a means of consumption and pleasure. You can't put lipstick on that pig and call it a sexual purity strategy. You've got to get rid of the pig. You can't accept Satan's terms that sex is about body parts and orgasms and urges and then try to reshape and funnel those toward surface-level obedience of biblical commands for purity.

Sex unifies two people into a lifetime one-flesh union where vulnerability and trust prevail in *all* aspects of life.

The apple is the fruit of the orchard. It doesn't exist without the orchard. It's beautiful, but it can't be experienced in isolation. Taking sex out of its one-flesh context and experiencing it isolated from the rest of the marriage union is in clear contradiction to God's design. Like pouring lemonade into a car's gas tank, it causes disaster. No wonder our sex lives, our struggles with purity, and our culture are in such a mess. Satan's hollow perversion of sex simply cannot compare to God's full recipe.

If you're using the Forty-Day Devotional Guide in the back of this book, turn now to **Day 24.**

CHAPTER 8

GOD'S RECIPE

One Flesh

Did you ever play with Play-Doh as a kid? Or, like me, do you play with it as an adult because you have small children? There is one cardinal sin of Play-Doh that every parent has ingrained in their child's mind: never mix the colors! (Well, mixing colors might be the second or third cardinal sin, behind eating it and failing to put it back into its airtight container, but I digress.) The reason we don't want our kids mixing Play-Doh colors is simple: once you mix them, you can never pull them apart.

The Bible tells us in Genesis 2:24 that this "is why a man leaves his father and mother and is united to his wife, and they become one flesh."

Bringing two people together to become one flesh is like mixing a yellow piece of Play-Doh and a blue piece of Play-Doh. As you mix them, the blue and the yellow cease to be, and they create a new color: green. There is no way to separate the yellow from the blue, or even to find the yellow and the blue. The two have truly become one in all facets.

The glaring problem with the Corinthian "anything goes" mindset that is so prevalent today is one we know from experience:

sex involves much more than just our physical selves. This is because God's design for sex is all about intimacy. Sex is meant to be just one aspect of the union of two people physically, emotionally, mentally, and spiritually. Anyone who has ever been used or dumped, or who can't shake the memories associated with previous partners, can testify to this. God's design for sex is for it to occur within an unbreakable bond between two people who are becoming one. It is an act of supreme transparency and vulnerability in which two people embrace each other's full humanity in an act of trust and faithfulness.

The New Testament often uses the metaphor of a bride and groom to describe the relationship Jesus has with us.[1] The intimacy God wants us to have with him is like the intimacy he designed us to have with one wife. No idols. No lust. Just pure love. Pure devotion. Pure relationship.

We find the marriage metaphor in the Old Testament too, but usually it's for the Israelites' tendency to cheat on God. God instructs the prophet Hosea to marry a prostitute to show the people what it feels like for God to be faithfully married or covenanted to them while they sleep around.[2] The book of Jeremiah begins with a reminiscence of when God and Israel were like a newlywed couple in a faithful marriage.[3] The rest of the book is essentially the tale of Israel's prostitution and affairs with idols. Israel is called a swift she-camel and a wild donkey in heat, sniffing the wind in sexual craving![4] She is called a prostitute with many lovers[5] and, worse than this, a prostitute with a brazen face, refusing to blush with shame about her unfaithfulness but only continuing in it.[6] God associates the people's idol worship with adulterous sex,[7] and he

---

1. Matthew 25:1–13; John 3:29; 2 Corinthians 11:2; Ephesians 5:21–33; Revelation 19:7; 21:2.
2. Hosea 1–3.
3. Jeremiah 2:1–3.
4. Jeremiah 2:23–24.
5. Jeremiah 3:1.
6. Jeremiah 3:3.
7. Jeremiah 3:6.

identifies himself as their husband, longing for his bride to return to him.[8]

Why does God relate sex to a relationship with him? Because sex is the deepest expression of intimacy in a relationship. It is the model of what faithful, committed, lifelong intimacy and love are supposed to look like. It's not simply one body entering another. It is the melding of two people full of hopes, dreams, goals, fears, likes, dislikes, insecurities, vulnerabilities, needs, personalities, family roles, responsibilities, faults, strengths, weaknesses, imperfections, and quirks. It is all strings attached. It's one person saying to another, "I will accept you and support you as a complete human being. You can trust me with everything that makes you human." This is called love.

In 1 Corinthians 6:15–16, Paul goes back to Genesis 2:24's Play-Doh mixing to prove his point: "Do you not know that your bodies are members of Christ himself? Shall I then take the members of Christ and unite them with a prostitute? Never! Do you not know that he who unites himself with a prostitute is one with her in body? For it is said, 'The two will become one flesh.'"

Paul argues that becoming one flesh is much more than a physical interplay. It is two people pouring their hearts and souls into each other, seeing one another the way God intended them to: as valuable, dignified, precious human beings created in God's image. It is saying to someone, "I accept 100 percent of you, and I will be here for you through anything." Nobody would argue that this is what happens when someone is having sex with a prostitute, yet Paul is saying that when you have sex with *anyone* you have just united yourself with them in this way. If you have sex with a prostitute, you'd better marry her. Or to be more accurate, in a theological sense you just got married to her.[9]

---

8. Jeremiah 3:14.

9. I sometimes hear people argue that the Bible does not say premarital sex is wrong. This passage begs to differ. What Paul is saying in verses 15–16 is that you don't become one flesh with someone when you get married (as you often hear pastors say at weddings), you become one flesh with someone when you have sex. His reference to a prostitute isn't

Of course, no one is making this sort of commitment when they have sex with a prostitute or with the person they just found on Match.com or even with the girlfriend they've been dating for five months and care deeply about. This lack of commitment helps explain the massive amount of relational heartache we see in the world. Like having a baby and leaving it to die, we are creating any number of "one fleshes" (a mathematical fallacy) without treating them as such. You can't ditch a one-flesh relationship and not have major fallout.

This dynamic sheds further light on Jesus' commands about lust. He tells us, "You have heard that it was said, 'You shall not commit adultery.' But I tell you that anyone who looks at a woman lustfully has already committed adultery with her in his heart."[10]

When we lust over someone, we are not accepting and supporting 100 percent of them, nor have we committed to be there for them in any way. Just as you create a one-flesh relationship when you have sex with a prostitute, a Match.com hookup, or your longtime girlfriend, Jesus is saying that whether you lust over a woman or her photograph, you're creating a one-flesh relationship with her. Talk about breaking God's design for sex. We haven't just broken it. We have obliterated it.

For the sake of illustration, let's say lusting over someone is the equivalent of accepting 10 percent of who they are. Jesus and Paul are saying that, when we lust, when we accept only this 10 percent, we are still creating a 100 percent one-flesh bond. They are saying that when we lust, even if we try to keep some of the yellow Play-Doh off to the side while only a portion mixes in with the blue, in truth, everything becomes intertwined. So what happens to the

---

referring only to people paid for sex. The Greek word for prostitute comes from the word *porneia*, which encompasses any sex that happens outside of wedlock. This isn't to judge or condemn you if you've had sex before marriage, nor is it to say that if two fifteen-year-olds have sex, they should immediately get married. It's to give us further biblical proof for God's design for sex and to give us a greater understanding of why sex and the "one flesh" concept must go hand in hand, a concept we desperately need to recalibrate our thoughts and actions to.

10. Matthew 5:27–28.

other 90 percent of the other person? Or the other 90 percent of our own selves? It's neglected, abused, and starved to death as we move from fix to fix to fix, hoping that a whole bunch of 10 percents will eventually add up to one hundred.

When we try to do our math by our rules rather than sticking with God's design, it's no wonder we end up with a mess on our hands. When talking about sex outside of marriage, Proverbs 6:27 sums this truth up well: "Can a man scoop fire into his lap without his clothes being burned?"

It is an illusion to think we can follow any design for sex other than God's (as individuals and as a culture) without getting burned. You can't make one flesh by adding ten different fragments of flesh, just as you can't scoop fire into your lap without being burned.

None of us has followed God's design for sex perfectly. Staring at our failure or being weighed down with shame is not the point of bringing his design to light. The point is to see with crystal clarity the contrast between God's design for sex and the fruit it produces compared with Satan's. We study the manual for the car so that, from this day forward, we can commit to doing what it says, as well as see any alternative for the folly it is.

When we approach our sexual purity by embracing a design that has a life-giving set of values, we start to become attracted to and desire those values. This is the beginning of true freedom.

> If you're using the Forty-Day Devotional Guide in
> the back of this book, turn now to **Day 25**.

Pour Some Sugar on Me

Our culture tells us you can isolate sex from the rest of the one-flesh relationship without consequence. "I can have sex (or lust, porn, etc.) now and marriage later" is a common way of thinking. As is the thought that we can be married and have a little lust on the side.

Def Leppard's 1987 rock anthem "Pour Some Sugar on Me" provides a good metaphor for what our culture has done with sex. The song is about the singer having sex with a woman and he equates the experience to her pouring sugar on him. She is sugar and he eats her up, which sounds a lot like the Corinthians' statement, "Food for the stomach and the stomach for food." Sugar is good, so eat it. Sex is good, so have it. Eating sugar and having sex have become synonymous.

Have you ever eaten sugar by itself? I mean lots of sugar. Once, when preaching a sermon on sexual purity, I asked everyone in the audience who liked sugar to raise their hand. Hands shot up all over the room. Sugar is great. We love candy, cake, brownies, chocolate, ice cream, pie, and hundreds of other delicious foods made possible by sugar.

I held up a twenty-two-ounce container of sugar I'd pulled from our coffee bar (a large cylinder with a pour spout) and offered twenty dollars to anyone who could eat the entire thing. The only hands that shot up this time belonged to middle-school boys. I decided to pick the one who had already jumped to his feet exclaiming, "Oh, this will be easy!" He came on stage and took the sugar container with confidence and began to pour it into his mouth.

It didn't take long for a mound of sugar to pile up on his tongue, and eventually the inevitable happened: sugar sprayed from his mouth all over the stage.

I used this object lesson another time with a group of college students, and what do you know, a college freshman (a guy, of course) was determined to defeat my challenge. Full of determination, he sat there chomping down mouthfuls of sugar for the final fifteen minutes of my sermon. He had ingested just under half the container when I had to wrap up, so I gave him the money and mercifully told him to stop. I found out later he ended up with chronic headaches that he had to seek medical attention for. And yes, that was the last time I ever gave that challenge in a sermon!

The thing about sugar is that, as wonderful as it is, it is not meant to be eaten on its own. Whether it's in coffee, peanut brittle, or cake, sugar is meant to be included in a recipe with other ingredients and flavors. It is too potent on its own and needs to bond with the other ingredients to be palatable.

What are the other ingredients needed in a relationship to bond with the potency and power of sex?

Trust.

Faithfulness.

Commitment.

Vulnerability.

Patience.

Perseverance.

Selflessness.

Love.

Commitment . . . did I already say that one?

Commitment.

If you have sex without these supporting ingredients, its immense weight and raw power will break hearts and crush hopes.It was never meant to be consumed on its own. It was always meant to be a complementary ingredient in the much larger recipe of marriage, needing all of these supporting ingredients to give it balance and support.

Let's say a cake represents a healthy marriage and sugar represents sex (as Def Leppard sings so eloquently). What Def Leppard and the rest of our culture do (and have conditioned us to do) is to eat a piece of cake and say, "Wow, this cake is great. What makes it taste so good?"

We are told it's the sugar. We decide that if sugar is where the good taste comes from, then why bother with the rest of the ingredients? If sugar is where it's at, let's just eat sugar and skip the boring, inconvenient, difficult, bland, and time-consuming ingredients like flour, butter, yeast, and eggs. If we can get the pleasure of sex without taking on the responsibilities and inconvenience of marriage, then count us in. This is a pretty easy sell, because there's no denying that sugar is good. When it can be packaged in so many quick, easy, bite-sized portions, it's no surprise so many of us are hooked on it.

> If you're using the Forty-Day Devotional Guide in
> the back of this book, turn now to **Day 26**.

More Than Animals

One of the most popular songs of 2014 was Maroon 5's "Animals." In it, A-list celebrity Adam Levine[11] sings about preying on a woman and hunting her down to eat her alive, just like animals. He continues to sing that things are good as long as he's inside of her, just like animals. It even declares what is obvious: that this animalistic sex is a drug that is killing him. Yet Levine isn't calling out this death drug for the havoc it's wreaking on his soul, the woman's soul, and on our culture. Or how the whole concept of the song could be considered sexual abuse. Oh no, the song is a celebration of carnal pleasure, with our culture applauding the entire time, embracing the full-on pornographic lust of both the song and its sexually explicit music video. I'm not pointing out "Animals" as something unique, I'm saying that this is our culture now. It's everywhere and is the prevailing view of sex today.[12]

Many men have stooped to an animal-level existence when it comes to sex and life. This is so prevalent in our culture that the only way to cope with its trauma has been to celebrate and normalize it. For many guys, their entire lives revolve around eating and casual sex.[13] What is the difference between this existence and a stray dog's? Are we not meant for more than this? Yes! We are.

After Paul quotes "food for the stomach and the stomach for

11. Levine was declared Sexiest Man Alive in 2013 by *People* magazine and was a cohost of NBC's *The Voice* for sixteen seasons.

12. I wonder how Levine would feel about someone singing this song with one of his two daughters in mind, of whom he said on *The Ellen DeGeneres Show* (October 7, 2019), "I'm obsessed with them. I genuinely just adore them in a way I never knew I could adore any person." Yet another reminder that all women are sacred daughters and not the objects Satan tells us to consume.

13. If they pursue money or power, it is often only because money and power make it easier to get sex.

food," he writes, "God will destroy them both. The body, however, is not meant for sexual immorality but for the Lord, and the Lord for the body."

Paul essentially says, "No, you don't understand, your body is meant for *so much more* than sexual immorality." This is like saying, "Sugar is meant for so much more than to be eaten alone." Can you imagine if all you ever did was eat sugar on its own and you'd never tasted homemade chocolate chip cookies or cherry pie or a Chick-fil-A peach milk shake?[14] Imagine the poor soul scooping a mountain of sugar into his mouth by the spoonful, thinking he'd conquered the world. That image makes me break down and cry! I want to say to the guy, "What are you doing? Don't you know how good Chick-fil-A peach milk shakes are?"

We can't just cognitively assent to the knowledge that sex needs the marriage covenant or that the entire sex metaphor is really about our relationship with Jesus, yawn, then put it on the shelf to gather dust. When we look at the alternative—this empty, harmful, shallow, animalistic lifestyle—we need to sprint toward what is good and true. This picture makes for a classic plot to a sci-fi movie. The hero wakes up and realizes everyone around him is on drugs that are killing them, but they don't know it. He realizes they are all slaves to a giant machine. He has unhooked from the machine and from the drug, breathing fresh air for the first time. The scene shifts and now all of his fellow humans become zombies that start groping at him and chasing him, trying to get him back into the clutches of their animalistic slavery. Our hero is not going to stop to consider whether the disfigured zombies have it right and their drugged lifestyle is worth it. He's going to sprint toward life and truth for all he is worth—certainly using massive amounts of gunfire and kung fu along the way! (This is a sci-fi movie, after all.)

As we are waking up to realize, this isn't a movie. It's real life. And we need to hear Paul's war horn blowing: "Men! You are meant for more than being an animal. Run toward life. Run toward God's design."

---

14. Chick-fil-A peach milk shakes are proof that Jesus' kingdom has indeed come near.

"You are not your own; you were bought at a price. Therefore honor God with your bodies" (1 Cor. 6:19–20). Jesus bought your body out of slavery, and the price was his blood shed on the cross. He bought you for a purpose much greater than being a slave to sex, and he yearns for you not to go back to that cheapened existence.

When I lust after a woman, I do not take into account her hopes, dreams, insecurities, and vulnerabilities, and I am in no position to support these things. The same goes for animals. With rare exceptions, the majority of the animal kingdom experiences sex as nothing more than instinctual pleasure, doing their reproductive deed, then moving on with life, with never a second thought about supporting their previous partner.[15] Animals don't support the emotional needs of their partners because they don't have any. But humans do. Women do. God created us above the animals. We are created in his image,[16] the animals are not.

Only a husband is in position to support a woman's insecurities and vulnerabilities. When I lust over a woman, I am definitely not her husband and cannot offer her that support. I am only taking into account her body parts and how I can consume them, like an animal. I care nothing about the rest of who she is or my inability to support her full humanity. Instead, I have taken away her humanity. I have degraded her.

On the flip side, my wife is fully human (with hopes, dreams, insecurities, vulnerabilities), and I've made a commitment to her that allows her to trust me with her humanity and all her imperfections. When I lust over the girl working at the coffee shop, I break that trust by spilling my marriage's intimacy. As Proverbs 5:15–17 states, "Drink water from your own cistern, running water from your own well. Should your springs overflow in the streets, your streams of water in the public squares? Let them be yours alone, never to be shared with strangers."

Our streams of marital intimacy are not meant to spill over into

---

15. Or if you're a praying mantis, the female bites off your head during sex and devours your corpse for nourishment. Does anyone still want to cast their vote for animal sex?

16. Genesis 1:27.

the public square. I've just given the barista something intimate, something meant only for my wife, and I've also taken something intimate from her.

Yes, I am designed to be attracted to the body of a woman, but it's meant to be attached to all the other aspects of our one-flesh relationship, so that the other ingredients of the relationship can support and shape this experience. When I indulge in this attraction at the coffee shop counter, I tarnish both the barista (by degrading her) and my marriage (by enjoying something meant to be enjoyed with my spouse). Now when I go to be sexually intimate with my wife, I am bringing in another flesh, a flesh I cannot support and a flesh that pollutes the trust we have established. This is the trust that allows my wife to be vulnerable with me. It is the trust and faithfulness needed to make a marriage healthy, strong, and sexually thriving.

Have you ever done a trust fall as part of a team-building exercise? One person stands on the edge of a picnic table or similar platform and the rest of the team gets behind them at ground level. Team members make two parallel lines facing one another with their arms extended, alternating to form a "zipper" of arms. The person standing on the tabletop has their back to their team. When signaled by the team, this person tips backward toward the earth.

The sensation of falling is a rush. The reason this exercise is called a trust fall is obvious: the person falling trusts their team to safely catch them. Without the team's commitment to catching the person, the fall could be disastrous. If the teammates get distracted by their smartphones or by a squirrel, the results could be deadly. One person must trust, and the others must commit to a laserlike focus on guarding and honoring that trust.

In the same way, sex is meant to take place only within a trust relationship, when one partner is committed to supporting the other. Would you ever do a trust fall with people you aren't sure care enough to catch you? Or with animals? Certainly not. And if someone is falling into your arms, are you the type of person who cares enough to keep them safe? I hope so.

The potency of sex needs this type of support or it will produce cataclysmic results in the long run—both to the individuals involved and to culture at large.

What damage has been inflicted on you by falling into the wrong set of arms? What damage have you inflicted?

Meanwhile, your wife is falling, trusting you to catch her and keep her safe.

Will you?

> If you're using the Forty-Day Devotional Guide in
> the back of this book, turn now to **Day 27**.

Bland Bread

God's recipe for sex is a great reminder of the truth that God created sex, and he created it to be very good.

Sex is God's, not Satan's.

What is the purpose of a car? Why does its creator make it run on gas and oil and design thousands of moving parts to work efficiently together? The car's creator does this so it can take you places. And not only take you there but also take you safely and comfortably.

God didn't randomly create sex and then add a bunch of rules to make it as difficult as possible for us to enjoy. He created it with great intentionality. And the part of that intentionality we so often overlook is that sex is about much more than what happens between the sheets. God-honoring sex produces strong, incredible families, which produce incredible societies and incredible legacies. God-honoring sex upholds all humans with dignity and love, rather than relegating humans to be objects that are consumed and discarded. God-honoring sex shapes our hearts to love the way Christ loves us. God-honoring sex teaches us what real love is. God-honoring sex models to our children how they are to view people. God-honoring sex produces lives of substance, character, and integrity.

God-honoring sex produces better people and a better world. It produces a life free from the emptiness and destruction of betrayal that Proverbs 5 speaks so passionately against.

The purposes and benefits of God-honoring sex are limitless, but they are all the benefits of tending an apple orchard—of careful planning and preparing, of sweat equity and self-discipline, of hard work and diligence, of strings attached, of the long term, not the short term, of endurance and perseverance, not selfishness, of the big picture and the final harvest, not instant gratification.

These benefits come from reading the recipe and investing the time each step takes. We go to the store to buy all of the ingredients, most of them bland. We wait for an oven to preheat, then get our hands and clothes dirty mixing everything we need. We let a bunch of ingredients work together as one, then let them go through the 400-degree fire for a long period of time. Finally, we wait for the cake to cool down before we add the frosting.

But it's worth it, isn't it?

The beauty of God's recipe for sex is that it provides the perfect place for sugar. Imagine you made a cake without the sugar. A marriage without God-honoring sex isn't a delicious cake. It's bland bread. Have great sex in your marriage, not a bland utilitarian life partnership. The butter, flour, eggs, and milk that go into a cake aren't nuisances to be tolerated. They are inseparable companions for the sugar and are to be celebrated. The other ingredients of marriage allow us to lovingly say to our wives:

You are the only person I do this with.
You are the only person I say these things to.
You are the only person I trust myself to.
You are the only person I will support through thick and thin.
When you fall, I will catch you.
You are safe with me.

God created sex to cement a relationship and provide experiences and pleasure that only spouses share. Marriage was created to be the space where sex shines, not fades into oblivion. Remember that Proverbs 5:18–19 points out we are meant to enjoy sex long past our youth: "May your fountain be blessed, and may you rejoice in the wife of your youth. A loving doe, a graceful deer—may her breasts satisfy you always, may you ever be intoxicated with her love."

Breasts and body parts and sex are a beautiful, God-ordained ingredient in the overall recipe of marriage, but lose their meaning and purpose when they are removed and consumed as a side dish.

How do you get more and better sex in your marriage? Books like *Sheet Music*[17] by Dr. Kevin Leman are helpful, for both you and your wife. Just be careful not to let "more and better" be your motivation, lest you fall into the traps of entitlement and consumption. But by all means, see what help you can find from these tools.

See all of your marriage as an act of worship.

God created sex.

God created marriage.

God sovereignly brought you and your wife together.[18]

Trust him.

Be faithful.

Pray unceasingly for God's approval to fill you up and be your power source. Double your intentionality here if your marital sex life is struggling.

Remind yourself of God's voice over and over again: "You are my son, whom I love, and in whom I am well pleased."

Pray unceasingly for your wife.

Pray unceasingly for your marriage.

Pursue your wife as a full person, not as a set of body parts. Love her soul as your highest priority.

Tend the orchard.

---

17. Kevin Leman, *Sheet Music* (Carol Stream, IL: Tyndale, 2003, 2008). I highly recommend this book for Christian instruction on the mechanics of sex, but be aware it is also full of the kickback-love approach.

18. If your wife is holding out on you and it's leading you to sin, go back and reread chapters 2 and 3. Thank God for using this lack of sex to sanctify you and draw you closer to him.

And stick to the recipe.

Listen to the advice of the wise old man in Proverbs 5. When you look back on your life as an old man yourself, you won't regret it.

> If you're using the Forty-Day Devotional Guide in
> the back of this book, turn now to **Day 28**.

Below the Surface

The purpose of this chapter is to help you see how God's design for sex brings incredible benefits that, if put on a scale, outweigh the benefits of Satan's design for sex. Proverbs 5–7 testifies to this powerfully. But often we look only at the surface level of Satan's design for sex and the surface level of God's, and we end up fighting the battle for purity with the deck stacked heavily against us.

In this chapter we tried to zoom out to view God's design for sex and see how lust and extramarital sex are destined to fail, regardless of how they make us feel in the moment. This chapter also reminded us that God is in control and he knows what he's doing, even if it doesn't always feel like it.

This leads us to the place God controls, the place we are to live: reality.

In Your Small Group

Scan this QR code or go to www.beyond thebattle.net/videos and watch "Session 5 (Chapters 7–8): God's Recipe." (All small group resources are free.)

CHAPTER 9

THE NEED TO EMBRACE REALITY

The Death Grip of Fantasy

Have you ever seen someone run into a pole as they walk while texting? It is hilarious! Texting is hazardous—people run into poles, a woman fell into a mall fountain, and a man almost walked into a bear. Thankfully, all of these mishaps were caught on video so the rest of us could be entertained.[1] A woman even walked off of a pier into Lake Michigan and had to be rescued by the Coast Guard. Fortunately, no one was seriously hurt in any of these instances.

But not all of the stories are as funny as these. In 2014, more than twenty-five hundred people had to go to emergency rooms because they were injured while texting and walking.[2] Every year, there are even texters who die because they walk out in front of cars while texting.[3]

---

1. See ABC News, "Texting while Walking Accidents: Video," May 14, 2012, https://youtu.be/wl0JojWH1rQ.

2. Michael Addady, "Texting while Walking Is Sending People to the Emergency Room," *Fortune*, February 18, 2016, http://fortune.com/2016/02/18/texting-while-walking.

3. ABC News, "Texting while Walking Accidents."

127

These stats don't even include all of the zany stories about the Pokémon Go mobile phone game. These include two men who fell off a seventy-five-foot cliff, and people being robbed at gunpoint, getting hit by cars, crashing their cars into trees, and falling into ponds.[4]

A continual complaint from older generations is that Gen Z and millennials are unable to be present. The feeling is that these generations have been raised on video games and smartphones, so they aren't equipped to have conversations in real life with real people. While it's not fair to stereotype an entire generation, some young people (in fact, people of all ages) fit this description—adults who would rather play video games for twelve straight hours than get a job or who constantly comment on the social media pages of their friends without having any real friends they can share their real lives with.

A word that sums up this way of life is fantasy. I'm not talking Lord of the Rings–style wizards and elves. I'm talking about a false reality substituted for actual reality. While people walking into poles while playing Pokémon Go can be funny, the consequences of this trend in our thought lives are no laughing matter.

What is the opposite of life? The obvious response is death, but a viable alternative is fantasy. Think about it: Life is real. Fantasy is not. Life is the dirt beneath you. It is gravity. It is oxygen. Fantasy is dragons, galactic adventures, and unicorns. Life is your job, your bills, your responsibilities, real relationships, and conflict. Fantasy is thinking about punching your boss, desiring to live in Tahiti, and indulging in unreal sexual scenarios. Fantasy is the belief that the person you are infatuated with has no flaws and that you will always have the butterfly feeling you had when you first met.

Life simply cannot compete with fantasy. While life is full of letdowns that are out of our control, we can shape fantasy however we see fit. Fantasy can seem irresistible. Once we get a taste of its fruits

---

4. Josh Luckenbaugh, "Pikachu's Sinister Side: A Compilation of 'Pokemon Go' Fails and Wrongdoing," MRCTV, July 14, 2016, https://www.mrctv.org/blog/pikachus-sinister-side-compilation-pokemon-go-fails-and-wrongdoing.

(which do not exist in reality), it reels us in again and again to sip from its magical chalice. But as we look at fantasy with an experienced eye, its glass jaw appears. For all of fantasy's appeal, its weakness is so obvious we may miss it: it is not real. And for those who failed their vocabulary tests in elementary school, real is all we have!

Imagine you ate only fantasy food, drank only fantasy water, and breathed only fantasy air. What would happen to you? You would die. To remain alive, you must eat, drink, and breathe in reality, not just fantasize about doing such things. If this is true of these components of life, why wouldn't it also be true of sexuality and human relationships? Fantasy in our sexual lives will kill us, while living in reality will bring us life. This truth is the secret weapon we need to conquer the giant of sexual immorality.

In John 10:10, Jesus tells us, "I have come that they may have life, and have it to the full." He prefaced this with, "The thief comes only to steal and kill and destroy." We all want life, and Jesus is offering it, yet there is a thief who is trying to deceive us and take it from us any way he can.

Because God created sex, it makes perfect sense that following his design for sex will bring life, whereas Satan's cheap substitutes will bring only empty imitation and dysfunction.

Our sexual sins take many forms, but they all deceive us into living in fantasy rather than reality.

It's amazing how realistic video games are nowadays. I remember playing games on the Atari 2600 with my brothers as a kid. We'd play "football," which consisted of a collection of beige squares moving against another collection of beige squares, using a black square to represent a ball. Nowadays sports games, war games, and adventure games all offer us a picture as close to reality as possible. Games are also getting more and more interactive, with motion-sensing controllers and other sensory apparatus, trying to offer as lifelike an experience as they can. It doesn't take much imagination to foresee how virtual reality will be incorporated into every mainstream video game system soon, complete with visors and an array of body sensors.

The scary part about today's video games is they are such a far cry from the innocent days of squares and dots. Games today not only look and feel real, they are also filled with gratuitous violence and, yes, even fully nude sex scenes. It's easy to see how the virtual reality experience will soon take over the pornography industry as the go-to choice for endless sexual fantasies.

Imagine you created a video game so exciting and entertaining you never wanted to leave it. Think of how that would sell. And what would the impact be of a game like that? People all over the world would soon be dying at a rapid pace! They'd never actually eat. And they wouldn't care, because the fantasy experience would be so captivating.

Honestly, this is the experience many have already created in their minds. Whether it's porn or extramarital fantasy, we devote an incredible amount of time and energy to fantasy—a place of longing, a place that doesn't exist. Like a parasite slowly sucking the life from us, fantasy emaciates our reality until we become a shell of ourselves.

> If you're using the Forty-Day Devotional Guide in
> the back of this book, turn now to **Day 29**.

Marrying the Wrong Person (For Married Men)

Pornography isn't the only place we entertain fantasy.

If you're in a dry season in your marriage, you've more than likely had some of the following thoughts:

What if I'd married one of my ex-girlfriends instead of
　my wife?

What would life be like with the woman at work (or at the
　gym or at church)?

What if I had married someone who shares my recreational
　interests?

If only I hadn't felt pressure from my family to get married.
If only I hadn't gotten married so young.
If only I hadn't gotten my wife pregnant, I could have left her.
If only my wife gave me compliments the way other
    women do.
If only my wife had more of a sex drive.
If only I had married someone who was more attractive.
If only I had married someone who kept themselves in better
    shape.
If only I was single so I could flirt with and pursue this other
    woman.
If only I was single so I could manage my house, schedule, and
    finances the way I want to.

And the list could go on and on.

All of these thoughts have one thing in common: None is based in reality. Each one is a fantasy, a false reality. Each time we entertain one of those thoughts, we deprive our actual reality of much needed investment.

And even if we did act on one of these thoughts, making it real, it would create consequences and pain that we're not planning for in our fantasy worlds. Acting on these questions is like believing that time travel is real. Even though the 1980s Back to the Future movies predicted Donald Trump's presidency and the Cubs winning the World Series, I'm pretty sure time travel is still out of reach! The deception beneath all of these fantasies is that we are convinced we married the wrong person. We made some sort of error, and we need to go back and fix it. But we can't change the past. Attempting to only further scars our present.

The truth we must embrace is that no one marries the right person. There is no such thing. It's an illusion fed to us by pop songs and Hollywood love stories.

Leading marriage therapists Drs. John and Julie Gottman say that when we choose whom we will marry, we are choosing the set of perpetual problems we want to deal with for the next fifty years.[5] We could have an affair or get divorced and marry someone else, and we'd simply be marrying a different set of perpetual problems. The Gottmans' extensive scientific research shows that perpetual problems are as much a part of marriage as wedding rings and anniversaries.

It is ironic that we are so infatuated with Hollywood romance movies starring our favorite celebrities. These movies include fun, sexy women who fall in love with handsome, charming men. They go on exotic dates, have passionate sex, and of course, get married and live happily ever after. The wedding (with a corresponding group-dance scene during the credits) is always at the very end of the movie. Movies about marriage itself are boring, but movies about falling in love get our juices flowing. We watch them, then wish our love lives looked more like what we see on the big screen.

The irony is that in reality, celebrities are often notorious for having the worst success in marriage, yet we model our relationships after the fictional characters they embody. They make gossip headlines for their fifty-five-hour marriages,[6] their constant breakups, and their cheating escapades. If it weren't for the tawdriness of celebrity relationships, the $3 billion[7] celebrity gossip industry would go bankrupt.

Yet despite these impressive relational shambles, these are the people we fantasize about being with. We crave the illusions they depict in movies and songs. These celebrities' relational patterns are the patterns we strive to emulate, convincing ourselves we'd be better off with someone other than the one we made our vows to.

One of Satan's biggest lies is that you married the wrong person. What he wants most is to slowly suck the life out of your marriage and your life, and he is more than happy to offer you fantasy after fantasy to ensure this happens.

---

5. The Gottman Relationship Institute, *The Art and Science of Love*, DVD set, https://www.gottman.com/product/the-art-and-science-of-love-home-dvd-workshop/.

6. Britney Spears in 2004.

7. Jim Rutenberg, "The Gossip Machine, Churning Out Cash," *New York Times*, May 21, 2011, http://www.nytimes.com/2011/05/22/us/22gossip.html.

A year or two into our seventeen-year marriage, my wife and I were having a hard time agreeing where to go on vacation and what to do together in our free time. We realized we didn't have as much in common as when we were gushing over one another during our dating and engagement years. We decided to take a compatibility test in a premarriage resource—one of those surveys with around a hundred options of things you like to do. Each spouse works privately to check the boxes that apply to him or her, then together they compare answers. When my wife and I took this survey, we discovered that we had zero matches! Proof that each of us had married the wrong person, right? By the world's relationship metrics, yes. But because we were operating under a higher authority, we did not see our marriage as doomed. Instead, we invested in each other and in our marriage.

Honestly, what ended up saving our marriage was finding our individual fulfillment in the love, acceptance, and approval Jesus had already shown us on the cross, rather than looking for our spouse to meet those needs. If we say we've married the wrong person, we are really saying we've finally discovered that our spouses can't give us what only Jesus can.

There is no such thing as marrying the wrong person. There is only marrying the person you married. Love your wife and invest in her. And when it feels as though you've married the wrong person, get married to Jesus (or "renew your vows" with him). He is the only one whose love will truly make you whole.

> If you're using the Forty-Day Devotional Guide in the back of this book, turn now to **Day 30 (For Married Men)**.

Pick Your Poison (For Single Men)

As a single man, you don't have to struggle with the fantasy that you'd be better off with someone other than your wife. But you have a variety of other fantasies to choose from.

You might have a girlfriend and fantasize that she is the best thing since sliced bread. You are intoxicated with her. You get a rush of endorphins whenever she is around. You worship her and she worships you. You've sinned sexually with her time and time again, forsaking God's commands for your sex lives, because frankly, she feels like a much better god than God does.

But the news flash is in: reality bites. Reality will hit with every girlfriend in one way or another. One option is that you'll break up and she'll become an ex, a far cry from the perfect human doll you worship now. Or you'll make it long enough to get married, and then reality will hit. A different transformation will take place—she'll become a wife. Every woman who has ever married has become a wife. Not a single one remains a permanent butterfly-inducing doll.

Every woman who gets married changes from the date who always has her hair and makeup done, who always is in a good mood, and who always puts her best foot forward. She changes from the flirtatious woman who does whatever is necessary to keep you around. Now that she has you, her real self comes out, a self you will never see until you get married. Don't get me wrong: this isn't a bad or scary self that comes out. It's just her real self. Her real self which lives in real life.

Dating isn't real life.[8] Marriage is real life. It's a life of bills and planning and teamwork and obligations and responsibilities and childrearing. This woman you dated has turned into a wife. She once was one thing, and now she is something else—too busy or too stressed out to always put her best foot forward, too much real life to work on together to be constantly playful and flirtatious. She doesn't need to flirt or primp to keep you impressed anymore, and frankly, you're no longer that impressive to her either (sorry to burst your bubble). She has gone from worshiping you to trying to get you to clean up after yourself, from batting her eyes at you to balancing the checkbook with you.

This is why guys serial date. This might be why you are serial

---

8. I like to joke that dating was part of the Genesis 3 fall of humankind. It never existed in the perfect world of Genesis 1 and 2. God made a man, then made a woman, and that was all there was to it.

dating as you read this. Guys date a girl for up to a year or two, until reality hits—conflict, flaws, responsibility, boredom—and then they move on to the next Golden-Haired Woman. This is Fantasy 101. Some of these guys settle down and get married to whomever they happen to be dating when they start to feel old or when they decide to have kids. Others just continue to date around into oblivion.

For other single guys, the fantasy is quite different. Living alone or with little Christian community, the fantasy of pornography reigns. Pixilated and airbrushed depictions of women adoring them keep them coming back for more. Every time they go back, their minds get more hooked and more warped. Reality becomes more and more distant as the onslaught of porn has them swallowing the bait hook, line, and sinker.

For some, the fantasy turns to despair. The desire for marriage turns into despair about never being married.[9] Rather than embrace singleness as a gift (see "A Note from the Author" at the beginning of the book), they allow frustration and feelings of failure to reign. This is a much more cloaked way Satan sucks the life out of our reality, but it's just as effective. Rather than embrace the reality of being single and all the blessings it can bring to God's kingdom and to their individual lives, they toil in misery for the rest of their days, basing their identities on the fantasy of marriage, a fantasy they don't need but have been duped into thinking they do.

Whatever your spot in life as a single man, you need to see marriage for what it is. Like your married brothers, if you get married, you too will ask the same doubting questions about your wife someday. Get rid of the mindset that marriage is a happily-ever-after experience. It isn't for your married guy friends now, and it won't be for you. If you get married, fine—have realistic expectations. If you don't get married, fine—you're not missing out on what you think you are. As it is, you are single now, so live fully in this reality.

Get rid of the mindset that any form of sex is a happily-ever-after experience. Get rid of the mindset that sex is the most powerful

---

9. This is different from choosing not to be married or to be content in submission to God's sovereignty regarding your relational status.

force in the universe. Get rid of the mindset that you get a sin pass in this one area. Get rid of the mindset that your current Jesus-soaked reality is somehow subpar or a consolation prize. Get rid of the mindset that God made a mistake when creating you or that God is holding out on you. Get rid of the mindset that it's okay to devour women. Get rid of the mindset that a woman can be a better god for you than God can. Get rid of the mindset that there are no repercussions for your lust and fantasies, even if you remain single. Get rid of the mindset that everything in your life should revolve around your romantic life or that a romantic life is the only type of life that matters. Get rid of the mindset that you're entitled to sexual sin because you're single. Get rid of the self-pity that often accompanies singleness and see your singleness for what it is: the only reality you have, a reality worth investing in.

The reality God gave you.

For a purpose.

If you're using the Forty-Day Devotional Guide in the back of this book, turn now to **Day 30 (For Single Men)**.

The Grass Is Greener

At the age of twenty-four and three years into my marriage, I let the world of fantasy take me all the way to the edge. I was convinced I had married the wrong person. I was convinced I couldn't continue in my marriage. All I could see was divorce, followed by a season of promiscuity.

Satan is crafty in getting us to think that a quick decision like divorce is easy and will bring us immediate and absolute relief from all problems. The illusion is that these decisions let us rewind to the days when we were free. Like breaking one Lego piece from another with no strings attached. You go your way and I'll go mine. Clean, quick, and painless.

He is so good at duping us with fantasy.

I remember the day I pulled out my journal to assess all of my options before making a decision.

I'm so thankful I did.

I wanted to put Satan's Lego theory to the test and see how easy and painless a break like this really would be. I knew I had three choices, and I wanted to write down each choice's ripple effects to envision what each one would be like in reality.

It's amazing what happens when we bring reality into Satan's fantasy equation. Like a morning sunrise evaporating the fog, the scene changes quickly. What was supposed to be simply one Lego piece separating from another turns into the crashing down of an elaborate house of cards. What follows are excerpts from my journal, dated August 3, 2007. As I look back on these words more than a decade later, they feel raw and even shocking to me now. I wrote them during a difficult season, but perhaps you can relate to where I was at that time.

Choice 1: Listen to the little voice. Get a divorce. Quit my job. Move to San Diego. Work at Starbucks. Get a master's degree. Live near the beach. Play sports. Try to pick up attractive women. Try to find attractive women who'd want to have sex with me. This choice involves: I would have hollow sex with insecure girls who don't really care about me. I'd get a reputation as a player, as a people user. I'd wreck friendships. I'd be lonely. I'd end up getting married to someone eventually anyway, and I'd be right back where I started. I would be severing myself from pretty much all of my current friendships. Having everyone, including my family, look at me with shame for the rest of my life. I'd have to completely start over with zero friends. No one to talk to about my struggles. Isolated. All the friends I currently have would basically be gone. I'd no longer be able to work in ministry—for the rest of my life, most likely. Crossroads [the church I founded] would be kaput. I'd be disobeying God's calling on my life to lead this church. I would segregate myself from kingdom work, and my concern would now be to make sure my needs got met.

Divide up my possessions. Have memories with Jen the rest of my life. Risk never having a family or support system. Risk no career stability ever. Break covenant with God and witnesses I made on my wedding day to stay married. I will look like a hypocrite to everyone I've ever ministered to or preached to, causing them discouragement in their walks with God.

Choice 2: Persevere and make my marriage work. The risk here is I will go on being unfulfilled and feel like half a man for the rest of my life. Feeling empty. Hollow. To change that, I decide to fully dive into the current life I'm living. I gear all of my efforts around investing in Jen and in our marriage. Whenever I'm tempted to do something for myself, like fantasizing or porn or checking a woman out, I instead dive into my life and invest something into Jen to make her life better. I submit to knowing God brought Jen and me together for his reasons and he is in control.

Choice 3: Go on living conflicted. Put on a good front by preaching the sermons you get paid to do. By slipping every now and then into porn, yet wanting it always. Always wishing Jen would divorce me. Never feeling close with Jen.

Choice 3 is definitely the worst choice of the three and is what I feel right now.

Reality is powerful.

Repercussions are powerful.

I chose choice 2.

What I realized was that all the time I spent in fantasy was preventing my heart from investing in reality. When my heart was somewhere else, it couldn't be present in my marriage. I had no desire to humbly love my wife and invest in what we had. As a result, reality just continued to shrivel up.

I realized that fantasy does not exist. My only choice was to reject reality or embrace reality. I chose to embrace it, not begrudgingly or out of obligation but truly with joy, like taking a deep breath of pure oxygen after being underwater too long. I chose to embrace it as the only thing I have, as the undeserved mercy God gave me.

Imagine you never mowed your lawn.

Or you never shaved, brushed your teeth, and showered.

Not a pretty picture, right?

Yet why is it we think our marriages will just take care of themselves? And why are we so surprised when we fail to invest in our marriages and then find they aren't going so great?

You've likely heard the statement, "The grass is greener on the other side of the fence." This is the reason people pursue affairs and divorce. This is the fantasy we buy into.

A better and truer statement comes from Christian community developer Neil Barringham: "The grass is greener where you water it."

Or, "Take care of your lawn, because it isn't going to take care of itself."

Or, "Water and mow your lawn and the other lawns won't be as appealing."

This mentality saved my marriage. If I was tempted to look at porn, I did the dishes instead. If I was fantasizing about a woman at the gym, I bought my wife flowers. When my flesh wanted to run away to fantasy, I chose to make a deposit in reality. I didn't want to make these deposits. I made them as a newly programmed response whenever I felt discontent in my marriage, which was often.

Looking back, I'm so thankful for this practice, but I have to admit my mentality was still stuck in "I scratch your back, you scratch mine." But I discovered that there is beauty in embracing reality. Reality is the only place where freedom dwells. Living in fantasy only sucks the life out of us. Fantasy enslaves us, leading us deeper and deeper into despair until we finally snap.

Fantasy starves reality. However bad your reality is now, fantasy will only make it worse.

Every time.

Without fail.

What I'm trying to get across is a simple truth: every ounce of energy you spend away from your marriage is an ounce of energy you could have invested in your marriage. Let those temptations to run away fuel you to serve your wife, to enroll in counseling, to buy her flowers, to write her thoughtful notes, to do the laundry, to go on dates, and to do whatever is needed to take care of your marriage. Tell yourself, "If my marriage is so bad that I want to run away from it, I will invest in it and make it better so that I won't want to run away from it."

Once you start investing in reality, don't keep track of the score. You'll be tempted to, but if you cave in to this, you'll end up worse off than when you started. You might not receive an immediate return on your investment, but for that void, you have the all-sufficient grace of Jesus, your power source. Your primary engine. Your groom.

Don't do this for the kickback. Do it out of worship and gratitude. Your investment of sacrificial worship and sanctification *will* produce lasting fruit and green grass in God's way and in God's timing, so persevere in it.

And single guys, we're all in the same boat. You're going to be tempted by fantasy. You don't have a marriage to invest in, but you do have a reality. Invest in it. I can't emphasize this enough. Invest in connection and community. Like marriage, these aren't going to bear fruit all by themselves. You have to put forth effort, take risks, and be courageous.

Fantasy produces barren apple orchards overrun with weeds. Investing in and embracing reality brings bountiful orchards full of fruit not only for you but for your wife, your children, and all of those your life touches.

Fantasy kills. Reality brings life. Which one will you embrace?

If you're using the Forty-Day Devotional Guide in the back of this book, turn now to **Day 31**.

CHAPTER 10

HOW TO EMBRACE REALITY

It's Not Real

The term "glass chin" or "glass jaw" comes from the world of boxing. A boxer can be the biggest, baddest behemoth on the planet, but if he has a glass jaw, one square hit to the chin puts him down for the count.

Fantasy can also look like the biggest, baddest behemoth on the planet. Whatever your cup of fantasy is, there are valid reasons it is so alluring and overpowering. Fantasy lets you eat a dozen donuts a day but never put on weight, or bring home a six-figure paycheck without having a job. You can make fantasy whatever you want. If you can think it, you can have it. When it comes to sexual and relational fantasy, how on earth can this enemy be defeated? What you have in reality can't even come close to what you can conjure up in fantasy.

But like the behemoth boxer, fantasy has a glass chin. Fantasy's glass chin is that it's not real.

The only way to deliver a knockout punch to fantasy's glass jaw is to figure out what *is* real.

What is real is your wife, your children (or future children), your job, your reputation, your ministry, your Christian testimony, your home, your marriage vows, your pets, and everything else you share with your wife. What is real is your life.

When we are attracted to someone other than our wives, we begin picturing a life with the other woman that is just that: a picture. And guess what? Pictures aren't real. You can put a cardboard cutout of someone in your house, but that picture is not the living, breathing person themselves. You can't live in a picture. Pictures are fantasy, and fantasy will kill you.

As we noted in chapter 3, it's not a good idea to watch television commercials when you're really hungry. The food in commercials, even Burger King, ends up looking so good. The onion, lettuce, and tomatoes glisten as they bounce through a cascade of water droplets to land gracefully on the exquisitely soft, golden-brown bun. The juicy burger looks gigantic and mouthwatering as its toppings billow out beyond the edges of the bun.

You decide you must have this delectable burger, so you get in your car and drive quickly to the nearest BK.

At the restaurant, what is this burger like in reality? The squished bun is shiny from the greasy handprint of the sandwich maker. It's flat as a pancake, the tomato is a pale pink, it has a single shred of shriveled lettuce, and the ketchup has made a mess of the inside of the wrapper. You take a bite and get all bun and ketchup because the meat and toppings are not stacked evenly.

Not exactly how the TV commercial pictured it.

It's pretty hilarious (and disturbing) to type "Burger King burgers" into Google Images and contrast the pictures that come up from official BK ads with the photos customers have taken of actual burgers. Viewer discretion is advised.

The fact is that the food you see in any TV commercial is typically not even edible. The deep red you see on strawberries is actually lipstick, and the milk you see in cereal is heavy cream, or even glue! Sounds scrumptious, doesn't it? And remember that mouthwatering BK burger you saw before you hopped into your car and headed to the drive-thru? The beef patty was cooked for only twenty seconds on each side, then branded with a skewer, painted with food dye, and cut up and spread out to enlarge it. It's resting on a piece of cardboard to keep the bottom bun looking perky. The sesame seeds are glued onto the bun, and the lettuce, tomato, and pickles are all held on by pins.[1] *Bon appétit!*

When we know what something would actually be like if it became part of our reality, it becomes much less appealing (like eating a pin-filled glue burger). If I were to pursue a relationship with this person I'm attracted to, it would destroy everything I have in my life. When I come to terms with this destruction, the allure of the fantasy fades away.

Some may say, "But my reality isn't good. The little high I get out of fantasy is better than what my reality can offer me, so I'm going to continue to indulge in it." This is a moot point, because no matter how good the food looks on TV, you can't eat it. You can bite into your TV screen all you want, but your stomach will remain empty. Whatever your alternative, you know for sure that fantasy will kill you. It will not do your body any good to eat fantasy food, so why invest any time and energy into it?

When we see these temptations as thieves that steal from, trap, and imprison us, their enchantment loses its power. I don't care how good looking an armed thief is or how low cut her dress is, I'm certainly not going to let her enter my house to harm my family and rob me of my valuables. I'm going to call the police and (if needed) physically fight her off before I allow this to happen, giving no thought to how alluring or seductive she might be.

Why not respond the same to a sexual thief?

If your reality is in rough shape, the solution is not to continue to fantasize about eating imaginary food. It is to learn how to cook. The solution is to make your reality better and to enjoy it. It's all you have, so you had better learn to enjoy it. The grass is greener where you water it.

The only thing that's real about fantasy is that it will suck your

---

1. Watch all of this for yourself: "Food Ad Tricks: Helping Kids Understand Food Ads on TV," a segment from *Buy Me That!* a 1989 TV show, http://youtu.be/fUjz_eiIX8k.

life dry and get you miles and miles off the path God intends for you, leaving you empty and worn out.

When fantasy calls your name, say aloud, "It's not real."

It's not real.

Live in what is.

Invest in what is.

Give the Flesh a Taste of Its Own Medicine

Those who struggle with lust know that it's often quite a wrestling match. Paul's description of the battle between the Spirit and the flesh comes to mind: "So I say, walk by the Spirit, and you will not gratify the desires of the flesh. For the flesh desires what is contrary to the Spirit, and the Spirit what is contrary to the flesh. They are in conflict with each other, so that you are not to do whatever you want."[2]

This passage, combined with Paul's testimony on the Spirit versus the flesh in Romans 7, gives a picture of the Spirit and the flesh grappling on an Olympic wrestling mat.

The flesh is lying to us, telling us that what we are seeing and feeling when we lust is real. A key wrestling move against the flesh is to give it a taste of its own medicine. Use its own force and momentum to throw it out of the ring.

When a woman comes our way that we're tempted to lust over, it feels like a magnet has grabbed us and is drawing us in, despite anything we are thinking or desiring to the contrary. Something physiological switches on inside of us and the Star Trek tractor beam pulls us in.

Even if we bounce our eyes, every part of us except our eyes is still being drawn by the tractor beam. We still *really* want to keep looking, even though we have trained ourselves to do otherwise. Certainly a partial win, but not real freedom. I've always thought, "Wouldn't it be better if we lost our desire to look altogether?"

There is legitimate pushback to this idea. Most guys are hard-wired by God to be attracted to the female body. And vice versa, I

---

2. Galatians 5:16–18.

suppose. There really isn't a way around this. So then the million dollar question arises: what's the difference between looking and lusting?

I'll pause here to remind everyone that attraction is not a sin.[3] The problem is when we act on it sinfully. Beating yourself up for being attracted to women is like beating yourself up for being hungry or thirsty or for desiring fresh air. If a pretty woman walks into the room, I'm going to be attracted to her. So are you. This is not a sin. The sin of lust is when we indulge our attraction and linger over and objectify and crave what we see.

I'm not giving you a license to look but not lust. What I'm saying is the look is going to happen naturally and inadvertently. But your flesh is going to want you to keep looking and to *long* for. That's really the definition of lust: wanting something that isn't yours.

Let's look again at Jesus' take on this discussion in some verses you are likely familiar with if you've been battling lust as a Christian for any length of time: "You have heard that it was said, 'You shall not commit adultery.' But I tell you that anyone who looks at a woman lustfully has already committed adultery with her in his heart."[4]

To the Pharisees, it was good enough not to have sex with someone who wasn't their spouse. This gave them license to lust and think about it all they wanted with no repercussions. But Jesus comes along with one of the heaviest doses of reality ever. He says the reality is that when you lust, you are having sex with that person in the *spiritual* reality, which is the truest reality. Try to wrap your mind around that for a second. Imagine you had sex with every woman you have ever lusted over. I honestly don't think any of us would want that. Not in real, ultimate, oxygen-breathing reality.

---

3. I'll give this same encouragement to my brothers in Christ who are attracted to the same sex. We don't choose our attractions and they are not sinful. It's what we choose to do with them that is either sinful or not. I can make a strong biblical case for this, but that is outside the scope of this book. For a full explanation, see "What Does the Bible Say about Same Sex Attraction?" July 21, 2015, https://www.noahfilipiak.com/what-does-the-bible-say-about-same-sex-attraction.

4. Matthew 5:27–28.

Imagine all the heartache, broken marriages, kids separated from parents, people feeling used and abused, fatigue of trying to balance so many intimate relationships, loss of the very idea of what intimacy is, waste of time, horrific reputation you'd get—the list could go on and on. Sure, you'd have some physical rush associated with these experiences, but I think we'd all agree that scenario would be a real nightmare.

Your flesh knows this.

Your flesh knows you don't want to actually have sex with all these people. There's way too much collateral damage involved, let alone time and effort. What it wants you to do is just think about it, to glean the good parts of the experience, so to speak, without having to pay for it. It wants you to think about touching that person and having sex with that person, but it doesn't want you to go through with it.

This is a weapon we can use against the temptation to lust. If we want to think about having sex with a person, but don't actually want to have sex with that person, can you see how we can short-circuit the flesh's lie? We can throw lust right out of the wrestling ring, using its own bullying weight to propel it.

What I'm telling you is you don't actually want to have sex with the woman jogging down the street in the tight spandex. You don't. You don't actually want to pull your car over, ask her to get in, take all your clothes off, and have sex with her in your back seat. You want to think about that, but you don't want to do it. That would be hell on earth. For one thing, there's a good chance you'd be accused of rape. Even if she went with it, now you have to tell your wife. Picture that conversation. Picture your wife sobbing, vomiting from the stress, wailing, shattering household objects against the wall (and against your head!), and cursing at you like no sailor has ever cursed before. Picture her pain. Picture her telling you that she never wants to see you again and that you can never see your kids again. Picture the custody battle and divorce court. I am telling you, you don't want that! Neither does your flesh.

Even if none of that bad stuff happened, even if you somehow hid your deed from your wife, or you're single and don't have a wife, I am convinced you still don't want to have sex with that woman. You don't want that guilt festering inside of you. You don't want to be the type of person who randomly grabs women and has sex with them in cars, closets, or hotels.

Have you seen *Saving Private Ryan*, *Hacksaw Ridge*, or *Black Hawk Down*? War movies like these have wide appeal and are box office hits. But any soldier who has been in battle will tell you that going to see these movies is nothing close to the intense and often hellish experience of real combat.

The difference between watching a war movie and being in a war is like the difference between lustful fantasy and the experience of having sex with that person in reality. Your flesh is all about the movie and wants nothing to do with the real thing.

Lust is the movie; actual sex is the war. You're fantasizing about being in a war, but you don't want to be in a war. You're fantasizing about something you do not want. That's not even a fantasy anymore. Who fantasizes about doing calculus homework or getting a root canal? Nobody! When your fantasy becomes something you don't actually want, it loses its power and is no longer a fantasy.

Your flesh isn't going to fantasize about things you don't want.

Are you tracking with me?

Do you think I've lost my mind?

The key is to convince yourself, and thus your flesh, that you truly don't want these things in reality. And I don't believe you do. Just like you don't want a root canal.

This is all based on Jesus' words in Matthew 5:28. He is saying you *are* having sex when you lust over that woman. If that's true, when lust comes your way, you know what you can say to your flesh (aka to yourself)? "I don't want that." And you are being 100 percent genuine. This is not a fabrication. This is not a "look away" while still craving it. This is even acknowledging the physical beauty of a woman's body parts, something you can't control, yet you do not want to lust because lust is sex and you don't want to have sex with her.

You might push back and say, "Well, I do want those body parts or else I wouldn't be looking." Jesus says you don't get the war movie without the war. Jesus says there is no movie at all, there's only the war. You are attracted to the body parts, but you don't want them. If you do, then go over there and get them! Did you go? Why not? Because you don't want the war. You don't want those body parts. You just want the thought of them. You don't want that sex. So you can look lust in its face and speak directly into its tractor beam, "I do not want that." And it's the truth.

In these moments of attraction, I often visualize the conversation I'd be having with my wife if I jumped into this war. "Jen, I had sex with that barista." Even typing that gives me nausea. I then picture my beloved wife's reaction after I describe to her how our encounter unfolded. My nausea increases. I no longer want to lust over that barista, because I do not want to have sex with her. She becomes a normal, pretty woman whom I want nothing to do with sexually.

You can simply detach from the magnet and move on with life, and let her move on with life.

When that spandex-clad jogger bobs your way tomorrow, say to yourself, "I do not want to have sex with that woman." You're not trying to convince yourself of this. You are stating what is true. Sure, a part of you wants to have sex with her, but that's not the same thing as your actually wanting it. You can say this truth confidently. And in so doing, she will run along as a pretty woman in spandex. You're attracted to her, but you have no desire to take it any farther than that. Because there is no middle ground. There is no best of both worlds. There is no war movie. There is only war or no war. Jesus says taking it further in your mind *is* sex. Even your flesh doesn't want to pursue something that it doesn't want.

The last battle to get over is to believe that Jesus is right. We've been taught our whole lives that there *is* a war movie we can be entertained by, yet as you look back at all the porn and lust and fantasy you've engaged in, it has left a lot of warlike collateral damage, hasn't it? That's because it has always only been the war, just like Jesus said. Take this truth to the next level, to Jesus' level, and dodge the bullets being fired at your face. You won't need to read a book to convince you that you don't want those.

> If you're using the Forty-Day Devotional Guide in
> the back of this book, turn now to **Day 32**.

Lusting Over Plastic

I do not pay thirteen dollars for a movie ticket so I can see Hugh Jackman mow his lawn, take his kids to the doctor, and floss his teeth. I pay thirteen dollars because I want to see Wolverine shoot claws out of his wrists and fight against Magneto, Sentinels, and the evils of the X-Men universe.

Fantasy sells. Reality doesn't.

As entertaining and innocuous as this truth is when it comes to sci-fi and comic-book movies, it's also what makes sexual temptation's destruction so widespread throughout society. When a man stares at pornography, a Victoria's Secret fashion show, or a racy HBO sex scene, he does not want to know about the actress's or the model's seasonal allergies, family history, or kids. He doesn't want to think about how she would never let him touch her or even talk to her in a real human encounter. All the man wants is for this woman to tell him how much she wants him sexually (while in reality, what she really wants is her paycheck).

When a man looks at the cover of a beauty magazine, he doesn't want to know how the photo has been altered to eliminate wrinkles, to cut inches of flesh off, or to erase cellulite,[5] or how the model starves herself and works out six hours a day to maintain the unhealthy body she is displaying. All he thinks is, "Wow, she is attractive (and I wish my wife were that attractive too)."

It's worth repeating: it is truly amazing how the digital age has

---

5. For a before-and-after look at how this works, see the video "Dove Evolution" created by Tim Piper at http://youtu.be/iYhCn0jf46U.

separated women's body parts from whole human women and conditioned us to engage sexually and relationally with the parts but not the human herself. Never before in history could anyone imagine this sort of warped disconnect, yet today it is the formula for sex ingrained into the deepest core of our brains.

Men's brains have become preoccupied with finding sexual partners who have superhuman qualities created by Photoshop and fantasy, and we won't rest until we do. Because fantasy trumps reality every time. Who wants a regular woman when you can create a woman with perfect breasts, skin, and sex drive? You can even have sex with a custom-made robot doll nowadays.

Our digital age has conditioned us to be attracted to something that is not human. This is disturbing when you think about it. If you took a survey and asked whether we were meant to be attracted to (a) human beings or to (b) mutants, silicone, ink, megabytes, and pixels, it's a safe bet we'd all agree we are meant to be attracted to human beings. But the digital age of sex has trained us to be attracted to something real human women simply cannot compete with.

Even the real-life women we lust over often fall into this category. My wife and I recently attended a minor league hockey game on what happened to be college night. The place was packed with college girls who were dressed to impress. My wife commented that she, too, used to spend hours in the bathroom getting done up the same way in college, yet knows how unrealistic (and unneeded) that is in everyday married life. The singles scene is just as much an act as the cover of *Playboy* magazine is, and men chase both with abandon.

Imagine you meet a thirty-year-old man who is sincerely attempting to track down the real Santa Claus. He has made a travel plan to the North Pole, purchased hundreds of thousands of dollars worth of arctic camping and exploration equipment, and won't rest until he finds the man in the red suit, Rudolph, and all the little elves. Insane, correct?

Yet we are no different when we chase the fictional women of fantasy. The woman you are fantasizing about is not any more real than Santa Claus.

It's no wonder people get bored with their spouses. Even the celebrities who marry the picture-perfect models and movie stars we lust over get bored and end up ditching them. The woman in the picture is much more exciting than the same woman in real life. You can fall in love with Katniss Everdeen of the Hunger Games movies, but I promise you that marrying Jennifer Lawrence in reality would not be what you are picturing as you are chomping on popcorn in front of the silver screen.

The magic of fiction is that none of the characters exist, yet we see them as if they do. In a sermon on prayer, a friend's pastor shared how he caught himself sincerely praying for Jack Bauer of the TV show 24.[6] This is hilarious. It shows how fictional characters can feel so real to us, even though we know they're not. This makes for a funny sermon illustration, but it is sad and scary when so many men are trading in their relational and sexual realities for imaginary characters. Imagine this same pastor quit his job and moved to Los Angeles[7] so he could help save Jack Bauer's life. That sort of distortion and waste is what sexual fantasy is doing to us.

With pornography, you can have millions of electronically altered nude "women" at your fingertips. Red hair, blond hair, or dark hair, and all Photoshopped and airbrushed to perfection. It's like visiting an all-you-can-eat buffet that changes every five minutes. Later you go to be with your wife, and it feels like the same old brown-bag lunch you've had for years. Real women cannot become shape-shifters, yet that's what the digital age has conditioned us to desire.

Even for those who aren't attracted to the creations of airbrushing, lighting, and breast implants, Hollywood and the internet still have plenty of lures for you. Whether it's the girl next door or even romantic movies that get you fantasizing about the perfect relationship or the charm you wish your wife had, these films are just as fictional as their more obvious counterparts. These subtler

---

6. Played by actor Kiefer Sutherland, Jack Bauer is the main character in the popular TV show 24, which aired from 2001–10.

7. Los Angeles is where many of the 24 plot lines were set.

deceptions can be even more dangerous because they can easily get you thinking about a comparable person in real life. And we typically haven't prepared any defense against them. Although we might use an internet filter to screen out hardcore pornography, we figure we can handle these lower-level stimulants, so we let them run free. They pile up and redirect us before we even realize it.

The models and actresses we lust over are playing a role, as is the cute girl who is batting her eyes at you. What we are seeing is not real. The relationships, attraction, and seduction they promise are not real. The stories they are playing out and the characters they are portraying do not exist.

It's why strippers use stage names. It's why actors and actresses get annoyed when they are recognized in public by their character's names rather than their actual names. It's why the woman who wants to have an affair with you shows you only her fake good side, hiding all of the collateral damage an affair will bring to your life.

If a woman dresses up in a hamburger costume, it doesn't change the fact that she is still a woman and not actually a hamburger. These models and actresses are paid to put on costumes and act out parts. Just as Hugh Jackman is paid to wear his Wolverine costume. He's not actually Wolverine. He doesn't actually have any superpowers. (Sad, I know.) He doesn't wear his costume to the grocery store, and you should not address him as Wolverine if you run into him there.

We need to take what we already know about our TV and movie fantasies and apply them to our sexual and relational fantasies. To fail to do so is both insane and disastrous.

> If you're using the Forty-Day Devotional Guide in
> the back of this book, turn now to **Day 33**.

Fading Beauty

What is sad and ironic about the way our culture conditions us to view sex is that it's designed to fail. Like building a pyramid upside down or an airplane with only one wing, this approach obviously isn't going to work.

Consider: A man's wife *was* a goddess when he first fell for her. It may be hard to imagine now because of years of strife, wrinkles, and weight gain, but it's true for almost every married couple. Find a photo from the time when you and your wife were dating or engaged, or pop in your wedding DVD. (You really have the cards stacked against you if you're watching your ceremony on a VHS tape!) What do you see?

Let's say you met when you were in your early twenties. Your wife was at the peak of her physical beauty, and you were swept away. Whatever your story is, there is no doubt that physical attraction (and your blindness to her flaws) played some role in your romance. There's no sin in this: God designed women to be pretty so we'd fall for them. But when we camp out there for the long term, what inevitably follows is the classic tale of chasing the Golden-Haired Woman. Your wife used to take your breath away when she walked into the room. Now she's just a person with a whole bunch of issues. Meanwhile, your engine still revs for the sleek, youthful goddesses who cross your path, but not for the hassle and monotony of your wife.

Depending on what research you read and what angle the research takes, it is often reported that around 50 percent of all marriages end in divorce.[8] We have to push the pause button and figure out how we got here. Nobody plans to get a divorce when they say their vows, yet here we are.

The system we operate under when it comes to love, sex, and marriage is obviously flawed. Imagine a restaurant where only 50 percent of the food is edible, or a car company where only

---

8. Avvo Staff, "Marriage and Divorce Statistics," Avvo, April 12, 2010, http://www.avvo.com/legal-guides/ugc/marriage-divorce-statistics. You may hear it said that this is an inaccurate statistic because only around one-third of *first-time* marriages ends in divorce, with second and third marriages having exponentially higher divorce rates. But second- and third-time marriages and divorces still count in my book. So since the 50 percent divorce-rate stat refers to *all* divorces, it remains accurate and helpful.

50 percent of the cars produced work. Nobody would buy what those businesses are selling. No one would invest in them. Their failure not only would be national news but would make them the laughingstocks of their industries and the butt of jokes worldwide.

Yet when it comes to the romance industry (everything in our culture that conditions us to see sex the way we do), despite its colossal failure to produce results, we continue to buy, invest in, gorge on, and obsess over what it's selling.

This broken system can be explained anecdotally: A young man is conditioned by pornography, flirtation, and premarital sex to believe that young, beautiful women are goddesses who bring men ultimate pleasure and satisfaction. When the man goes to college, he lives the high life, partying and having sex with young, attractive women in the prime of their physical beauty. He finishes college, lives this type of life a few more years, and eventually decides to settle down with one of these young, beautiful goddesses. Then comes the major drag—the beautiful goddess gets older every single year. Every year adds a few more wrinkles, a little more weight, and another year's worth of relational conflict. Before the man knows it, he and his once-young goddess are now both thirty-eight. With a body changed by birthing the three kids they've had, his one-time goddess has devolved from the nubile young thing she used to be. But like any red-blooded American male, the man hasn't stopped watching the NFL and its buxom cheerleaders, perusing *Sports Illustrated* swimsuit editions, watching *Game of Thrones* and other television dramas full of young, naked bodies (which are commonplace on Netflix and other streaming TV services nowadays), and watching movie after movie starring the most beautiful young women on the planet. All of these stimuli reinforce the message he learned as an adolescent: the pleasure-filled romance he longs for will be found with a woman whose body looks like a twenty-one-year-old's.

Part of the allure of pornography is that these women never age. No matter how old the man gets, he can always find a fresh batch of photos of naked young women ready to seduce him. When a woman becomes too old to model, five young models are right there to step into her place. It's as if the attractive-women factory is stuck in a time warp that keeps churning out beautiful, perpetually young twenty-five-year-olds.

It's only a matter of time before our man with the wrinkled, stressed-out, thirty-eight-year-old wife becomes consumed with porn, strip clubs, or cheating on his wife with someone younger and prettier.

This is the reason rich old guys in their seventies and eighties are known for marrying hot young women in their twenties. (Show me one time that has ever happened the other way around.) This "sugar daddy" relationship reflects the mentality *we* have when we lust after someone who's younger and prettier than our wives.

People magazine's annual "Sexiest Man Alive" and *FHM*'s annual "100 Sexiest Women in the World" editions offer a great example of this broken message played out for all to read at the magazine rack.

Beginning in 1995 and running through 2016, the average age of *FHM*'s sexiest woman in the world is 26.1, with ages ranging from twenty-one to thirty-seven. Beginning in 1985, the average age of *People*'s sexiest man alive is 38.4, with ages ranging from twenty-seven to fifty-nine. Do the math and you see how quickly these numbers don't add up. If you're a thirty-eight-year-old man, you have a great chance of being viewed as sexy by the women around you. If you're married to a thirty-eight-year-old woman, she doesn't have a chance of making the sexy list. She has aged out of the sexiness competition, while you still have another twenty years left to strut your stuff.

It doesn't take a rocket scientist to figure out why so many men feel trapped in their marriages and yearn for prettier, more youthful women. And it doesn't take a rocket scientist to see the damage this broken system does to the self-worth of women who don't embody the young-twenties body shape anymore (or perhaps never did). It's no wonder the global market for anti-aging beauty products is esti-mated to reach 191.7 billion USD.[9] The demand couldn't be higher, aging women couldn't be sadder, men couldn't be more deceived and discontent, and the big cosmetic companies and plastic sur-geons couldn't be happier.

We don't live in a reality where women stay in their twenties for-ever. Yet this is the fantasy men are sucked into and can't find a way out of. It's the illusion we are offered again and again by our oversex-ualized culture, and it is the illusion we have traded in everything for to try to attain.

Even if you don't struggle with lusting over the twenties body shape, the societal principle still applies. Our culture worships female youthfulness as the definition of beautiful, sexy, and romantic.

But this definition simply isn't real. Turning someone into a collection of body parts isn't real.

Who are you allowing to define your reality? Stop living in a world of fantasy. Dive headfirst into God's design and reality for your marriage—and for how you view all women.

> If you're using the Forty-Day Devotional Guide in
> the back of this book, turn now to **Day 34**.

It's Not Important

The sad thing about reading through *FHM*'s 100 Sexiest Women in the World list is it shows just how temporary and fleeting youthful beauty really is. You're 26.1 years old only once. One has to wonder what happens after that. We put so much emphasis and value on young, beautiful women. What do these former winners think of themselves now? Some of them are in their late forties and early

---

9. "Global Anti-aging Market for Anti-wrinkle Products—Snapshot," Transparency Market Research, n.d., http://www.transparencymarketresearch.com/anti-aging-market.html.

fifties, a long way from the time when the world thought they were so amazing.

This ought to remind us that physical beauty simply isn't very important, and we need to start treating women with this in mind. It holds some importance and was created by God and has its time and place, but it has nowhere near the importance our culture puts on it. We can use this truth as our ally when combating sexual temptation.

When we are lusting over a woman or are tempted to have an affair based on someone's looks, we are betting the farm (or the orchard) on one temporary characteristic. We get swept away by someone's beauty and become intoxicated by the idea that this single trait is important enough to risk everything on. For at least that moment, it becomes the most important attribute in the universe.

But as we can all attest, physical attractiveness isn't all it's cracked up to be. There's a reason almost all the women on the 100 Sexiest Women in the World list have gone through breakup after breakup, with many of their men eventually cheating on them or leaving them for newer, prettier ladies. The most attractive woman in the world will never fulfill the promises fantasy sells.

Many of us can think of the prettiest girl from high school and how she was also the most selfish or most obnoxious. Many of us have gone on dates with women we met online or met casually; we liked what we saw but quickly realized there wasn't much else to like. Some have gone as far as to marry a woman simply because she was pretty, only to find out they got much more (or maybe much less) than they bargained for.

If we can minimize the value of physical beauty, we will be better able to thwart its attempts to seduce us. If physical beauty really cashed out in the end, it would be much harder to resist. But when we realize that this fleeting characteristic is worth only nickels and pennies, it becomes a lot easier to walk by the dirty coin looking up at us from the sidewalk. It's just not valuable enough to trade for what really matters.

A helpful tool is to audibly tell yourself, "It's not important" (referring to looks) when you're feeling tempted.

When you see an attractive woman, just see her as a woman, a human being. Nothing more than human and nothing less than human. Imagine her hurts. Imagine her struggles. Know that she needs grace, mercy, and compassion. This is as practical as can be. If you want to loosen lust's grip, do this: when you see an attractive woman, view her as you would an average woman. You know what I'm talking about. When a man sees an average woman, he just treats her as a person. There's no worshiping. There's no dehumanizing. There's no fantasy or hope. There's just normal conversation, with dignity and respect. There's a respect that this woman is human just like you. This isn't the case with an attractive woman. A man's heart rate goes up. The flirtatious smile widens. Jokes are attempted. These are all symptoms of overvaluing physical appearance and in not seeing someone as fully human.[10]

Just allow an attractive woman to be human without giving her extra power. Remember, it's not her fault she's attractive. Some attractive women get tired of being treated differently. They're tired of the extra attention. They're tired of being objectified. Allow yourself to see attractive women without fantasizing about what they're like or what you'd be like together. You can retrain your brain to do this. Attractive women are just as human as the rest of us.

My middle daughter is five years old. She recently moved on from watching only cartoons to watching movies and TV shows that have human actors and actresses in them. It has been hilarious to help her young brain navigate what is and isn't reality whenever she sees computer animation show up on the screen alongside the

---

10. Elna Baker tells her fascinating and sobering story of losing 110 pounds and how she was treated in society before and after she lost this weight. On a radio program, she confronts her husband (they'd been married ten days) as she realizes he never would have dated her if he had met her when she was heavier. He has no answer. You can listen to episode 589, "Tell Me I'm Fat (Act Two)" of the *This American Life* radio show and podcast at https://www.thisamericanlife.org/589/tell-me-im-fat/act-two-4. Note: Elna Baker is not a believer and is a former Mormon who pokes fun at her old faith. I do not endorse her worldview or everything in this radio program. I do recommend you listen to it because it's a unique look into the mind of a woman as she wrestles with her personhood and copes with men's objectifying her, including her own husband. I think you will grasp reality more clearly after listening to this.

human cast. She thinks the computer animation is real. Imagine thinking every alien, monster, or talking animal you ever saw in a movie is real and living in your back yard. It's always fun to try to explain to her what a movie is, what acting is, and how computers are used to create things on the screen.

We were watching *The Chronicles of Narnia: The Lion, the Witch and the Wardrobe*. She was astounded that the lion could talk and terrified by the thought of ax-wielding half-man–half-bulls lurking in our neighborhood. My explanation of reality was falling short, so we decided to watch the DVD extras on the making of the movie to help her understand.

Think of one of these "making of" specials that you've seen. Isn't it surprising how hokey the cast often looks as they film a scene with a green screen behind them? There's something about the editing and camera work that makes a movie fly off the screen and causes "the making of" to look almost silly.

This is especially pronounced when two actors are yelling at each other with fake intensity, only for one of them to crack and start laughing, adding another clip to the gag reel. Or when you watch a choreographed fight scene. It looks so fake and contrived, it's hard to believe that you get sucked into thinking it's really happening when you're watching the film. Same goes for fake blood, fake guns, and fake deaths. To see them behind the scenes removes their power. Nobody is sucked in by a green screen, big fans blowing, and actors swinging around on heavy cables.

You'd never pay thirteen dollars to watch a green screen "making of" production sitting on the edge of your seat, in utter suspense, for two and a half hours. And the Hollywood studios would never be so foolish as to put these into the theaters. They know the dull and boring mechanics of reality will never sell.

Your lustful temptations know this as well.

Just like I walked my five-year-old through what is real and what isn't, we can learn to do the same thing when sexual fantasy knocks at the door. We can use reality to expose our temptations for the frauds they are. When you see an attractive woman and start to lust, when you are drawn in by that tractor beam, you are seeing the movie. Your mind is filling itself with all sorts of things that aren't true about her and about you. Go "behind the scenes" to get yourself grounded in reality again.

There aren't two species of women. The women you are attracted to are not a different species than the women you aren't. Attractive women have the dignity of being whole people, full of problems and pain and complexity and, well, normalcy. And the women you aren't attracted to have the dignity of being whole people, valuable as God's image bearers, a value that isn't based on appearance at all. We need to bring the former down to earth and elevate the latter.

Your wife is to be cared for, protected, and fought for. Freedom comes in realizing she is equal to these magnetic women. They are the same.

There is incredible power in this.

Not only is physical attractiveness not nearly as important as we are deceived into thinking, it also fades. As it does, some other pretty cool traits grow as you spend more and more time with someone. As the years go on, a relationship matures. The one-flesh bond gets stronger. Two lives become united in deeper and deeper ways. Shared memories, secrets, children, family, inside jokes, mutual hobbies, and myriad other shared experiences create an attractiveness and a loyalty that run much deeper and are more substantial than surface-level attraction.

The surface draw will still be there. The difference is that we choose to remember that it's not what's important, and we choose to appreciate and enjoy the things that are.

There will be days when working the apple orchard is difficult. The sun will be hot, your back will hurt, and the temptation to leave your responsibilities for an escape will seem overwhelming. See the strings attached. Remind yourself you don't actually want that. Then run to Jesus, the one whose grace is all-sufficient for you. Call out what isn't important, and ask Jesus to remind you of what is. Ask him how you can worship him by embracing reality and investing in the good grass he's given you to tend. See your longing to escape as the flashing red light you need to get you to invest in your reality, diving deep into who you are in Jesus.

> If you're using the Forty-Day Devotional Guide in
> the back of this book, turn now to **Day 35.**

Total Exposure

The purpose of this chapter is to expose living in fantasy for the lie it is, to allow you to see what fantasy is and what it is doing to you. The only thing real about fantasy is the reality that it will enslave and imprison you. You will long for fantasy while you feel stuck in your everyday shriveled-up reality.

The only way to fix this is to turn the tables.

If you are longing for fantasy, it's because you aren't investing enough in your reality. If the grass looks greener on the other side of the fence, it's because you're investing time and thought across the fence, rather than investing in the grass beneath your feet. The grass under your feet is shriveling from neglect while you tend to and nourish the grass beyond the fence. This is true whether you are married or single. God gave each of us one reality to attend to.

Is there a guarantee your marriage will become better if you embrace reality and water the grass you're standing on? No, not necessarily (though that subtitle would sell a lot of books). This very well may happen, but it also may not, or it may take a long time for the green to appear. The point isn't that you can count on the rewards that reality will bring. The point is that you need to get out of the destructive cycle fantasy always produces. Yearning for fantasy is a surefire guarantee that your reality will get worse and be filled with increasing heartache and pain. It's as if you have a nail stuck in your foot. Taking it out is a really good idea. Taking it out doesn't guarantee you'll heal beautifully and be able to walk farther than ever, but leaving it in guarantees you will continue to be miserable. There's no surefire, quick-fix formula for making your reality better, but there is a surefire formula for making it worse. And that is to keep living in fantasy.

Fantasy's pull is strong and it's not going to stop trying to draw you in. You can't avoid this pull simply by reading this book and telling yourself you'll be strong enough to do these things now. That's as foolish as thinking you can build a house with your bare hands. Are you really that strong? Can you really drive a nail into a two-by-four using only the strength of your fingers, forearms, and biceps? Of course not. Think of how ridiculous it would be to try to build a house without tools. Only an arrogant fool would try such a thing. Building your house of purity is no different. Thankfully there is a box full of tools at your disposal. It's time to open it and get equipped for the steps you need to take once you finish this book.

In Your Small Group
Scan this QR code or go to www.beyond thebattle.net/videos and watch "Session 6 (Chapters 9–10): Embracing Reality." (All small group resources are free.)

CHAPTER 11

TOOLS

The Truth about Tools

Some men really love tools. Do you remember the television show *Home Improvement*? Like *Home Improvement*'s Tim "The Tool Man" Taylor, you may have a garage full of tools that would put the local hardware store to shame. But these tools don't do you any good if you don't know how to use them (like Tim didn't!). Knowledge is more important than the tool itself.

I started a job as a youth pastor when I got married. I was twenty-one years old and altogether clueless when it came to using tools. My church threw a big wedding reception for my wife and me, and some of the men set me up for life with an abundance of new, shiny tools. More than a decade later, many of those tools are still new and shiny.

While I've gained some handyman knowledge by necessity over the past seventeen years, I know where my strengths lie, and that's not in the world of tools. If I want a job to take four hours and cause me tons of stress, I'll do it myself. If I want it to take thirty minutes while I hang around and watch or read a book, I'll call a friend. It really doesn't matter how many tools you own, if you use a hammer to tighten a screw or a screwdriver to seal a pipe, you're going to make a big mess of things.

The same is true of tools in a man's battle for sexual purity. Great tools like accountability partners, Bible memorization, and internet software definitely have their place, but there is a reason this is the eleventh chapter in the book. Tools are essential. But they are not going to transform your heart, teach you God's design for sex, or free you from the allure of sexual temptation. Tools must be used with the knowledge you've gained in the first ten chapters, along with time spent with the Lord, letting your soul marinate in those truths.[1]

Opening the Toolbox: Talk

One of Satan's most devious lies is, "You are the only Christian who struggles with this." We believe that if we shared our struggles with trusted Christian friends, their mouths would drop open in disbelief, and they'd be disgusted with how dirty and sinful we are. So we keep our struggles bottled up inside in shame and isolation, the spiral of addiction, confusion, and despair pulling us in ever deeper.

Some of us lie to ourselves, convincing ourselves that our sin isn't bad enough to bring into the light and deal with. We reason that we stumble into porn, lust, or fantasy only every now and then. We're working on it, and we really will eventually get rid of it without help. After all, this kind of sin isn't the worst kind, so it's not worth confessing to anyone or getting help for.

Still others figure God's commands for purity don't really apply to men in the twenty-first century. They give themselves a pass to indulge in lust here and there, as long as they don't get carried away. Or they simply define lust on their own terms. Sure, porno videos and *Playboy* are wrong, but *Game of Thrones* and *House of Cards* are just TV shows.

---

1. If you did not use the forty-day devotional guide as you read this book, challenge yourself to reread the book over the next forty days using the devotional as your guide.

These lies serve to keep us entangled in our sin and allow life to slowly seep out of us, never truly free.

When I first started sharing about my past addiction to pornography in sermons, I was hesitant. As I did my sermon prep, I felt a strong sense of fear and timidity (coming from Satan). What would people think of me? What if I truly was the only person in this crowd who struggled with this?

But every time I shared my testimony, and I mean *every* time, I'd have at least one Christian man in the church send me an email saying he was so glad to hear my story. Often this man was a mature Christian, married with kids, and had found himself wrapped in a net of porn addiction he couldn't find a way out of. After having a few of these conversations, I realized that not only should I not be surprised to hear of a man's struggle with sexual temptation, I should be surprised to find a man who doesn't struggle in this area.

Yet to this day, many churches remain silent on the topic, giving Satan exactly what he wants. A friend of mine worked on staff at a megachurch. He asked the lead pastor if the church could address pornography in a sermon, sensing it was an issue with many of the men in the church. The lead pastor told him the church wasn't ready for that. Chalk it up as a victory for Satan.

James 5:16 tells us, "Therefore confess your sins to each other and pray for each other so that you may be healed." There is power and healing when we have the courage to tell someone about our sin. Often, we confess our sins only to God but keep them a secret from those around us. While confessing our sins to God is necessary, he gave us the church, the very body of Christ,[2] for a reason. He calls the church his body because he has equipped the church to do his works. We have Jesus in bodily form at our doorstep, yet we remain captive in our sexual sins because we won't reach out to him.

Imagine your problem is that you need to get a nail all the way into a two-by-four. You've been trying to push the nail in by hand with all your might, to no avail. You take the two-by-four and the nail to God in prayer, telling him you need him to take care of your

---

2. 1 Corinthians 12:27. See all of 1 Corinthians 12 for context.

problem and hammer it in for you. Meanwhile, he has already provided you with a box full of tools (the church) and an instruction manual (the Bible). Here in this toolbox are brothers in Christ whom God has equipped to bring you his healing when you open yourself up to them.

It's powerful to speak our sexual temptations into reality in front of other Christian men. When our fantasies remain in our heads, they make sense to us. But when we speak them out loud to another person, their distortion and destruction become real as we see them for what they truly are. We have to hear ourselves describe how twisted our minds have become, not so we can feel shame but so we can see how we've veered off course and, with the help of a brother, can recalibrate our vision of life, reality, and truth.

Proverbs 27:17 is right on when it says, "As iron sharpens iron, so one person sharpens another." A piece of iron needs another piece of iron in order for it to stay sharp. What happens when a piece of iron goes it alone? It becomes dull and ineffective.

Have you become dull? Is this dullness fueled by the fear that you're the only one who struggles with sexual sin? Call Satan's bluff and speak your temptation out loud into the real world. Find a Christian brother or brothers and share your story. Read through this book together. Sharpen one another. Pray together. God works miracles through prayer.

Satan has a great poker face, but Scripture reveals he's holding an off-suited 2 and 7 in his Texas Hold'em hand.[3] Call his bluff. Speak your story and make him show his cards.

I will never forget leading a sexual purity Bible study my sophomore year of college. Twenty guys gathered in a room for our first week of the study, which was most of the guys in our section of the dorm. I began by sharing my sexual sin struggles and temptations, and I invited the rest of the guys to do the same. Eventually all twenty of us did. It was beautiful to experience. Nineteen out of twenty of us struggled with pornography, and this was at a Christian college.

---

3. That is the worst hand you can be dealt.

Many of these guys were studying to become pastors. Confessing our sins to one another and learning that we weren't alone was the beginning of many life-changing miracles.

The church is meant to be a place for broken, bleeding, hurting people. It is meant to be an emergency room, not a country club. It is meant to be a place of grace, not condemnation. Utilize it as such. Don't keep walking alone in your pain when healing is only a conversation away.

If you're using the Forty-Day Devotional Guide in the back of this book, turn now to **Day 36**.

Purity Software

Our world has been oversexualized for a long time, but the digital revolution has multiplied that intensity by a thousand. We live in the most oversexualized society that has ever existed. Sex comes at us from every technological nook and cranny, yet most of us have set up our lives like we reside on *Leave It to Beaver*. It's like shooting fish in a barrel for Satan as his tech bombardment ensnares men, women, and children sexually en masse. You wouldn't light a fire in your living room without a fireplace. You don't store your kitchen knives next to your toddler's stuffed animals. Nor should you bring the internet into your home without accountability software that can keep pace.

Enter Covenant Eyes.

For years, the best thing purity software companies could offer was tracking the keywords and websites you typed into your computer and either blocking those pages or emailing notices to accountability partners. This service was great in the internet's early years, when online activity was confined to the family desktop computer, like in my middle school days. (That's right, kids, there once was a day when smartphones and tablets didn't exist.) This old dinosaur didn't even have a cell phone until after college. (Walked to school uphill both ways, barefoot in the snow as well.)

We all know that times have changed a lot since then. Smartphones have taken over the world, allowing almost everyone a buffet of pornography to carry around in their pockets at all times. With the evolution of apps, internet access points have multiplied exponentially as well.

It used to be your purity software only had to monitor your web browser. Think Chrome, Safari, Firefox, Internet Explorer. (Is Internet Explorer still a thing? It's so hard to keep up nowadays.) When the internet came out, there was only one way to access it, and it was through your browser (Netscape Navigator, anyone?), so it was relatively easy for purity software to keep track of that one doorway.

Today you can get on the internet through any app on your phone or tablet, such as Instagram, YouTube, and Tinder. Anytime you open an app, you're opening the internet. Purity software that can monitor only your web browser is almost useless today. It's like cassette tapes in a Spotify world.[4] You could be monitoring your web browser while looking at all the porn you want through your apps, and nobody would know.

And we all know that it's not just porn that is the problem. Instagram, Facebook, Tik Tok, Match, YouTube, and a bajillion other apps are full of images of scantily clad women, sensual depictions, and all kinds of other snags and triggers in our sexual purity battle. These apps also have changed the game for purity software that tracks keywords. It used to be that if you were viewing a pornographic or sensual image online, that image would have its own website attached to it, called a URL. It'd be likely that words like sex or porn or nude would be in this URL, or it'd be the name of an actress or some other word that a computer program would flag and attach to your report. But with photos on apps like Facebook

---

4. For all the other dinosaurs like me out there, Spotify is an app used by anyone who is cool to stream music on. Instead of buying CDs or individual songs, you just subscribe to Spotify, where you can search for and listen to any music you want. I am not that cool yet. A college student recently helped me move and wondered what my CD collection was. He was fascinated. It was like he was visiting a museum. He had never seen such a thing. It might as well have been a live stegosaurus. He didn't own even a single CD.

or Instagram, the URL doesn't have any words on it at all. It's just a bunch of letters and numbers. And what words would it catch, anyway? It's a college student who took a selfie in a bikini. She's not going to punch the word bikini into the name of that photo. She is just going to snap it and post it and that's it, and your purity software has no way to distinguish it from a photo of a puppy or of your family's Christmas celebration.

What's needed is something that tracks everything on your screen, no matter what app you're in. This is what Covenant Eyes' Screen Accountability does.

Covenant Eyes uses an artificial intelligence algorithm that detects pornography and inappropriate images on your phone, tablet, and computer screens. It takes screenshots, blurs them, then emails them to your accountability partners. There's no extra charge for putting Covenant Eyes on all of your family's internet devices. You can even set up individual users so you can have separate reports for each person in the household, with different reporting settings for each. Covenant Eyes also offers top-of-the-line customer support via email and phone.[5]

What I love about using Covenant Eyes is I am never online alone. What a relief this is! My accountability partner (my wife, in my case) will be seeing everything I see. This takes away all the temptation to go down the wrong path online or even to linger on a revealing thumbnail at the bottom of an ESPN article.

Your accountability partners receive an email at an interval you choose (daily, weekly, etc.). Each email will have ten blurred-out screenshots on it from your online activity. Even if you didn't look at anything inappropriate, they will still get the report with ten of your random screenshots on it. This shows them that you still have the software installed and that it's working properly.

None of the screenshots are ever stored by Covenant Eyes. The images are blurred out enough so your accountability partner can't see or read any sensitive details like usernames or numerical information. There is also enough blurring so as to not cause the accountability

---

5. Covenant Eyes: support@covenanteyes.com, (877) 479-1119.

partner to lust, but clear enough that he can tell what type of image you were looking at and follow up with you with a conversation.

A thirty-day free trial of Covenant Eyes Screen Accountability is required for anyone going through a Beyond the Battle small group. I am that serious about it.

I honestly don't know why a person desiring purity wouldn't want this protection. Why go through the trouble of reading this book, being in a group, praying for freedom, but then not doing something as simple as allowing others to view what you are viewing online? Yes, we want to apply the cure to the root of our sexual temptations, but that doesn't mean we should make it easy for Satan to keep tripping us up along the way. Don't become prideful in your pursuit of finding the cure, thinking are too good or too strong to need help with the symptoms. We never graduate from needing help. If we think we have, we have lost. Covenant Eyes won't cure you, but it is an essential tool for your journey.

If sexual sin is a bonfire, every time we slip into porn, fantasyland, lustful gazes, or a movie with nudity in it, we simply throw more fuel onto the fire. We reaffirm the mental conditioning that women are objects to be dehumanized and give our brains more visual memories to draw on. The only way to get a fire to go out is to stop feeding it. Though there are more ways to access porn than online, the internet is the most readily accessible avenue and needs to be snuffed out as a first priority.

If you've been hooked on seeing women as objects and you're trying to reverse your mindset, why would you continue to allow alluring images to have unchecked access into your life? If there's a stream of gas flowing onto your bonfire and you can block the stream, what would possibly prevent you from doing so?

What's ironic is that a guy will pay for satellite or cable TV, Netflix, home internet, and a data plan on his phone (all things that stream porn into his life), but then say he doesn't have the money for Covenant Eyes, which is cheaper than most of these services. Pack your lunch one day a month instead of eating out and you've just paid for your Covenant Eyes. Now go find a new excuse.

I think some men's rationale for not using Covenant Eyes is pride mixed with shame. If a man has to add purity software, he feels he is admitting that his sin is bad enough for drastic action.

This mindset can be remedied with a proper view of sin and grace. To act like a little bit of sin is okay ("Well, sure, I sin—but not enough to need Covenant Eyes!") is a tragic blunder. Any sin is enough to separate you from God.[6] Any sin is a rebellion against a holy God.[7] Any sin is living in death rather than life.[8] The sin of porn is especially dangerous because even those "little slips" embed in our minds for years, and we all know they just increase our appetite for the next hit.

After Jesus teaches that lusting over a woman is the same as having sex with her, he tells us that lust is so serious and dangerous we ought to cut off our hand and gouge out our eyes if it would help us to avoid it.[9] If adding simple and inexpensive software to your laptop, tablet, and smartphone will prevent a huge swathe of sexual temptation from entering your life, wouldn't this be a much easier solution than chopping off your appendages? If Jesus were teaching in the twenty-first century, he might warn that many guys need to cancel their TV packages, their Netflix and HBO (yes, *Game of Thrones* is porn),[10] and their ability to add apps onto their smartphones.[11]

Honestly, sexual sin is so prevalent across society there's nothing drastic about adding purity software anymore. It's not just for extreme addicts, it's for anyone who wants to protect himself and his family against harm, even if no one in his family currently has

---

6. Romans 3:23.

7. Romans 5:8–10; Colossians 1:21.

8. Romans 6:11–14.

9. Matthew 5:27–30.

10. See Noah Filipiak, "If You Are Watching 'Game of Thrones,' You Are Watching Porn," Covenant Eyes, February 2, 2016, http://www.covenanteyes.com/2016/02/02/if-you-are-watching-game-of-thrones-you-are-watching-porn.

11. Most smartphones can be password protected so apps can't be added. If you're looking at porn on Instagram (or a number of other apps), you need to delete the app and have a trusted friend set up a password that stops you from adding apps. If you're not willing to do this, stop saying you want to be free from porn.

a problem. It's not even a matter of whether you or your kids go looking for porn anymore, it's a matter of when porn eventually finds you or your unsuspecting kids. Nearly 27 percent of teens have received a sext and around 15 percent are sending them.[12] Without Covenant Eyes, you'd have no idea whether your child is one of them.

Covenant Eyes ought to be seen as essential, not as extreme.

I always tell guys that adding Covenant Eyes is a lot cheaper than getting a divorce. And the expense is certainly worth it to save your heart and mind from the spiritual bankruptcy of destruction that is lurking for you as well. Saying you can't afford to buy it really isn't an excuse. The truth is, you can't afford not to.

Head over to covenanteyes.com or get the app from your app store right now if you haven't already. Punch in the promo code BEYOND to get your first thirty days free. You have nothing to lose and everything to gain.

More and More and More Tools!

VidAngel is an amazing service that allows you to filter out sex and nudity from movies and TV shows. (You can also filter profanity, violence, and other objectionable elements, if you desire. And I'm not kidding you, you can even filter out all Star Wars scenes that contain Jar Jar Binks!) It's has a low monthly fee and connects to your existing streaming accounts.

IMDb is another great resource to use before you watch any movie.[13] Every movie and TV show on IMDb has a parents' guide on its page. Click this and it will describe any sex or nudity scene in the movie or show.[14] I always check whatever I plan to watch using this guide. If something questionable is listed, I simply don't watch

---

12. Covenant Eyes, "Pornography Statistics," https://www.covenanteyes.com/porn-stats/. "Sexting" is sending or posting a sexually suggestive nude or nearly nude photo or video of oneself.

13. See www.imdb.com.

14. I think the movie details are more comprehensive, whereas it's harder to track the many episodes of a TV series.

the show. Now, thanks to VidAngel, I can still watch a lot of these shows or movies, but the IMDb tool is still helpful.

I'm just not going to watch any movie or TV show that has nudity in it. I don't comprehend why so many Christian men think this is okay. These scenes are the same as porn and affect our brains exactly the same way. If you want to continue to objectify women and always be lust's slave, then I guess go on ahead. But for me, it's a no-brainer. I don't want to go anywhere near that stuff.

You can find porn almost anywhere today, including video game consoles. While Covenant Eyes doesn't cover these devices (yet!), they do offer great tutorials on how to set up parental controls for Xbox, Netflix, and much more, which you can check out at https://www.covenanteyes.com/?s=parental+controls. And I can't stress it enough, sometimes you just need to get rid of some of this technology from your life. You really can live without it.[15] A friend recently told me how he smashed his Xbox to bits with a hammer because he kept looking at porn on it. *That* is what Jesus was talking about when he said to do whatever it takes to be pure!

> If you're using the Forty-Day Devotional Guide in the back of this book, turn now to **Day 37**.

Talking to Your Wife (For Married Men)

Talking out loud about your sexual sin with trusted Christian men goes a long way toward disarming fantasy's power. Doing this with your *wife* takes your transparency to a whole new level.

If you decide to have this conversation, you will experience the full brunt of reality in a way you likely can't imagine. You will feel guilt, pain, and shame as you realize what the secret acts you've

---

15. I know some guys who have ditched their smartphones altogether. This is a way of ridding themselves of one of porn's highways into their lives, but also it is an effort to be more present with the human beings and the world around them. Check out www.thelightphone.com for one example of these phone models that offer only basic services like texting, phone calls, and an alarm clock.

rationalized are doing to your life. When your struggles stay in your head, they are easy to justify. Even when you talk to other men for accountability, there is still a level of empathy and grace that comes from another man who can relate to the allure of your temptation. But when you share it with your wife, the one you have betrayed, you will feel the pain your sinful actions cause. We need to feel this pain because it makes us understand our sin is far from harmless. We need to see our sin the way God does, and feeling this pain helps move us closer to that reality.

I encourage you to talk to your wife about your sexual sins and to include her in your accountability team, but do so at the right time. I strongly encourage you to have some successes down the road of purity before confiding in her. If you are in the middle of a long-standing porn addiction that your wife knows nothing about and you suddenly tell her what you looked at last night and have been looking at your whole marriage, she is not going to know how to react. Some women panic and overreact, feeling as though all trust has been eroded and it's time for divorce. Others may want to forgive their husbands but will struggle to trust them not to fall back into old habits again. And frankly, there's no reason they should trust them at this point.

The solution is to first put a plan of action into place and develop a record of purity before you talk to your wife. It will certainly soften the blow if you are already meeting with some male accountability partners, and possibly your pastor as well, and you've put Covenant Eyes on your internet devices, especially since you are asking for her help and want to include her in your accountability reports.

Your wife will still feel hurt, and rightfully so, but knowing that you have a plan in place and that you have already had some success with it will show her you mean to carry out your new commitment and you truly do love her. I don't recommend going into gruesome detail on what or who you've been looking at or thinking about. Generalizations will be painful enough and should be all that is needed to get the help you need from her. The most important thing she will need is to see that even though it hurts to learn these things, it is much better than your keeping secrets and not doing anything about it (which lots of men do).

Allow your wife to grieve the trust that has been broken and expect her to pull away for a little while. Don't use this response to rationalize going back to your sin. It's only natural for her to respond this way, and it's all part of the healing process. It will take perseverance on your part to keep growing stronger in your purity, and you'll need to lean heavily on Jesus' approval as your power source, because your wife might shut her approval off for a season. As you persevere, your wife's trust in you will grow accordingly, as will her willingness to be close with you once again.

Also, be careful not to blame your wife for playing a role in your sexual sin, as if she pushed you to it. You are 100 percent accountable before God for your choices. Contributing circumstances within your marriage are not an escape clause that allows you to sin. Be convinced of this in your heart before talking to your wife, because any attempt to point to her contributions will shut down the process of repentance and growth you are pursuing. Don't even bring it up.

Talking to your wife will be a great strengthener, but she shouldn't be your main accountability partner. She doesn't need to know every time you are tempted and what's going through your mind every second of the day, but having her in your corner will be invaluable for the long haul. There is no greater accountability than knowing your wife is watching you. It is unlikely you would look at pornography or flirt with your coworker if your wife were standing right next to you.

It may also be helpful to share with your wife some purity resources such as this book and websites like www.CovenantEyes. com and www.XXXchurch.com.[16] Then she can see that you aren't the only Christian man struggling with sexual purity and that you are taking the Christ-centered steps of getting your heart and

---

16. XXXchurch.com even has a forum for wives of men who struggle with porn. They also have a prayer and advice wall. Covenant Eyes' blog has a category for women whose husbands struggle with sexual sin.

mind right, both for her and for your relationship with God. These resources may help equip her with a spirit of grace and healing rather than of judgment and alienation. They will also show her how much better off she is to have a husband who is tenaciously fighting against temptation than to be married to one of the scores of men who have become apathetic, even welcoming temptation.

Talking to your wife won't be easy, but it is worth it in the long run. After you've built a record of strength and purity, bring your wife in as your ally in this fight. You need all the help you can get.

> If you're using the Forty-Day Devotional Guide in the back of this book, turn now to **Day 38 (For Married Men)**.

Love Letters (For Single Men)

Some of you are nearly positive you will get married someday, some are nearly positive you won't, and some have no idea. Whatever your situation, you don't have a wife right now, but you might someday. The previous few pages for married men discuss how men's wives can be powerful allies in their fight for freedom from sexual sin. Wives take what feels harmless and easy to rationalize in our minds and make it real. They take what is fantasy with no repercussions and turn it into reality, revealing the full force of lust's collateral damage.

You don't have this powerful ally at this point in your purity journey, but there are still some helpful exercises you can do. This will feel a little corny, but trust me on this. Take out a pen and paper and write a letter to your future wife.[17] Tell her about the steps you are taking and your fight to be pure for her. Tell her about the type of marriage you'd like to have, one that embodies Jesus' love for you. Tell her about

---

17. I first encountered this idea in Eric and Leslie Ludy's book *When God Writes Your Love Story* (Colorado Springs, CO: Waterbrook Multonomah, 1999). And yes, I wrote many of these letters to my future wife during my single years and gave them to her on our honeymoon.

how far you've come and about the goals you've made as you move forward. Tell her you are praying for her now, even though you may not have even met her yet. Pray for her. Save this letter and give it to her someday. Whenever temptation comes around, pull out another sheet of paper and write another letter. And another.

Writing to your future wife now is much easier than talking to your wife someday about the sexual sins you are still fighting because you never dealt with them during your single years. You will also enjoy freedom and a clean conscience in your single life and will have more to celebrate with your wife if and when you do tie the knot.

Writing these letters and praying these prayers will remind you that your sexual sin involves more than just you. Your sin patterns affect your future wife and the children you might have together. (And again, even if you never get married, your sexual sin still affects all the relationships you have with the women around you.) The key to bursting the bubble of fantasy is to expose it to as much reality as possible. Writing letters to your future real wife will certainly help with that.

If you are convinced you will not be getting married and writing a letter to a fictional wife feels too far-fetched, use the same exercise to write letters to Jesus. Tell him why you are submitting to his will. Tell him you are turning to him for love rather than to the temptation facing you. Tell him why and how much you love him. Be personal with him and allow him to be personal with you. Share these letters to Jesus with your pastor or your men's accountability group.

> If you're using the Forty-Day Devotional Guide in the back
> of this book, turn now to **Day 38 (For Single Men)**.

Excuses

I know not everyone struggles with the same type of sexual temptation in the same way, but as I mentioned, it's difficult for me to know my Christian brothers watch popular movies and TV shows with explicit nude and sex scenes in them. If a video with people having sex in it is called porn and we all agree we shouldn't watch it, how does it become justifiable because there's an artistic plot underlying it and movie stars we've heard of are featured in it?[18]

There has always been a debate about what is porn and what is art. Nude modeling, which has been around for centuries, is seen by many as art. But there's a huge difference between nude modeling and seductive nude modeling. Seductive nude modeling is what you will find in *Playboy* magazine and a million other porn outlets. If you look at the nudity found in Hollywood blockbusters and HBO dramas,[19] can you really argue that it's not meant to be seductive? And let's be honest, there are plenty of sex scenes that wouldn't technically count as nude because an actress is wearing lingerie, but the orgasmic noises and sensual looks on their faces are vivid enough to haunt your mind for days (if not months) afterward.

If our biggest problem in maintaining sexual purity is that we've been conditioned to objectify women and live in a fantasy world, how on earth is watching some of the most attractive women on the planet have unrealistic sex done up with lights, makeup, seductive sounds, and background music going to help us in our journey toward purity?

It's just like Satan to take something so poisonous and wrap it up in a bunch of seemingly harmless or even enjoyable trappings: action, drama, movie stars, artistic stories, heroes, villains, kings, knights, dragons, soldiers, comedy, sports.

Is it enough that you cover your eyes during the nude scenes? Ask yourself honestly, are you still catching an eyeful prior to getting those lids shut, and does that eyeful and its accompanying sounds stick in your memory? You don't even need to ask whether your flesh enjoyed the eyeful or the moaning you still hear. Of course you

---

18. Visit www.noahfilipiak.com/vidangel to see how you can watch TV shows and movies without the sex and nudity scenes.

19. See Noah Filipiak, "If You Are Watching 'Game of Thrones,' You Are Watching Porn," Covenant Eyes, February 2, 2016, http://www.covenanteyes.com/2016/02/02/if-you-are-watching-game-of-thrones-you-are-watching-porn.

enjoyed it. Your brain is hardwired to enjoy it. You also don't need to ask whether that eyeful will continue to teach you to objectify women. Of course it will. It's simply more fuel for the same old fire.

Jesus wasn't messing around when he told us to cut off our hands and gouge out our eyes if they are causing us to sin sexually. While I don't think he was being literal, he was underlining the urgency of doing whatever is necessary to stay sexually pure. He sets up drastic examples—gouging out our eyes or cutting off our hands—so we can compare these steps to the sacrifices he is going to call on us to make.

Will you miss out on some gripping entertainment if you don't watch the latest racy HBO series? Yes.

Will you miss out on watercooler talk about the latest Hollywood blockbuster with nudity in it? Yes.

Will you miss out on some sports if you get rid of HBO? Or if you get rid of the level of cable service you are using? Yes.

But are these sacrifices anywhere near that of cutting off your hand or gouging out your eyes? No.

Are they anywhere near the painful damage these seeds of sin will cause in your life?

You can continue your HBO, Netflix, and movie viewing habits and short-circuit everything you've learned from this book. Is it really worth it?

We deceive ourselves by downplaying the effects these stimulating images have on our minds. These images are teachers. They are professors. They teach us to see women as objects. They teach us our sex lives should be like what we see in the movies. They teach us our wives should look and act like the actresses on our screens. They teach our brains to long for *that* type of sex with *that* type of woman. They teach us to be attracted to a *that* instead of a *her*. If we are viewing the images, we are being taught and shaped by the images.

This all comes back to Jesus and the gospel. You'll never get this if you don't get the gospel. In the inner-city park ministry we do, we always take one week out of the summer to talk about sexual purity and how God's design is for us to save sex until marriage. The teens never take us seriously. We can give them every benefit in the book about why to do this: from avoiding STDs and pregnancy, to not objectifying women, to the benefits of having a stable family, to even the spiritual benefits of submitting to Christ because he designed us.

But these teens don't know Christ. They are still their own gods and kings. Their hearts have not been softened and penetrated by the grace of Jesus to trust God's way over their own ways. So no matter what we tell them, they are simply going to do it their way because their way feels better.

I'm hoping readers of this book are followers of Jesus whose lives have been transformed by the gospel. If you're not, please turn to the afterword immediately and read it. Only men who have surrendered to Jesus will courageously do whatever it takes to follow Jesus' plan instead of their own.

My hope and prayer is that men of God will stand up, stop making excuses, and start fully obeying Jesus. Not because we will receive an amazing benefit from it. In reality, we are making a huge earthly sacrifice. No, I pray for this because of what our sin does to God's heart, to our hearts, and to the church's witness. I pray for this because Jesus knows what he is doing, and because Jesus is worth it.

Stop making excuses. Stop letting Satan slowly drip poison into God's beautiful design and plan for your life and your marriage.

If you're using the Forty-Day Devotional Guide in the back of this book, turn now to **Day 39**.

Weightlifting

Growing strong in your sexual purity is akin to weightlifting. If you lift weights one time and then stop, your body remains weak. But if you lift weights consistently over a long period of time, you will see results as your body becomes stronger and the discipline of lifting becomes easier and more natural to maintain.

Making a onetime commitment to be sexually pure is as effective as buying a gym membership for the new year but never using it. Reading this book once won't cure you of sexual impurity. I wish it would. I wrote it, and I still need to be reminded of its principles regularly. Reading this book sets you up well with a lot of pages of weightlifting, which is a great start. The most frustrating thing about weightlifting, though, is that you really can never stop doing it. Once you reach your fitness goals, it doesn't take long for those results to vanish if you stop maintaining your workout regimen.[20]

As is true for any area of spiritual maturity, sexual purity is not something you achieve and then store on the shelf. We are forgetful people. We can hear a great sermon, be convinced of its truths, then go home the next day and forget what we learned, reverting right back to our old routines. This is the burden of being human.

What compounds this natural forgetfulness is that we have been conditioned for our entire lives to do things a certain way sexually. Decades of conditioning aren't reversed overnight, no matter how moving the altar call or how helpful the book.

I take comfort in knowing that Jesus knows this about us. When he instituted the Lord's Supper the night before his crucifixion, he broke a piece of bread and held up a cup of wine—the bread signifying his body, broken for us, and the cup his blood, shed for us. He said, "Do this in remembrance of me."[21] He knows we are forgetful, so he gave us the Lord's Supper to remind us of him and his truth. If Jesus thought we'd need to learn this message only once, he would not have told his disciples to regularly remember his life, death, and resurrection through this revered sacrament.

In our quest for sexual purity, we also need reminders. Satan will not stop bombarding us with lies, so we need to never stop bombarding ourselves with the truth. This book contains the truths

---

20. Obviously, this is not a perfect analogy. God is the one who transforms us. We don't do this by our own strength. But we do need to remind ourselves of the truths of the gospel (Luke 22:19–20) and remain in them (John 15:4), which takes discipline. Spiritual weightlifting is a way of fighting against our forgetfulness so that we are able to bear fruit by the Holy Spirit.

21. Luke 22:19–20.

we need to reprogram our hearts and minds from the enslavement of sexual immorality to the freedom of living fully in God's design for sex and life. It is like a room full of weights and exercise equipment. But these weights won't do us any good if we let them just sit around and collect dust.

The key to the journey is to remember that you cannot do it alone. If you read this book and resolve to stop the sexual immorality in your life but never talk to anyone about it, you are doomed to fail.

Athletes, to be successful, need coaches and trainers to continually provide training, discipline, and accountability. They need teammates to train with, bond with, and be spurred on by. They need fans to cheer for them while they are on the field. They need to be able to look at the crowd and see that they are part of something bigger than themselves, that others are rooting for them and are looking up to them. They need to look around and see teammates and coaches who are depending on them to do the right thing so that the entire community can thrive.

This is a picture of what the church is meant to be.

Even the best athletes in the world have coaches. We are much stronger and can achieve exponentially more when we have others around us, stretching us past our limits. The only way we can successfully reprogram our hearts is if we enlist reliable coaches, teammates, and fans. While we can expect to have this supporting cast on the athletic field, it is less common on the battlefield of spiritual growth. As Christian men, we are much more likely to keep our guard up. Like the proud, uncoachable player, we assume we don't need the help of others.

We must change this mindset.

Spiritual personal trainers come in many shapes and sizes. The key is to have them. The only qualities they need are that they love you, love the way of Jesus, and are trustworthy.

Personal trainers come at a cost. So do life, health, and freedom. And that cost comes to us as a choice. Will we choose to do what it takes to become sexually and spiritually healthy? Or will we choose to continue to take the easy way out, allowing sexual sin to bog us down and bury us alive?

Not only do spiritual personal trainers help us with accountability, they also help us restructure the rhythms of our lives to make sure we are staying in the stream of God's healing. The solution to sexual sin is not cognitive processes and accountability practices but a heart in love with Jesus—and more important, a heart that knows that Jesus loves it. The only way to get these concepts from your head to your heart is by spending time in Jesus' presence.

You have all the concepts you need now. You know Jesus loves you and accepts you and gives you value. You have Scripture after Scripture to back these truths up. You now need to sit with Jesus and ask the Spirit to infuse these truths into your life.

It's the difference between a wedding and a marriage. Yes, you had the wedding with Jesus, but do you have a marriage? Yes, you know these truths, but are you spending time with Jesus so that he can hold you within them? I challenge you to commit thirty minutes a day, five days a week to spend time in Jesus' presence. Rest in Jesus' sufficiency. Rest in his authority. Rest in knowing that he is Almighty God and that any idols you have pursued are puny and worthless. Rest in these facts on a heart level, not a head level, for this is the path of transformation. This isn't something you can do alone. We can always think of something better to do than spend thirty minutes with Jesus, so get some guys to help you stay committed to this.

If you didn't go through this book with a group of men, recruit some friends and go through it again with them. You can also head over to www.beyondthebattle.net and join an online small group led by me and my Beyond the Battle team.

Make a covenant with your group to commit to this thirty-minute time with Jesus for at least the next thirty days. If you are white-knuckling it as you fight off temptation, you need to spend more time in Jesus' presence, asking him to show you that his truths really apply to you. Hold the Scriptures open, ask him, and listen to what he says. Then soak in it. Allow his love for you to fill you with peace, joy, and fulfillment.

Instructions: Set aside thirty minutes each day to spend time in solitude with the Lord. Light a candle. (Actually try this part. No, I'm not a candle guy either, but I have found it to be a powerful reminder of God's presence. It has made the time much more focused and intentional for me.) Set a timer for thirty minutes. Keep a Bible and a journal handy. Start the time in silence and listening, applying Psalm 46:10's exhortation to be still. Listen to what God wants to speak to you and transition into a time of prayer or journaling concerning what he says. Focus on God's holiness and majesty, and then on his undeserved mercy toward you. God will do the rest![22]

If you're using the Forty-Day Devotional Guide in
the back of this book, turn now to **Day 40**.

Finishing Strong for Married Men

The biggest fans in your life are your wife and your children. Your kids long for a father they can look to as an example of what it means to live out God's design for sex so they can follow in your footsteps.

Your wife longs for a husband who will be true to her, who will be there for her with love and faithfulness, for better or for worse, for richer or for poorer, in sickness and in health. Who will see her soul and love her as a full person, not as a collection of body parts. A husband who thinks she is worth it. A husband who thinks his kids are worth it. A husband who thinks freedom in Christ is worth it.

Your wife and kids are doing the trust fall, hoping you will be there to catch them.

Will you be?

---

22. Read *Sacred Rhythms: Arranging Our Lives for Spiritual Transformation* (Downers Grove, IL: InterVarsity, 2006) by Ruth Haley Barton for great inspiration and guidance on this sort of spiritual formation practice.

Finishing Strong for Single Men

Singleness is the prime season of life to surround yourself with other Christian men who can spur you on in your sexual purity. It's also the prime season of life to bury yourself into a deep hole of isolation, where no one can know how deep and dark your sexual sin problems are.

Living in a dorm at a Christian college was the closest thing I've ever experienced to the type of community the first-century church had in Acts 2:42–47. Most everyone's door was always open, welcoming whoever wanted to pop in and say hi, catch a game of Madden on the PS2, or share how things were going in life. These conversations often led to prayer and discipleship, and even some lifelong friendships. We did small group Bible studies together and read through sexual purity books together. My roommate Steve and I had an especially close brotherhood. We were able to constantly check in with each other and support each other on how we were doing in our walks with Christ and particularly with our sexual purity.

This is a season of sharpening a married guy will never have again.

There were also a few guys in our dorm who decided not to take advantage of these growth opportunities. Behind their locked doors, they buried themselves in video games. They never showed up for the Bible studies or prayer groups or for sexual purity discussions. More than likely, their sexual sins were spiraling out of control (and still are) as they remained alone in the dark, something so easy to do when you're single.

I'm not advocating that you move into a Christian college dorm, but I do think you can simulate some of these Christian community elements as a single man in a way no one else can.

Go to church.

Seek out other guys who are single and befriend them.

Hang out with them regularly.

Have strong Christian housemates or roommates.

Don't wait to be invited to someone's house. Invite people over to yours.

Set up regular times to study Scripture together and to have conversations about life and sexual purity.

Strengthen one another.

Coach one another.

Cheer one another on.

The choice you face as a single man is whether to take advantage of the opportunities for community given to you by singleness instead of allowing singleness to drive you deeper and deeper into isolation and enslavement to sexual sin. The choice really is yours, but you have to take the initiative.

The only thing that will happen on its own is the dark spiral of isolation. Community will not. Both of these options feed off of themselves. If you've been buried in isolation for years, it's unlikely you'll want to take steps to get out of it. If you're enjoying a flourishing community of Christian brothers, it's unlikely you'll ever want to go it alone.

A path of freedom and a path of darkness lie before you.

It's your choice as to which one to walk down.

Choose freedom.[23]

It is well worth it.

Whether married or single, we all need this path of freedom. What we often have to learn the hard way—I know I did—is that no matter how far down the path of freedom we get, we never graduate. You can clear out the jungle path with your machete and think you've arrived because you are living in freedom. But the jungle always grows back. The only way to keep it at bay is to keep your machete sharp and never stop stomping out your path. We never get to a point where we no longer need authentic community. We will always need a place to share our struggles and vulnerable selves and be reminded of the truths of gospel freedom over and over again. This is true for all of us, even pastors and sexual purity authors.

---

23. This line reminds me of Deuteronomy 30:19, "I have set before you life and death, blessings and curses. Now choose life, so that you and your children may live." These were some of Moses' last words before his death.

CHAPTER 12

BREAKAWAYS AND TAKEAWAYS

Iwrote this chapter two years after the first edition of this book was published, and around eight years after I first sat down to write the original manuscript. One of the beauties of getting to publish a second edition of a book is you get to make it better. You get to add a ton of improvements and new ideas that came from people wrestling through the content on their own journeys, exposing gaps and offering new solutions. Many of those solutions have already been peppered into what you just read, and more will be peppered in here. This new chapter breaks away from the format of the rest of the book, focusing on crucial takeaways you must grasp before you put this book on the shelf.

Takeaway 1: Isolation Kills, Vulnerable Community Brings Life

When I first wrote this book, I thought I could solve men's desire for sexual sin by replacing it with Jesus. I still believe this is partly true, that Jesus is the cure for our desire for sexual sin. We'll never find what we're looking for from sex and women, but we will find it in Christ. But where I was wrong is it'll never be that clean cut.

You can't get that from a book. You can't get that from any onetime experience. Jesus is our cure. But he's less like a vaccine and more like filling up your empty stomach with a hearty meal.

And then meal after meal after meal.

As I said in chapter 11, in weightlifting, you have to keep doing it or you're going to lose what you gained. Reading this book was a great workout, but if you stop now, you'll lose your new muscles. This is the point I want to make the loudest.

After leading dozens of guys through Beyond the Battle groups, after discovering I'm in the same boat as everyone else, I want to speak loudly here, both to you and to myself:

I believe in the church. I love the church. The church is Jesus' wife. The church is me and you. A Christian who is not active in a church is like a football player with no teammates and no coach.

The church is also fallen and broken, as you and I are.

I used to think the church could pick up where this book left off. I thought you could read chapter 11, then go to your church and say, "Hey, let's keep talking about this. Let's preach about it. Let's get some groups of guys gathered around this."

I thought you could nudge your small group to start talking about these things and the group could become a place to share your deepest temptations.

But after two years of guys trying this, I want to be a responsible leader and cast a vision for something with a higher success rate.

You need guys you can be 110 percent transparent, vulnerable, and honest with about what you have done, what you are doing, and what you are thinking about doing, and who can remind you of the truths in this book. It is up to *you* to create the context for these conversations.

I believe in the church and I believe in small groups. You need to continue to put your heart and soul into them. They are fertile ground for relationships to grow in, relationships you need.

But can we please stop fooling ourselves when we're asked how we're doing in small group and the only things we share are about how our kids are doing in school or about a surgery someone has coming up?

This is not the planet I live on.

This is not the planet any of us lives on.

I'm not throwing stones at church small groups. I think they are a great place to make friends and to be cared for and to learn about the Bible. They are also a great way to connect new people with others. But I honestly don't think your small group is the place for you to dump your guts on the living room floor. It's just not built for that. Nor is it what the others in the group signed up for. It's built for socializing and Bible study, not for you to confess that you can't stop looking at the cleavage of the woman who brought the snacks.

Awkward.

But you need a place to dump your guts on the living room floor, and *you* need to create it.

Two years after publishing the first edition of *Beyond the Battle*, I realized it was becoming natural for me to hold back about the areas I was struggling in. And I didn't have any structured places to share these things. How can the guy who "wrote the book" on sexual purity still struggle with sexual purity? Doesn't that make his book a fraud and him a phony? I had to be the expert and the answer man, and in so doing, I stopped cultivating places for me to be gut-wrenchingly honest with others.

And let's be honest, it's hard to find these spaces. I tried cultivating accountability relationships with several guys, and it wasn't working. It wasn't their fault. Guys are busy. And frankly, as a whole, guys are soft. What I mean is, it's a rare thing to find an assertive man who will ask you the hard questions. To ask you how you're doing in an area of purity you have confessed to struggle in, without your asking him to ask you. To get up in your grill like an old-school football coach. I don't mean in order to shame you or lecture you. I mean someone who is going to keep coming at you. To spur you on toward love and good deeds like Hebrews 10:24 commands. (A spur is a sharp metal weapon attached to a boot, designed for kicking into an animal's flesh to make it go forward. Yikes!) To send you obnoxious text messages. To ask you probing questions. And most important, just to listen without judgment. To absorb and listen and be present and love. To allow you to expose your darkness to the light, something that is impossible to do on your own. And then to regularly check in with you about it and encourage you.

This just isn't our culture. Our culture is filled with busy men, myself included, many of whom are uncomfortable having such deep conversations.

The other factor is that this type of relationship takes up a lot of bandwidth. If you asked me to do this for you, I'd say no. If I'm to do this well, I can do it for only a very small number of people. And it must be done well. There's too much at stake. Everything is at stake.

I'm tired of hearing from guys how their church isn't providing a structure for vulnerable relationships or how they can't think of anyone to ask to share their struggles with. If you are amped up after reading this book, you must commit now to finding guys you can have honest conversations with and not stop until you've succeeded. You need to get past the learned helplessness of quitting because you can't think of anyone or because the first guy you asked said no, or said yes but is doing an insufficient job.

I'm not telling you to find an accountability partner whose job is to motivate you not sin and to shame you when you do. I'm talking about people you can be vulnerable with and share all of yourself with, with whom you can get stuff out into the light before it grows legs.

The difference between a church small group and an Alcoholics Anonymous meeting is that people show up to AA knowing they will be sharing their deepest, darkest secrets. It's normal. It's what is expected. It would be strange if you showed up and didn't share or if you held back and talked only about surface-level things.

AA is the type of vulnerable community you and I need.

After several failed attempts to reach out to friends to get a community like this going, here's what I did. I emailed fourteen guys I felt comfortable baring the darkest corners of my soul to. You might be saying, "I don't know fourteen guys I can share the darkest corners of my soul to." I disagree. You do know fourteen guys. Everyone knows fourteen guys. And if you really don't know enough guys, join a church small group. Getting to know new people is what church small groups are really good at.

But the underlying problem isn't that we don't know enough people. It's that we don't want to share the darkest corners of our souls with the people we know. It's up to you to believe in grace enough to be vulnerable in cultivated contexts of trust.

If you don't think you're up for this, I challenge you to believe more deeply in grace, to believe that grace is the antidote to shame. If Jesus has shown us all grace, how could we not show grace to one another as well?

Jesus' grace kills shame. Yes, you can experience this in your personal time with him, but you must also experience it in bodily form. You need brothers in Christ who can look you in the eyes and tell you they love you and accept you, no matter what you've done or thought, to model in-person the love and grace that Jesus pours out to you every second of every day.[1]

Where grace lives, vulnerability abounds.

So I emailed fourteen guys and I laid it out for them. I told them exactly what I needed. I set up the expectations just like an AA meeting does. Because I didn't want anyone to feel bad if he had to say no, I told them I would say no if someone asked me to do this for them. I also told them I didn't want them all to say yes, because fourteen would be too many.

I told them not to say yes to being on this team if it wasn't something they could follow through on. I knew I needed some guys I could share everything with when it happened, guys who could remind me of the gospel truths taught in this book, and guys who

---

1. Jim Wilder and Michel Hendricks describe how showing this type of love to another physically changes and heals our brains (*The Other Half of Church: Christian Community, Brain Science, and Overcoming Spiritual Stagnation* [Chicago: Moody, 2020], 79-90).

would pray for me and check in with me. I asked for a one-sided relationship, making it known in advance I would not be doing the same for them.

I'm not saying you need to do it the way I did. I'm telling you what I had to do to make sure I don't become the next pastor-author who cheats on his wife, particularly after writing a book on how not to cheat on your wife. Particularly because Satan's attacks increase when you write a book like this, and you're an utter fool if you think you can fight them off in your strength or maturity. I didn't stop until I found a vulnerable community of guys who would defend me and counterattack Satan with the supernatural power of prayer, because I knew I need this community in the same way I need oxygen, the way a drowning man needs his friends to jump in to save him.

You need this too.

I now have a team of five guys whom I tell everything to. For me, it's over email, followed up by text messages.

Do you have a group of guys you can tell everything to?

I am not talking about a group of guys to talk to if you look at porn. That's important, but as you get farther on this journey of freedom, you'll find that looking at porn almost becomes superficial. I'm not making light of it, I'm just saying it's nowhere near the finish line. Praise God for the freedom of not looking at porn, and I know many of you reading this long to get to that place. And you will! But Satan isn't going to stop attacking you and twisting your thoughts once you get there. The temptations just go to a deeper level.

Let me put it like this: do you have a group of guys you can confess to if you look at porn? I think many of you do. Or if you don't, you could generate that with a pretty good degree of success.

But do you have a group of guys you can confess to when you're watching a Star Wars movie with your kids and your eyes get stuck on the breasts of an actress in a revealing outfit? We're talking about a PG-rated movie here! And I don't mean confessing as a way of being legalistic or beating yourself up for being attracted to a pretty woman. I mean confessing it because you indulged in that look. You had the choice to be pure and look away, but you didn't. You savored the objectifying look. That image embedded in your brain and it took you down a path of lust and fantasy, one that you couldn't get out of your mind even hours later.

I'm telling you right now, that's one of the situations that caused me to seek the help I did before things got any worse.

I don't like typing that here. It's much easier to tell you about the porn I looked at twelve years ago than it is to write about this recent episode.

While the ramifications of looking at porn are far greater, it is harder to confess that Star Wars led me into deep, lustful sin. This is embarrassing. Seriously, can you imagine sharing that with your small group during the next prayer-request time? That's actually a pretty hilarious scene if you play it out in your mind.

But here's the thing, if you don't confess it and get it into the light, it will grow legs and start running places you can't control.

Do you have guys you can confess to when you wish you weren't married?

Do you have guys you can confess to when you've been browsing Tinder or Match.com?

Do you have guys you can confess to when you've developed a lingering attraction toward a woman at work or church? Even though attraction itself isn't even a sin? But as we all know, it will lead to sin in a hurry if it goes unconfessed and unchecked. Which it almost always does because we don't have lay-your-cards-on-the-table relationships.

Like the cat who finally gets the hairball out, man it's good to be free! Exposing this gunk to the light is what we are called to do: "But if we walk in the light, as he is in the light, we have fellowship with one another, and the blood of Jesus, his Son, purifies us from all sin."[2]

When thoughts and temptations stay in our minds, they fester

---

2. 1 John 1:7.

there. Things that should not feel normal become normalized. You need to say them out loud to other people, exposing them to the light. You need men to remind you of the gospel truths in this book, all the while utilizing Covenant Eyes to keep temptation at bay as much as possible.

This is the formula for success:

1. Correct theology about who we are in Christ and how to view women (the contents of *Beyond the Battle*)
2. Being reminded of these truths over and over in our daily rhythm time and throughout our day (see takeaway 2)
3. Experiencing these truths in vulnerable community (allowing others to be the hands and feet of Jesus, experiencing God's acceptance and love through his people)

I've been applying this formula long enough, both in my own life and in helping others, that anything short of following it is arrogance. Arrogance to think we can do it on our own. Arrogance to think we don't need others. Arrogance to think we're above having screen accountability. And arrogance to think we don't need Jesus to satisfy our deepest longings.

Don't be that guy.

You aren't that guy. If you were, you never would have read to the final chapter of this book.

If you'd like a vulnerable community that is already set up for you, check out Samson Society, Pure Desire Ministries, Undone Redone, or BraveHearts University.[3] If you'd like to experience a shorter group commitment that will get you hooked on the beauty of vulnerable community, check out www.beyondthebattle.net for one of the online small groups my team and I lead through this book. All beyondthebattle.net online group alumni are then invited to join a free weekly video call with me as we remind each other

---

3. See the Resources section in the back of the book for details.

of the truths of this book, have confession and accountability, and remind each other we are beloved sons of the Father. I need this as much as the next guy.

I am telling you, if you don't take the step of finding gut-level community or if you don't think you need to take this step, you have wasted your time reading this book. You might be okay in this moment, but it's only a matter of time before all of those little paper cuts add up.

The most important takeaway is to know that isolation kills, but vulnerable community brings life. If you have this community, all the other takeaways will fall into place.

Takeaway 2: Learn to Feed Off of Jesus Deeply and Daily

The church tradition I grew up in stressed daily devotions. Also called quiet time. Also called "God and I time." But at the end of the day, it was copious amounts of Bible reading, plus prayer requests.

I am all for Bible reading, even copious amounts of it. I have read the *One Year Bible* multiple times and am in the middle of reading it again (at my own pace). And I'm all for prayer requests. But that is not what I'm talking about here.

Our typical idea of daily devotions is cognitive, meaning it is a brain-powered activity. We go to the Bible to learn lessons from it or to learn *about* God. We then take these relatively impossible lessons (be patient, love sacrificially, don't lust) and try with all our might to apply them. We fail more often than we succeed, but we keep trying. The path to righteousness is to try harder. We try harder in our choices and in the amount of Bible we read.

It's no wonder most of us don't do our daily devotions, even though we know we should do them.

When we read the Bible to learn information about God, we forget that this is different from spending time *with* God. I can know a lot of information about LeBron James or George Washington, but that's not spending time with them. I can know a lot of information about my wife, but that's different from spending intimate time with her. The cognitive approach creates a malnourished marriage; the same is true of our approach to God.

Let's look at prayer requests as a case study. Prayer requests are cognitive: "God, give me this. God, give this person that. God, help me with this." They come from the head. Even if we really want them at a deep, heart level, saying the words is a cognitive act. We say them and move on.

Now let's look at a prayer you have likely prayed a thousand times: "God, take away my desire to lust." Or maybe after reading this book you've switched it to, "God, replace my desire for lust with a desire for you."

These prayers are like going to the grocery store and asking the food to nourish your body: "Hi, food, please nourish me."

It's treating God like a genie in a bottle, expecting him to perform for you because you said some magic words, rather than treating him as the very food you need to survive.

What do you do with food?

You eat it! You don't study it, categorize it, quantify it, or try really hard to be like it. You eat it. And you eat it over and over and over. You might also grow it, prepare it, study it, cook it, and smell it, but you always eat it.

A prayer like that looks and sounds something like this:

On your knees, hands raised to the sky, or face planted on the ground:

Jesus, I am broken. I come humbly before your throne. You are Almighty God, King of Kings and Lord of Lords. Jesus, I am so in need of you. I am so in need of your grace. Thank you for giving it to me freely, even though I don't deserve it. I know I deserve your wrath, but you give me your grace instead. You make me whole. Thank you! What a gift. You love me and embrace me as your son, loved, holy, righteous. You made me a new creation. There's no more condemnation. Not because of what I've done but because of what you've done for me. I am weak and feeble. I cannot produce fruit without you. Forgive me for all the times I've tried to do things on my own rather than relying on you. Help me to rely on you now. I'm struggling with lust right now. There's something deep in me that wants to feel loved, approved of, and validated. God, I confess that it feels like a woman can give this to me. I know that will never satisfy. God, I rest in you. I rest in your love for me. Thank you for loving me. Thank you for adopting me. Hold me in your arms, Jesus. I am your son, whom you love, in whom you are well pleased.

I am your son, whom you love, in whom you are well pleased.

I am your son, whom you love, in whom you are well pleased.

Be still. Stop "doing" anything, and let him "do." Meditate on his love for you. Raise your hands to him in surrender. Receive his love. Let the Father's arms wrap around you.

Do you see the difference?

Do you feel the difference?

One is prayed from the head and is looking for a genie-in-a-bottle answer. The other is prayed from the soul. It is experienced. It is not looking for an answer. It knows it is praying *to* the answer.

You must take this daily rhythm with God away from this book to have a fighting chance going forward. I know I've said it several times already, but you must carve out a daily time to be with Jesus to feed off of him. To get from him what you are looking for from women. You need to be alone. I recommend getting up before anyone in your household does, in the stillness of the morning. You need to do this daily, not out of discipline but out of desperation. Use your vulnerable community to help hold you accountable to do this.

Jesus *is* the cure, but he's not a onetime vaccine. He's not in the magic potion business. Nor does he expect you to walk in purity using your own willpower. He wants you to abide in him.[4] Jesus is so clear on this in John 15:4: "Remain in me, as I also remain in you. No branch can bear fruit by itself; it must remain in the vine. Neither can you bear fruit unless you remain in me."

What do you think he is talking about here? When we try to obey in our own strength, we are a branch separated from the vine, lying on the ground in a pile of brush, trying with all its might to produce fruit. What a ridiculous picture!

If you grew up in the evangelical tradition, like I did, you are at a disadvantage. Our strength is also our weakness. Evangelicals are strong in theology and doctrine, things that are of utmost importance. But theology and doctrine are cognitive. They are beliefs and truths. We have been so trained to have mind-based relationships with God that we've never been taught how to have an emotional, heart-based relationship with him. Evangelicals want to know a lot and want to get a lot done, but these admirable traits work against what Jesus wants from us here and what we need desperately from him.

Jesus wants us to rest in him. To be still. To stop doing and to be. To be his sons. To be with him in his love.

It's pretty common in evangelical circles that everyone knows they should be doing their devotions, but very few actually do them. We feel shame about this and don't talk about it much. When we do, we often hear a common reassurance: You can pray and spend time with God at *any* time. When you're driving in your car, when you're working out. You don't need to beat yourself up for not sitting down at a desk and reading your Bible for thirty minutes every day.

You certainly can spend time with God any time, which is beautiful. And you certainly don't need to read your Bible for

---

4. My friend and mentor Kevin Butcher wrote an entire book about this concept titled *Free* (Colorado Springs, CO: NavPress, 2021).

thirty minutes every day to appease your guilty conscience, nor do I think a thirty-minute cognitive exercise is going to bear much fruit anyway. But do you see the tragedy here? In this approach, a person is too busy getting things done (and often getting things done for God) to just sit and be with God. They can't sabbath. (That's a verb, friends.) They can't stop their doing in order to let God do in them.

To feed off of Jesus to receive the love, validation, acceptance, and approval you are looking for from women, you actually have to feed off of Jesus. How will you go through your day knowing deep in your soul you are loved by Jesus if you aren't stopping and resting in this love? This is not a cognitive reminder. It is something you experience as you rest.

This is the difference between believing the beach exists and is a restful place (cognitive) and lying in the sun on your beach towel, listening to the waves lap the shore and the seagulls squawk in the distance (experience).

I'm telling you, you can't experience this restful love when you are driving to work, cruising in and out of traffic, even jamming to the worship radio station. The mindset of spending time with God anywhere is beautiful and it has many benefits, but it is like snacking. Snacking is awesome. You can snack anytime and always have snacks on hand. But you can't live on snacks. You can't eat three hearty meals of snacks per day, nor can you buffet on snacks. You can try, and you will end up sick and undernourished.

By all means, snack. But not at the expense of allowing Jesus to transform your heart in the stillness when you aren't doing anything else but letting him speak to you. Feeding off of Jesus deeply and daily is the core of our hearts' transformation. It's the core of being filled up with his affirmation of us, so we don't end up looking for it elsewhere.[5]

---

5. To learn more about developing restful spiritual rhythms in your life, I highly recommend the book *Sacred Rhythms: Arranging Our Lives for Spiritual Transformation* by Ruth Haley Barton (Downers Grove, IL: InterVarsity, 2006).

Takeaway 3: See the Full Personhood of Women

This final takeaway gives you something simple to put in your toolbelt, or maybe to replace your toolbelt with altogether. As I've mentioned, I'm not good with tools. They confuse me. There are too many options. Sexual purity tactics can often be the same way.

You've learned a lot of great stuff in this book. Parts of it, I'm sure, were more helpful than others, but there's no way you'll remember all of it. In these final pages, I want to give you a simple weapon you can keep in your pocket, a simple tactic you can use in the heat of any temptation to recalibrate your mind. Some of this will be review, but I hope the result is memorable, simple, and effective.

If you make it your goal to see every woman's full personhood, you will not go wrong. The state we find ourselves in is like a person with double vision. Stick up your index finger a few inches in front of your book's pages right now and focus your eyes on the book. What do you see? You see two fingers, but in reality how many fingers are there?

Of course, there's only one. This is where we find ourselves in the way we've been conditioned to see women. We know that in reality there is a full person there, but our vision separates her body from the rest of her and makes that the new reality.

A scene from the Johnny Cash movie *Walk the Line* stands out to me. There's nothing exceptional about the scene. It's as familiar as end credits or a catchy soundtrack. But for me, it stands out as a good example of how and why we divide a woman's body from her personhood.

Cash's career is starting to take off. He is married to his first wife, Vivian, who is back home while he is touring. He's performing on stage and an attractive woman near the front row catches his eye. She's wearing a tight-fitting shirt and gives him a seductive look. She later meets him backstage and starts to kiss him. Sex is implied. We then see a few more backstage rendezvous with other women, fore-shadowing Johnny's long struggle with infidelity as a star musician.

As Hollywood goes, the scene is pretty vanilla and doesn't show anything. It wasn't the mild visual stimulus of the scene that enticed me, it was the message our culture tells us about women and sex: hot woman ⇨ wants sex ⇨ wants me ⇨ sex. And my mind believed that as truth—not about that woman in the movie but about *women*.

My flesh went a step farther: *I want that.*

I feel I should nuance what I mean by "I want" here. I'm referring to my flesh. I'm referring to the inner urges inside of me that I don't really choose. What I choose to want is my wife and to obey God and this dictates my actions and my priorities. I want to be clear about that. But I also want to be gut-level honest and say I want to have sex with that woman in the movie. I don't *want it* want it, but I want it at some level, or else it wouldn't capture my attention.

That flesh part of me wants Johnny Cash's lifestyle. I want to see attractive women and have sex with them. I would go as far as to ask, Who doesn't want that on some level? I feel like that's what we are all trying to work through, myself included.

It sounds so dark and insidious to hear a married pastor write something like that, but that *is* the lifestyle of countless star musicians, athletes, and movie stars today, whom we idolize. It is the lifestyle attempted by most guys in college today, which our culture doesn't bat an eye at. I have friends from high school in their late thirties who began such a lifestyle as fourteen-year-olds and are still living it, with the Facebook photos to prove it.

My point is, you and I have been brainwashed to believe this message is true. That the woman in the front of the Johnny Cash concert is just a body. That her body is removed from the rest of her and we can experience it sexually apart from the rest of her, no strings attached.

What do you need to tell yourself to get the double vision to go back to being singular? To get the two fingers to rejoin as one? Figure that out, and tell it to yourself early and often. That's the final takeaway you need.

Whether it's porn, a fantasy, or even any number of issues with your wife, I think this is the truth and tactic we need to master. I have to choose that Johnny Cash was wrong. That that's not what a woman is. I can slow down and go over each option: this woman as body only, or this woman as full person. Then I can cast my lot with one or the other of those choices.

If I go with personhood, I'm snapped back into reality by the power of its strings-attached complexity. The body-only formula simply doesn't compute. Johnny Cash's life spiraled out of control because his wife Vivian had full personhood, as did each woman he slept with. Your life will spiral out of control too, turning into a living hell. Use this to your advantage when you play out each fantasy into reality.

I don't want to continue to train my mind to think in such a false reality that brings a tsunami of destruction onto my actual reality.

Figure out a way to see a woman's full personhood. When you start to see her as body only, reattach the person to the body. See her soul. See the strings attached. Repeat this over and over in your mind. Take out a piece of paper and write down truth after truth after truth. We can choose this truth.

You can also use this tactic in your marriage. If you are disappointed with your wife's body or with something in your sex life, use this tactic to see her as a whole person again. Overlay her body with her soul and love her for who she is as a person. Lean into her soul to overcome the way you've been conditioned to see only her body. Base your attraction on all of who she is, not just her appearance. You will begin to see beauty and personhood in a way you never thought possible.

Jesus said, "Do this in remembrance of me," because he knows how forgetful we are. I wrote chapter 12 because I know how forgetful we are. These three takeaways will save your life. They will put you on the path of freedom. But it's not going to happen overnight. Celebrate every single small win along the way. Don't get discouraged when you struggle. Just keep walking the path. Stick with these takeaways. You'll be stronger in six months than you are now, and even stronger six months after that.

Like a stone in the middle of a stream, keep letting God's truth wash over you and the lasting change will happen over time.

Isolation kills, vulnerable community brings life.

Learn to feed off of Jesus deeply and daily.

See the full personhood of women.

> "Come to me, all you who are weary and burdened, and I will give you rest. Take my yoke upon you and learn from me, for I am gentle and humble in heart, and you will find rest for your souls. For my yoke is easy and my burden is light."
>
> —JESUS (MATT. 11:28–30)

In Your Small Group

Scan this QR code or go to www.beyond thebattle.net/videos and watch "Session 7 (Chapters 11–12): Tools & Takeaways."

AFTERWORD

Sexual purity will never be possible unless the grace of Jesus has transformed you and the power of the Spirit lives inside you. The path of sexual purity is the path of following Jesus as your King. It's following his ways, rather than making yourself king and doing things your way.

If you've never yielded your crown to Jesus as your King, you can do so right now. If you've never received his forgiveness for your sins, a forgiveness he purchased as he died on the cross, you can receive it right now. And if you have never escaped from the slavery imposed by your sins, sins he conquered and a slavery he freed you from as he was raised from the dead, you can find freedom right now. Confess to him that you are a sinner in desperate need of his saving grace and forgiveness.[1] He gives this to you freely when you ask him and put your faith in him.

Sexual sin brings with it a lot of guilt and shame. Lay your guilt and shame at the foot of the cross. Know that Jesus paid the price for your sins, killed your shame, and replaced it with a clean slate. He created the entire universe; he can handle your sins. Your sins are cleansed and removed as far as the east is from the west.[2] And he promises not to leave you there. He promises

---

1. Romans 10:9–10.
2. Psalm 103:12.

to give you everything you need to grow in the love and freedom he longs for you to have.[3] This is grace. Bask in it. Swim in it. Rejoice in it.

> It is for freedom that Christ has set us free.
>
> —GALATIANS 5:1

> Now the Lord is the Spirit, and where the Spirit of the Lord is, there is freedom.
>
> —2 CORINTHIANS 3:17

---

3. 2 Corinthians 1:20–22.

FOOD PRAYER

God,
Help me not to fantasize,
Help me not to objectify,
Help me not to deify.
Amen.

God,
Help me not to fantasize about women (for fantasy is the opposite of life),
Help me not to objectify women (dehumanizing them),
Help me not to deify them (or myself).
Amen.

(God, help me not to **F**antasize, **O**bjectify, **O**r **D**eify.
But instead, Jesus, may you be my food. May you fill me, sustain me, and bring me life. Amen.)

FORTY-DAY
DEVOTIONAL GUIDE

Day 1: A Freeing Truth (Beginning of Chapter 1)
Read Today: Romans 3:9–20; Revelation 14:10–13; Luke 16:19–31; Luke 12:4–5

Questions for Married Men
1. What expectations have you placed on your wife that she is not meeting?
2. How does it make you feel toward her when she doesn't meet your expectations? How does it make you feel toward God?
3. What have you tried to do over the years to get your wife to meet your expectations? What has been the fruit of these efforts?

Questions for Single Men
1. What expectations do you have for your future in regard to marriage? Do you feel entitled to marry someday? If so, what do you feel entitled to receive within that marriage?
2. Do you have peace about being single? Why or why not?

Prayer for the Day: God, show me how broken, rebellious, and deserving of judgment I am apart from your saving grace. Thank you for your saving grace.

Day 2: Thousands of Mercies
Read Today: Isaiah 6:1–8; Psalm 103; Revelation 4; Luke 18:9–14

Questions for Reflection
1. What are some of the things you've been given in life that are better than hell? (Yes, go ahead and begin answering this.)
2. How does your perspective change when you realize you don't deserve any of these gifts?
3. How does your perspective change about the additional things you ask God for? About the changes you want your wife to make? About asking God to change your singleness?
4. Do you believe the mercy of Jesus is better than anything you could ever ask God for?

Prayer for the Day: God, thank you for the thousands of mercies you have already shown me this day, mercies I do not deserve in any way, shape, or form. (List in thanksgiving some mercies God has given you. Anything better than hell will qualify here!)

Day 3: Kickback Love
Read Today: 1 Corinthians 13:4–7; Exodus 19:9–25; 20:18–21; Job 38–39

Questions for Married Men
1. Have you ever built a scoreboard in your marriage after reading a marriage book or attending marriage counseling? In what areas were you keeping score?
2. Today's Bible readings allude to self-righteousness. How would you define self-righteousness? Have you ever been

self-righteous in your marriage? (Be careful. Answering no is more than likely a self-righteous answer!)

3. God's desire is not for either spouse to be abused or cheated on. Where is the line between being abused and simply not getting our desires and expectations met?

Questions for Single Men

1. In what ways are you allowing your dating relationships to condition you to believe that love is all about getting your desires met?

2. How does today's reading give you pause about possibly getting married someday? Ask a married man you're close with to help you brainstorm how your girlfriend or fiancee might change in the way she treats you once you are married. Are you prepared to handle these changes and still love her selflessly?

3. What scoreboard do you keep track of with God? What do you feel he owes you?

Prayer for the Day: God, break down the scoreboards I've built in my marriage. Break down the scoreboards I use to compare myself with others. Break down my self-righteousness. Let me see that only you are righteous and that in my sin, I deserve nothing other than judgment. Thank you for all of the gifts of mercy you have given me.

Day 4: Living Pardoned (Beginning of Chapter 2)
Read Today: John 8:31–36; Romans 8:1–2; Galatians 5

Questions for Married Men

1. Which of the thoughts listed at the end of the reading have you thought most frequently in your marriage? Which have you thought most recently?

2. Do you ever feel your wife owes you something? If so, what?

3. How can living pardoned remove your feeling of entitlement?
4. How can living pardoned give you a physiological feeling of freedom and joy, regardless of your circumstances?
5. What does living as a new creation, resurrected to new life in Christ look like?

Married Men Prayer for the Day: Jesus, thank you for pardoning me from the death sentence I deserve, from spending eternity in hell. Thank you for taking my place and my punishment on the cross. Thank you for freeing me. Thank you for life. Thank you for making me a new creation, resurrected to new life in you. Thank you for the air I breathe. Thank you for my wife. I do not deserve her.

Questions for Single Men
1. You might not have a wife, but that doesn't mean you don't feel entitled. What do you feel God owes you?
2. How can living pardoned remove your feeling of entitlement?
3. How can living pardoned give you a physiological feeling of freedom and joy, regardless of your circumstances?
4. What does living as a new creation, resurrected to new life in Christ look like?

Single Men Prayer for the Day: Jesus, thank you for pardoning me from the death sentence I deserve, from spending eternity in hell. Thank you for taking my place and my punishment on the cross. Thank you for freeing me. Thank you for life. Thank you for making me a new creation, resurrected to new life in you. Thank you for the air I breathe. Thank you for my singleness. I do not deserve any of your mercies.

Day 5: From Entitlement to Appreciation
Read Today: Philippians 2:1–21; 4:10–13; Isaiah 40; Psalm 100

Questions for Married Men
1. In what ways have you compared your wife to other women?
2. What flaw of your wife's is holding you back from admitting you don't deserve her?
3. What do you appreciate most about your wife?
4. How will you show your wife you appreciate her?
5. How has your wife served as the glue of grace in your life?
6. What sins does marriage keep you from being involved in? What good things does marriage bring into your life?

Married Men Prayer for the Day: Lord, forgive me for putting myself above my wife on so many occasions. Forgive me for not seeking you to meet my needs. Forgive me for all the times I've held my wife's flaws against her. Help me to surrender all of her flaws to you and to soak in how undeserving I am of her. THANK YOU for saving a wretch like *me*.

Questions for Single Men
1. How does your life compare with other men's lives? What about other men's lives do you covet?
2. What do you appreciate most about the life God has given you?
3. How can you joyfully rest in God's sovereignty as a single man today?

Single Men Prayer for the Day: Lord, help me not to covet what other men have. Please fill any void I feel about not having a wife. Allow me to see with a fresh sense of appreciation all the blessings you have given me as a single man. Strengthen my married brothers in their marriages, and strengthen me in my singleness.

Day 6: Forgive, or Else
Read Today: Matthew 18:21–35; Ephesians 4:32; Colossians 3:12–14; Romans 12:14–21; Matthew 6:12–15

Questions for Married Men

1. Why do you think Jesus tells us that if we don't forgive our wives, he will not forgive us?

2. What is preventing you from fully applying this passage to your marriage and life? Are there any excuses you normally use to dismiss the potency of Jesus' point?

3. How do you need to reposture yourself before God? How will reposturing allow you to forgive and love in new ways?

4. How can you keep an active memory throughout your day of how much Jesus has forgiven you?

5. How does living as a new creation, resurrected to new life in Christ, allow you to walk confidently before God in the love and freedom of Christ?

Questions for Single Men

1. In Matthew 18, Jesus obviously isn't referring exclusively to the need for us to forgive our wives. He wants us to forgive everyone in our lives. Is there anyone you need to forgive? In today's prayer, swap out the word wife with someone close to you whom you need to forgive.

2. How does this passage help you prepare for a future marriage?

3. How do you need to reposture yourself before God? How will reposturing allow you to forgive and love in new ways?

4. How does living as a new creation, resurrected to new life in Christ, allow you to walk confidently before God in the love and freedom of Christ?

Prayer for the Day: Lord, allow me to feel the weight of the incalculable debt I owe to you. Then allow me to feel the immeasurable forgiveness you pour out on me as you make me a new creation. Allow me to feel the release and relief this forgiveness brings. Reposture me before you, Almighty God. Put me flat on my face so I can fully appreciate the wholeness you have given me. May I pour out mercy and grace to those around me because you have poured them out to me. Thank you, God!

Additional Prayer for Married Men: Allow me to see the way my wife has wronged me compared with the way I have wronged you, and allow me to show her continual forgiveness as a result. Thank you for the freedom I receive when I show continual forgiveness to my wife.

Day 7: Christ's Example
Read Today: Ephesians 5:21–33; Hebrews 4:14–16; Psalm 23

Questions for Married Men
1. How have you tried loving your wife using your own strength (even when trying to be like Jesus)? How has it worked?
2. What kickback do you expect from your wife when you do something loving for her? How do you feel when you don't get this kickback?
3. How does it make you feel that Jesus gave up what he was entitled to in order to reconcile his relationship with you?

Married Men Prayer for the Day: Fill me with your love, Jesus. Saturate me like a sponge with the power of your unconditional love. I do not deserve your love, but I desperately need it. Let it overflow from my life into my marriage. Help me love my wife the way you love me.

Questions for Single Men
1. You don't have a wife, so you might think this chapter about Jesus' example of love doesn't apply to you. But remember, Jesus was single, just like you. Memorize John 13:34–35, a command from Jesus for us to love one another (meaning to love our community of other Christians) exactly as he has loved us.

2. It is a myth that a wife will complete you. How can Paul's and Jesus' respective lives of singleness be a guide for you? What spiritual practices of theirs can you emulate to experience the Father's love?

Single Men Prayer for the Day: Fill me with your love, Father. Saturate me like a sponge with the power of your unconditional love. I do not deserve this love, but I desperately need it. Remind me that you, Jesus, the ultimate human, were single. Thank you for this example you've set for me. Thank you that the love of the Father is enough for me. Thank you for completing me.

Day 8: Our Power Source (Beginning of Chapter 3)
Read Today: Matthew 3:13–4:11; Psalm 63; Matthew 11:28–30; Numbers 6:22–26

Questions for Married Men
1. What things do men look for in our culture to find identity, approval, acceptance, and validation?
2. In what ways do you look to women to find your identity, approval, acceptance, and validation?
3. How do you feel when your wife isn't showing you approval and attraction, but other women are?

Questions for Single Men
1. How are you looking to women to find approval, acceptance, and validation? (This could be your current girlfriend, the girlfriend you wish you had, the women you flirt with, or even the women in the pornography you look at.)
2. What else do you look to, besides women, to find your approval, acceptance, and validation?
3. What type of approval, acceptance, and validation do you feel a future wife might give you?
4. Do you feel less valuable because you are single?

Prayer for the Day: Father, show me that all I need is you. Show me that all other sources of approval and acceptance are counterfeits. Show me that the only verdict with authority on who I am is your verdict. Let me live in the truth that I am your son, whom you love, and in whom you are well pleased.

Day 9: The Golden-Haired Woman
Read Today: Isaiah 41:5–7, 21–29; 44:9–17

Questions for Reflection
1. Have you ever found the Golden-Haired Woman, only to have her golden shine wear off later?
2. How have you looked to sex and to women to provide you with what only God can provide?
3. What promises does our culture make about what sex or women can give us?
4. What is your primary engine right now?

Prayer for the Day: Lord, let me see the emptiness of my pursuit of the perfect woman. Let me see that no woman, or number of women, can give me what only you can give. Forgive me for worshiping women and sex as idols. God, show me how your intimate affection, validation, and approval can be my primary engine of fulfillment. Thank you that you are the best thing in the universe, Jesus, and I get to have you. Forgive me for thinking that a woman could ever replace you.

Day 10: When Even Burger King Looks Appetizing
Read Today: Hebrews 13:1–6; Colossians 2:6–7, 10; Romans 12:1–3; Acts 14:8–18

Questions for Reflection
1. Have you ever had a spiritual high, perhaps at a Christian camp or at a time when you felt extra close to God? How did sexual temptation appeal to you during this time?

2. When has sexual temptation been the strongest for you? What circumstances have accompanied these seasons?

3. Have you ever considered whether sexual temptation and gratification make you feel more valuable, accepted, and desirable? Even godlike?

4. What regular spiritual disciplines (spiritual meals) can you add to your life to be reminded of and strengthened in the love, mercy, and acceptance God has for you in Jesus? (Along with regular Bible reading, I highly recommend the book *Sacred Rhythms* by Ruth Haley Barton for a life-changing guide on how to establish these rhythms of being in the presence of God.)[1]

5. What truths from God do you need to remind yourself of over and over again?

Prayer for the Day: Lord, give me an appetite for your love and truth. Fill me with the substance of your love, comfort, mercy, approval, and acceptance of me. Forgive me for desiring to be worshiped rather than living my life as a living sacrifice of worship to you. Let me see your awesome holiness and be humbled by it every time I desire a woman to worship me. Simultaneously fill me with the satisfying sweetness of your unconditional love for me as your son. Help me to want this so badly that I will do whatever it takes in my schedule to spend daily time with you.

Day 11: Stop Living like They Were Right about You (Beginning of Chapter 4)

Read Today (They're short, read 'em all!): Colossians 1:22; Psalm 139:13–14; Matthew 6:26; 1 Thessalonians 2:4; Proverbs 29:25; Galatians 1:10; 1 Corinthians 4:3–4; 2 Corinthians 5:17–21

---

1. Ruth Haley Barton, *Sacred Rhythms: Arranging Our Lives for Spiritual Transformation* (Downers Grove, IL: InterVarsity, 2006).

Questions for Reflection
1. What messages of inadequacy were given to you as a child and from culture?
2. In what ways have you sought to prove that you are valuable?
3. How do your sexual temptations falsely promise to enhance your self-worth?
4. How do your sexual temptations falsely promise to satisfy questions from your insecure past: "Am I lovable? Am I important? Am I acceptable? Am I valuable?"
5. Have you ever come to the conclusion that the people in your past who told you you're worthless and unacceptable were wrong about you? Name these people and their false messages. Reject the lies and declare the truth.

Prayer for the Day: God, let me live in your truth. Show me the lies I believe about my identity and the ways I buy into these lies, especially in the area of sexual temptation. Give me the courage to name those in my past who have branded me as worthless and to stop living as if they were right. Thank you that you are my Judge, not them. Thank you for fully accepting me and allowing me to rest in your approval and acceptance of me as your son. Thank you that I couldn't be any more valuable to you than I already am. Give me the courage to seek a Christian counselor to walk me through these questions and truths.

Day 12: Adopted
Read Today: Romans 8; Hebrews 4:14–16

Questions for Reflection
1. When you close your eyes and ask God who he says you are, what do you hear him say?
2. Do you have a community of other men who embody and remind you of the truths in this chapter? If not,

what steps can you take today to begin building this community?

3. How do you need to prioritize a daily rhythm with the Lord to prayerfully hear these truths from him?

Prayer for the Day: Father, show me what it means to be your son in all its fullness. Show me the wholeness I have in you. Show me how much you already love me because of what Jesus did on the cross for me. Show me that my identity, my value, and my desire for acceptance, approval, and validation are already fully met in my standing as your beloved son. Show me that I don't need to seek these things anywhere else. Thank you for loving me. Thank you for holding me. Thank you for protecting and cherishing my soul.

Day 13: My Wife Is Not God Either
Read Today: Deuteronomy 4:15–40

Questions for Married Men

1. What expectations have you placed on your wife to satisfy your heart's longing for approval, acceptance, and validation?
2. In what ways has she fallen short of your expectations?
3. What sexual or relational sources outside your marriage have you looked to in order to supplement your heart's longing for approval, acceptance, and validation?
4. How can you view your wife with compassion?
5. How can the way you treat your wife become an act of worship to God?

Married Men Prayer for the Day: Jesus, I repent of worshiping idols. I repent of looking to my wife to fill my heart's longing for approval, acceptance, and validation. Help me to love, cherish, and appreciate her for who she is and not to dwell on who she isn't. I repent of looking to sexual and relational sources to fill my heart's longing for approval, acceptance, and validation. Jesus, I run to you to do what only you can do. Let me worship you with every thought and action I display toward my wife. Thank you for approving of me, accepting me, and loving me. Fill me with the reality of this supernatural gift of mercy. Transform me, reformat me, and recalibrate me to operate in the strength of this great gift.

Questions for Single Men

1. Singleness and dating are fertile environments to make your girlfriend, or the girl you're seeking, into a god. The reason is because it is such an idealized phase of a relationship when you mostly see only the surface of who a person really is. Infatuation and hormones rule, while genuine conflicts are few and far between. It's only when the commitment of marriage is sealed that people (both husbands and wives) show all of the cards they've subconsciously been holding close to the vest. Knowing this, how do you need to reprioritize what you're looking for in a dating relationship?
2. What sins do you need to repent of? How have you trusted in sexual sin rather than God? What have you been trading God's will for?
3. Are your dating relationships (or desired relationships) oriented around getting what you want from a woman, or around worshiping God?

Single Men Prayer for the Day: Jesus, I repent of worshiping idols. I repent of looking to women to fill my heart's longing for approval, acceptance, and validation. I repent of looking to sexual and relational sources to fill my heart's longing for approval, acceptance, and validation. Jesus, I run to you to do what only you can do. Let me worship you with every thought and action. Thank you for approving of me, accepting me, and loving me. Fill me with the reality of this supernatural gift of mercy. Transform me, reformat me, and recalibrate me to operate in the strength of this great gift.

Day 14: Water Boys for Jesus

Read Today: 2 Corinthians 12:7–10; Hebrews 12:3–16; Romans 5:3–5; 6:16–23; 1 Peter 1:6–9; John 21:17–18

Questions for Married Men

1. Have you ever prayed for God to remove a problem in your marriage, as Paul prayed for his thorn to be removed in 2 Corinthians 12:7–10? Have you grown resentful toward God because of this?

2. In what ways have you taken your marriage problems into your own hands rather than trusting God's will and God's ways?

3. What have you learned about true love through the hard times in your marriage?

4. How can God use the hard times in your marriage to teach you that he is all you need? Does God's grace feel sufficient to you during the dry seasons of your marriage?

5. Why is there joy in spiritual maturity, even if it comes at a cost?

6. How do you feel about being God's slave (versus being sin's slave)?

Questions for Single Men

1. Have you ever prayed for God to remove your singleness, as Paul prayed for his thorn to be removed in 2 Corinthians 12:7–10? Have you grown resentful toward God because of this?

2. How is being single like fasting? How can your singleness draw you closer to Jesus? How can Jesus fill the vacancy of a spouse in your life?

3. In what ways have you taken your singleness or relational problems into your own hands rather than trusting God's will and God's ways?

4. Why is there joy in spiritual maturity, even if it comes at a cost?

5. How do you feel about being God's slave (versus being sin's slave)?

Prayer for the Day: Heavenly Father, hallowed be your name. May your name be the center of everything in my life, and most prominently in my marriage/dating life. May my life be about you and not about me. May your will be done, not my will. May the way things happen in heaven, the way you designed my heart to love, happen on earth right here in the middle of my life, in the middle of my marriage/singleness. May your kingdom come here. May you craft me into the person I'm meant to be within your kingdom. Please give me my daily bread. Give me the sustaining power of your grace to get me through today with joy and satisfaction, no matter what earthly trials I am facing. Forgive me for the ways I've taken things into my own hands, not trusted you, and rebelled against you. Help me to forgive my wife/girlfriend for the ways she has hurt me. Help me to forgive her just as you have forgiven me. Strengthen me against temptation. Give me the courage to reach out and seek help from the Christian men you have placed in my life. Deliver me from the evil traps of sin. For you are the King of this kingdom (not me), you are all powerful (and I am your unworthy servant,) and I give you my entire life for your glory, that you may be glorified through me forever and ever. Help me to trust you and know your goodness. Amen.

Day 15: Strings Attached (Beginning of Chapter 5)
Read Today: Genesis 1:27; Colossians 2:20–23; Ephesians 5:1–20

Questions for Reflection

1. Do you want to be attracted to a *her* or a *that*? What is disturbing about being attracted to a *that*?
2. Have you ever analyzed what you turn a woman into when your eyes dart to her body parts? How does this act define who and what she is to you (and where her purpose and value come from)?
3. Is this the same way God would define who and what she is?

4. How does objectifying women make you an unsafe member of a Christian community?
5. What "strings attached" can you train yourself to see when lust's tractor beam is pulling you in?

Prayer for the Day: Lord, I repent of what I have turned women into. I repent of what lust has turned me into. You have called me to bring life to people, yet my lust has taken life away. It has taken away what makes a woman the full, beautiful, and dignified creation you made her to be. Help me to see a woman's soul, not simply her body parts. Help me to see the strings attached. Teach me to see all people, most especially women, with honor and dignity. Help me to bring life, not take it away.

Day 16: Daughters
Read Today: Psalm 139:1–18

Questions for Reflection
1. When you lust over a woman, do you realize you are lusting over someone's daughter?
2. Did you notice that nothing in Psalm 139:1–18 mentions a person's value coming from their body parts? Where does a person's value come from?
3. If you now have or were someday to have a daughter, how would you feel about men lusting over her? How can your answer to this transform your inclination to lust over other people's daughters?
4. If you now have or were someday to have a daughter who got married, how would you feel toward her husband if he left her for another woman? How can this reshape your commitment to love, protect, and cherish your wife?
5. What can you do for your wife this week to show her you cherish her?

Married Men Prayer for the Day: Lord, let me see my wife as a precious soul you have created. Let me see her value the way I would see my own daughter's value. Let me protect her. Let me cherish her. Let me pour love over her imperfections. Let me not measure her value based on what she can give me, or on the world's standard of beauty or affection or performance. Let me love her as you love her. Let me love her as you love me—as a precious soul created in your image.

Single Men Prayer for the Day: Lord, help me to see every woman as someone's daughter. Help me to see her as your daughter, full of dignity and honor, rather than as a piece of meat to be consumed. Help me to see the sacredness of this. Help me to not take advantage of women for my own gain.

Day 17: Objectification All Grown Up
Read Today: Philippians 2:1–4; Isaiah 1:11–18; Amos 5:21–24

Questions for Reflection
1. How is the mindset of looking at women in pornography similar to the mindset of rape, molestation, or sex slavery?
2. How does pornography train and condition someone to view the women they see in real life?
3. How have you seen your own porn exposure become more advanced over time? Do you find the same type of stimulus doesn't bring you the same rush it used to, so you seek more intense stimuli? Where might this road lead?
4. How does it make you feel to know that your porn usage supports the global sex slave industry?
5. Will you visit www.SharedHope.org/become-a-defender and commit to helping end the sex industry by helping end the demand for its product?

Prayer for the Day: Lord, may the reality that porn usage supports the sex slave industry make me sick to my stomach. May I be so repulsed by the idea of a sacred human, created in your image, being raped over and over again for the sake of profit. May I mourn this travesty the way you do and vow never again to create a demand for this industry. May I vow never to view women as objects to be consumed. Lord, please end the human trafficking industry. Please bring justice and free the oppressed.

Day 18: When Women Want to Be Objectified
Read Today: Proverbs 7

Questions for Reflection
1. How does lusting over women who want to be objectified condition your brain to uncontrollably lust over women who don't want to be?
2. Why do you think women desire to be lusted over? What is lacking in their lives that they're trying to satisfy?
3. What is God's will for a woman who wants to be lusted over?

Prayer for the Day: Lord, help me not to reinforce the lie so many women believe about themselves. Help me not to continue to believe our culture's message that women's skin is what makes them valuable. I pray for the women I have lusted over. (Be specific with names here.) I pray they would know that they are created in your image, that you love them, and that you are the only one who can give them what they are seeking to gain through the attention of men. I pray that I can help deliver this good news to them rather than reinforcing and agreeing with the lies Satan has told them.

Day 19: Turning Your Wife into Porn (Beginning of Chapter 6)
Read Today: 1 Corinthians 6:12–20; Colossians 2:21–23

Questions for Married Men
1. How have you defined sexual attraction as being solely about bodies and body parts? How is this an incomplete picture of what a sexual relationship is supposed to be?

2. What value are you assigning to women when their only function is for you to consume their body parts?
3. How would it feel to be so rewired to God's definition of sex, and so filled up in him, that you simply lost the desire to lust after women?

Married Men Prayer for the Day: Let me see my wife for the beautiful creation she is. Let me see sex as the uniting of two lives, not the consuming of body parts. Let me see and define beauty the way you do, Lord: You see that a person is not simply skin and body parts. Let me see and appreciate all of who you made my wife to be. Thank you for the honor of protecting and cherishing this one woman. Thank you for the one flesh you have made us into.

Questions for Single Men
1. In the flawed theory of "eye bouncing," a single guy does not have a wife to bounce his eyes toward. How could redefining sex as something that involves all of a person help you to see women as God's creations, made to have dignity, rather than as objects?
2. How might seeing women as people with dignity and not just body parts help you conquer your tendency to lust?

Single Men Prayer for the Day: Let me see and define beauty the way you do, Lord. You see that a person is not simply skin. Help me to see women as human beings, not human body parts. Change my desire to selfishly consume women for my own purposes. Let me see sex as the uniting of two lives, not simply an act of pleasure.

Day 20: Turning Your Wife into an Object
Read Today: Proverbs 5:15–23; 1 Corinthians 10:13

Questions for Married Men
1. Do you think your wife knows whether you are less

attracted to her when she gains weight? How do you think this makes her feel?

2. Do you feel entitled to demand that your wife maintain a certain weight or shape for you?

3. Do you feel like you married your wife or her body? How should your answer to this dictate how you view attraction within your marriage?

4. How can what you believe about the purpose of sex help you have a more satisfying sex life with your wife?

5. How can what you believe about the purpose of sex help you or hurt you in your struggle against lust?

Married Men Prayer for the Day: Lord, help me see my wife as more than just a body. Teach me what love is.

Questions for Single Men

1. How do you feed the lie our culture tells women—that they must have A-level body shapes in order to be seen as valuable?

2. Even if you plan never to get married, how does your pattern of objectifying women make you an unsafe person for women to be around? How does it make you an unsafe friend?

3. If you do plan to get married someday, what sorts of sinful or unrealistic expectations do you have about the body shape your wife is to maintain for you? How will these set you up for failure?

4. How can what you believe about the purpose of sex help you or hurt you in your struggle against lust?

Single Men Prayer for the Day: Lord, help me to see women as more than just bodies. Teach me how to be a friend to the women in my life. Teach me to neither devalue nor exalt someone based on their appearance.

Day 21: Loving Sex or Loving Your Wife
Read Today: Ephesians 5:25; John 15:12–13; 1 John 4:7–21

Questions for Married Men
1. Which scenario would you choose: you lose your wife but get to keep having sex, or you are no longer able to have sex but keep your wife?
2. How have you viewed marriage as a way of getting your selfish desires met?
3. How does God want to use your marriage to sanctify you (to form your heart to be more like Jesus')?
4. What does God want you to long for in your marriage?

Married Men Prayer for the Day: Jesus, teach me what love is. I am to model to my wife the same love you have shown to me. Help me to grasp the selflessness of your love. Help me to grasp that the kickback you longed for was simply a relationship with me. Rather than longing for sex, help me to long for my wife. Help me not to make sex an idol in my life.

Questions for Single Men
1. If you do get married someday, have you been setting yourself up for failure by imagining sex as a utopia?
2. Do you have any way of foreseeing what sexual problems might arise throughout your marriage? (Answer: no.) How do you need to reframe what marriage is now so these future problems don't shatter your picture of reality?
3. Have you ever been envious of married men because it seems their problems with sexual temptation are solved? Know that this is simply not the case. The temptations don't go away. They just shift, become more complicated, and add layers you'd never expect. Allow God to rewire your view of sex and women now. Don't wait until you get married.

Single Men Prayer for the Day: Lord, help me to trust you with the expectations I put on my future marriage. Help me to trust you as to whether I'm even to be married. I surrender this to you. Help me to trust you with what my married life would be like and, specifically, what my sex life would be like. I also pray for my married brothers and sisters who are secretly struggling in their sex lives in their marriages. Strengthen my brothers to love their wives and to trust your sovereignty in whatever sexual expectations are not being met in their marriages. Help me not to make sex into an idol in my life.

Day 22: Who Made Sex? (Beginning of Chapter 7)
Read Today: 1 Corinthians 6:12–20; Genesis 1–2

Questions for Reflection
1. Are you envious of the way non-Christians can live sexually?
2. In what ways have you fought for sexual purity under Satan's design for sex rather than God's?
3. Have you ever considered the implications of the fact that God, not Satan, created sex? How does this encourage you? How does it frustrate you? How does it shape the way you approach sexual purity?

Prayer for the Day: God, thank you for creating sex. Forgive me for the ways I have contorted and polluted your wonderful design. Give me eyes to see your design and to submit and conform myself to it, trusting that you, the designer, know what you're doing.

Day 23: Apples and Oranges
Read Today: Proverbs 5; Psalm 27:14

Questions for Reflection
1. In what ways have you been taught that God's view of sex

will give you greater instant pleasure than Satan's? Have you found this to be true or false in your experience?

2. Why is it so hard for us to see past the dripping honey of temptation to the double-edged sword hidden within it?

3. Is the work needed to grow and operate an apple orchard worth it, when compared with simply grabbing and eating an apple?

Prayer for the Day: God, give me a broader view of the purpose of sex. Show me how shallow, incomplete, and incorrect Satan's idea of sex is. Help me to abandon it altogether. Help me to discover your design for sex—something that may not be able to compete in the moment but is far better over a lifetime. Help me to rejoice in and appreciate the ordinary life of health and purpose you've given me.

Day 24: Food for the Stomach and the Stomach for Food
Read Today: 1 Corinthians 6:12–20; Matthew 7:24–27; Proverbs 12:11, 24; 13:4; 14:23; 28:19

Questions for Reflection

1. How long have you been pouring lemonade into your car's gas tank, approaching sex via the world's design of consumption and objectification rather than through God's one-flesh design? Where has this gotten you?

2. Why is the "stomach for food, the body for sex" mentality so popular?

3. What are the repercussions of this mentality? How have you experienced them?

4. How will viewing the purpose of sex as uniting two lives help you in your struggle against lust, fantasy, and objectification?

Prayer for the Day: God, deconstruct my thinking that sex is all about consumption and objectification. Show me how flawed and destructive this mentality is. Rescue me. Help me to build my house on your rock.

Day 25: One Flesh (Beginning of Chapter 8)
Read Today: Matthew 5:27–30; Hosea 1–3

Questions for Reflection
1. How have you seen the one-flesh principle hold true in your marriage? If you're single, how have you seen this principle at work in Christ-centered marriages that you have observed?
2. Where did you see a healthy one-flesh dynamic in your parents' relationship? Where did you see a lack of this one-flesh dynamic in their relationship?
3. Are you able to see how temptations for sexual sin are of a different character from what God designed sex to be?
4. Why do you think our world has so blatantly exchanged God's beautiful one-flesh design for the illusion of physical-only sex?
5. How does a marriage symbolize our relationship with God? How do lust and affairs symbolize worshiping idols?

Married Men Prayer for the Day: Lord, thank you for the one-flesh relationship I share with my wife. Forgive me for when I haven't understood sex to be a part of this greater design. Allow this to reformat what I base attraction on. Help me to appreciate the wisdom with which you designed the bond between a man and a woman, and the beauty of this picture of your love. Thank you for being committed to me as my faithful and loving husband and I your bride. Help me to model this love and commitment to my wife.

Single Men Prayer for the Day: Lord, help me to see sex as much more than simply physical. Help me to see your commands for sex as a reflection of the intimacy you desire to have with me. Thank you for protecting me from polluting that intimacy by commanding me to stay away from sexual sin. Thank you for designing sex to encompass 100 percent of a person. Help me to see sex this way and not to buy the lie of Satan's concept of sex. Help me to see through this lie and to know it will never cash out the way it promises to.

Day 26: Pour Some Sugar on Me
Read Today: Proverbs 6:20–35

Questions for Reflection
1. In what ways have you bought the idea that sex is meant to be consumed on its own, like eating sugar without making the rest of the recipe?
2. What consequences has removing sex from the recipe of marriage had on our culture?
3. How can these consequences show you that your striving for sexual purity is about more than just you?
4. What influences in your life (movies, TV, music, friends) continue to send you the message that it's okay to remove sex from the recipe of marriage? What do you need to do about these influences?

Prayer for the Day: God, give me your wisdom to see the whole recipe. Give me the discipline and self-control not to binge on sugar without the rest of the ingredients you have provided. Show me what a sugar-only diet does to my heart. Show me how lust pollutes and contorts my heart. Show me your vision for my heart. Help me to see sex and women the way you want me to see them, the way you designed me to see them. Help me to remove the influences in my life that tell me sex on its own is okay.

Day 27: More Than Animals
Read Today: Proverbs 7

Questions for Married Men
1. What do you need to do to build trust, commitment,

vulnerability, faithfulness, and selflessness within your marriage?

2. Why can only a husband (versus a boyfriend or fiance) provide the support needed for sex? What happens when a husband's support isn't there?

3. Who have you been lusting over that you have no way of providing this support to, and thus have no business fantasizing about?

Married Men Prayer for the Day: God, help me to be someone my wife can trust to be faithful and committed to her, not just in my actions but also in my heart and my mind. Help me not to see the marital ingredients of trust, commitment, vulnerability, faithfulness, and selflessness as nuisances. Help me to see them as essentials to be the man you've created me to be and to see sex according to your design, not the world's.

Questions for Single Men

1. It's easy to rationalize lust as a single guy when you're "only looking" and not planning to actually have sex with someone. How does this pattern of misplaced intimacy make you an unsafe person if you are to get married someday? Even if you stay single, how does it damage the way you view women? How does it damage the woman you're lusting over?

2. Can you still be a faithful and trustworthy man of God even if you never get married? How does lust make you an untrustworthy man?

Single Men Prayer for the Day: Lord, reshape my definition of sex to include the essential ingredients of trust, commitment, and fidelity. Though I am single, remind me I don't have free reign to lust. Remind me I am not in a position to give trust, commitment, and lifelong fidelity to any woman I desire to lust over. I'm not her husband. Help me to stop damaging women, and in the process damaging myself, by disobeying your design for sex.

Day 28: Bland Bread
Read Today: Proverbs 5

Questions for Married Men
1. How can you make sure you are doing your part to ensure your marriage doesn't become bland bread?
2. What can you do to create a more comfortable and hospitable environment for your wife sexually?

Married Men Prayer for the Day: Lord, help me to see the fruits of God-honoring sex within a God-honoring marriage. Please bless me and my marriage in this way. Please give me the perseverance and faithfulness I need not to abandon the recipe when things aren't going the way I want.

Questions for Single Men
1. You may not ever get married, but how can you avoid looking back on your life when you're an old man and seeing a path of sexual ruin and regret?
2. Do you trust in God's sovereignty that if you are to be married, he will bring you your bride in his timing, for his purpose? And if you are not to be married, that he is in control of this for his purposes? Can you rest in him and trust him in this?

Single Men Prayer for the Day: God, help me to trust you. Remind me of your almighty power, your infinite wisdom, and your divine sovereignty. Remind me that you are in control and that your ways are higher than mine. Help me to rest in you and submit to your will. Help me not to covet marriage or sex. Help me not to worship marriage or sex. Fill me with your love. Saturate me with your all-sufficient grace and mercy. Thank you for walking this life with me, every step of the way.

Day 29: The Death Grip of Fantasy (Beginning of Chapter 9)
Read Today: Deuteronomy 30:19–20; Proverbs 5:3–6; 7:10, 16–18, 21–27

Questions for Reflection
1. What sexual and relational fantasies do you entertain?
2. What lies about fantasy have you bought into?
3. How has entertaining fantasy affected the way you view real women in your life?
4. How has your attention and investment in a sexual fantasy world negatively affected your marriage and your real world?

Prayer for the Day: Lord, help me to identify all the ways I live in fantasy instead of reality. Help me to realize how the investment I'm putting into these things is sucking the life out of my reality.

Day 30: Marrying the Wrong Person (For Married Men)
Read Today: Proverbs 31:10–11, 30; Hebrews 13:4; Matthew 5:31–32

Questions for Married Men
1. What are the "what if" and "if only" questions that go through your mind about your marriage?
2. Has any one of these ever helped to make your marriage better?
3. Where are you most susceptible to being persuaded to buy into a relational fantasy?
4. How would you be freer to love your wife if you let go of the fantasy scenarios that play out in your mind?

Married Men Prayer for the Day: Lord, help me to reject the fantasy thoughts that go through my mind. Help me to reject them as lies from Satan. Lies promising a reality which doesn't actually exist and never can or will. Lies that keep me from investing in my marriage and loving my wife with my whole heart. Help me to stop looking to the world for a model of relationships and to look to you and you alone.

Day 30: Pick Your Poison (For Single Men)
Read Today: John 10:10; Hebrews 13:4; Matthew 5:27–28

Questions for Single Men
1. Which aspect of fantasy do you fall prey to as a single guy?
2. How does God want you to invest in your reality as a single man? Reread the sections "The Gift No One Wants" and "Open the Gift" in "A Note from the Author" at the beginning of the book for ideas.
3. How does Satan get you to doubt yourself because you are single? Do you ever feel self-pity about being single? How does God see you as a single man?

Single Men Prayer for the Day: Lord, help me to invest in the reality of singleness you have given me. Help me not to covet what my married friends have, and help me not to use my singleness as an excuse to disobey you. Help me to trust you.

Day 31: The Grass Is Greener
Read Today: 1 Corinthians 13:7; Proverbs 12:11; 28:19; Philippians 4:4–8

Questions for Married Men
1. Have you ever considered divorce, or are you considering it right now? Write out every implication and repercussion of the possible choices that lie in front of you.
2. Have you decided to embrace reality in your marriage? (Whenever you want to run to fantasy, to make a deposit in your marriage instead.)

3. What would investing in your marriage look like for you?
4. Who else will be blessed if you invest in your marriage instead of running away from it?

Married Men Prayer for the Day: Lord, help me to embrace my reality. Whenever the temptation to waste energy in fantasy comes, help me to make an investment in my marriage. Help me to water my marriage faithfully.

Questions for Single Men
1. What does the bountiful apple orchard look like for you as a single man? (What will happen in your life if you invest 100 percent in the reality God has given you, obeying and trusting him in all things rather than wasting your life on sexual fantasy?)
2. What does your life look like when you allow fantasy to run wild? What are the repercussions of this on all aspects of your life? Be specific.
3. What will your life look like in five or ten years if you continue to allow fantasy to run wild?
4. What does investing in community and connection need to look like in your life?

Single Men Prayer for the Day: Lord, show me what it looks like to embrace reality as a single man. Show me how to replace destructive and distorted patterns of fantasy with constructive and life-bringing patterns of reality. Show me how to flourish in your will. Give me courage to invest heavily in connection and community.

Day 32: It's Not Real and Give the Flesh a Taste of Its Own Medicine (Beginning of Chapter 10)
Read Today: Proverbs 12:11; 28:19; Proverbs 5:3–14, 22–23

Questions for Reflection
1. Has fantasy ever fulfilled its promise to you? (Has it ever

turned out to be as good as it looked, without causing collateral damage?)
2. How has fantasy made you feel trapped and imprisoned?
3. Would you eat a pin-filled burger that was painted and uncooked? Obviously not. How can you reframe your sexual temptations to reflect this same mindset?
4. How can you change your mindset toward lust to match Jesus' teaching that lust is the same as sex? Can you weaponize this against your flesh, understanding you really don't want the sex your flesh is tempting you with?

Prayer for the Day: Lord, show me how to invest in reality. Continue to bring me freedom from the enslaving prison of fantasy. Help me to invest in my reality. Help me to embrace my reality. Show me how to make my reality better. Show me how to water the grass you've given me. Help me be so grateful and appreciative of the mercy-filled grass you have given me. I believe you. I believe that you are right and that what our culture has taught me about sex is wrong.

Day 33: Lusting Over Plastic
Read Today: Proverbs 12:11; 28:19; 1 Thessalonians 4:3–8

Questions for Reflection
1. Does it seem weird to discover you've been warped into being attracted to something that isn't actually human?
2. If you were a woman (specifically, a wife), how would you feel knowing you had to compete with so many "mutant," electronically created sexual images?
3. If you were a Hollywood actor, why would it be insulting (or at least strange) to you to be called only by your character name when in public or when doing interviews, with no one knowing your actual name?
4. How does God want you to pray for models and actresses rather than lusting over them?

Married Men Prayer for the Day: Lord, I lift up in prayer the models and actresses I lust over. Help them to find their identity and security in you. Help me to see fantasy for what it is. Help me to see the pins in the burger and the Photoshopping on the magazine cover. Help me to see how broken a system this is. Free me from it. Help me to be attracted to my wife, this precious human being, for who she is. Help me see her soul. Help me redefine what makes someone human. Forgive me for how I've made my wife compete with so many unfair sexual representations.

Single Men Prayer for the Day: Lord, I lift up in prayer the models and actresses I lust over. Help them to find their identity and security in you. Help me to see fantasy for what it is. Help me to see the pins in the burger and the Photoshopping on the magazine cover. Help me to see how broken a system this is. Free me from it. Show me how it's not your will for me to be attracted to plastic. Reshape my view of who women are, and help me to see women the way you see them. Help me to see their souls. Help me to give them the dignity, value, and respect you give them. Take away the allure of sexual fantasy's lie by showing me the reality of what I'm doing.

Day 34: Fading Beauty
Read Today: Proverbs 5:18–19; Psalm 62

Questions for Reflection
1. Who are you allowing to shape your reality?
2. What is bound to happen to us and our marriages if we continue to allow ourselves to be influenced by a culture that worships and exploits youthfulness as the definition of sexy and romantic? Where does this road end for you?
3. In what ways have you bought into our culture's broken system of romance? In what ways has it burned you?

Prayer for the Day: Lord, help me to see our culture's broken system of romance all around me. Help me to see it and pity it rather than continue buying into it like a mindless fool. Help me run to your design for romance. Thank you for your design for romance. A design that doesn't exploit. A design that doesn't dehumanize. A design that gives love and dignity and value all the days of our lives. Help me to see beauty and romance as broader and bigger and deeper and more selfless than simply consuming someone's body parts. God, I pray for the women in my life. I pray for my mother, my sisters, my wife, my daughters, and my friends. I pray these women would find their value in who they are in you, not in the enslaving pressure to look like they are twenty-five years old the rest of their lives. Forgive me for perpetuating this harmful system.

Day 35: It's Not Important
Read Today: Proverbs 31:30–31; Matthew 6:19–21; Hebrews 12:27–29

Questions for Married Men
1. What temptations do you need to call out in your life as not worth giving into? How can you help minimize what these temptations are promising you?
2. If you were to further act on your temptations, where would it lead?
3. If you are longing for an escape from your marriage, how can you use that yearning as a flashing red light to get you running toward Jesus and toward serving your wife and investing in your marriage?
4. What has developed over years of marriage that you can appreciate and be grateful for?
5. What messages can you give yourself when you see an attractive woman and start treating her differently than you would an average-looking woman?
6. How can you go behind the scenes of lust's facade and see women for who they really are?

Married Men Prayer for the Day: Lord, forgive me for the ways I've cast my wife aside after her beauty and charm faded—the same way

I cast aside one bit of porn or lust and move on to another. Forgive me for buying into our culture's lie that physical beauty is the be-all and end-all. Allow me to see the damage this does to women. Allow me to see the damage this has done to my wife. Allow me to see the damage this does to the way I view women. Jesus, show me how I can transform this yearning for escape into fuel to run toward you and toward my marriage, investing wholeheartedly, rather than running away from it and away from you.

Questions for Single Men

1. What temptations do you need to call out in your life as not worth giving into? How can you help minimize the value of what these temptations are promising you?
2. If you were to act on your temptations, where would it lead?
3. How has seeing physical appearance as the most important attribute of a woman gotten you into trouble as a single man?
4. What messages can you give yourself when you see an attractive woman and start treating her differently than you would an average-looking woman?
5. How can you go behind the scenes of lust's facade and see women for who they really are?

Single Men Prayer for the Day: Lord forgive me for seeing physical appearance as the be-all and end-all of value for women. Forgive me for how I treat physically attractive women better than women I don't find attractive. Help me to understand that your will for my life is so much more important than any quick fix an attractive woman can bring me. Help me to invest in my relationship with you and in my future, not in things that don't matter.

Day 36: The Truth about Tools and Opening the Toolbox: Talk (Beginning of Chapter 11)
Read Today: Proverbs 28:13; Psalm 51; Romans 8:1

Questions for Reflection

1. What Christian men could you share your sexual purity struggles with?

2. What's the culture of your church like when it comes to talking about sexual temptation? Are there outlets available for this type of ministry?

3. If your church isn't a place where you can confess your sexual temptations, don't use this as an excuse to let Satan win in your congregation. How can God use you to lead such an initiative in your church?

4. Do you feel condemnation when you think about your sexual sin? Read Romans 8:1 aloud. The truth is that there is no condemnation for those who have the blood of Jesus covering them. Know that God wants you to live in freedom from sin because he loves you so much, but your sin doesn't condemn you. Jesus' grace still covers you. Allow the Holy Spirit to convict you. Conviction leads to repentance, which leads to freedom.

5. If you aren't reading this book with a group right now, will you commit to recruiting a group of men to go through the book with you from the beginning or to join a beyondthebattle.net group?

Prayer for the Day: Jesus, help me to taste your grace anew. Thank you for your grace and forgiveness. Thank you that you don't condemn me. Thank you for giving me your church to help strengthen and sharpen me. Give me the courage I need to talk to brothers in Christ about my sexual struggle. Give me the courage I need to initiate this conversation. Give me the humility and courage I need to allow myself to be held accountable and to be prayed over by brothers in Christ. Thank you that there is freedom in you, Jesus.

Day 37: Purity Software and More and More and More Tools!
Read Today: Matthew 5:27–30; Job 31:1–12

Questions for Reflection

1. What slips do you allow on a regular basis? How do these have a detrimental effect on your quest for freedom from sexual sin?

2. If you don't have Covenant Eyes on your computer and mobile devices, what excuses are you making? Are these excuses worth the consequences of continuing to dabble in sin and the potential disaster continued exposure to porn will bring?

3. Even if you don't feel you need Covenant Eyes, what do you have to lose besides a few bucks if you start using it?

4. Who can hold you accountable to adding Covenant Eyes on all of your online devices? Who can you hold accountable to do the same?

5. If you are accessing porn in other ways than the internet, what other appendages do you need to cut off? Are you willing to cancel your satellite/cable TV or Netflix, or to remove your phone apps (and have a friend password protect your phone from being able to add them back on) in order to be free from porn seeping into your life?

Prayer for the Day: Lord, give me the courage to swallow my pride and put Covenant Eyes on all of my internet devices. Thank you for the freedom this will bring me. Forgive me for the ways I have rationalized allowing sewage and pollution into my heart, soul, and mind. Strengthen me, Lord. Help me to make the sacrifices needed to worship you wholeheartedly in the area of sexual purity.

Day 38: Talking to Your Wife (For Married Men)
Read Today: Proverbs 28:13; 31:10–12

Questions for Married Men

1. How would letting your wife know about your sexual purity struggles help you fight against temptation?

2. What things are you hoping your wife doesn't find out about?

3. What's the worst thing that can happen if don't tell your wife about your sexual purity struggles?

Married Men Prayer for the Day: Lord, thank you for giving me my wife as my ally in this fight for sexual purity. I pray that you will prepare her to hear my story and my struggles. Give her a spirit of grace and understanding and help her to see my heart in this. Give me the courage and humility to take responsibility and not blame her for the way I've acted out sexually. Help this to be a landmark step toward a stronger marriage and freedom from sexual sin.

Day 38: Love Letters (For Single Men)
Read Today: 1 Corinthians 6:19–20; 7:23; 1 Peter 1:18–19

Questions for Single Men
1. Are you under the impression that your sexual sin involves only you because you are single? Ask some married men how the mindset of your single years will affect the reality of your married years. Ask someone who has been single a long time how the mindset of their younger years has affected the patterns they live in today. Ask them if they could go back in time, what they would change about their behavior patterns.

2. Are you under the impression that the sexual sins you commit now will not affect your future and that it will be easy to switch off these patterns when you need to? Ask some married men whether marriage was an automatic cure for their sexual temptations. (Hint: it wasn't!)

Single Men Prayer for the Day: Lord, I lift my future wife up to you. Only you know who this woman will be or whether I will ever get married at all. If I am to marry, I pray you would help my wife with her sexual temptations at this very moment, just as you help me with mine. Let her know she is your daughter and she doesn't need to seek validation from sin or from this world. Help me to prepare myself now to be the husband you want me to be. In the meantime, help me to be a committed spouse to you, Jesus. Remind me that you purchased me with your blood, that I am yours. Help me to learn to trust you and submit to you. Help me not to make compromises or think it's okay to squander my single years away in sin. Help me to trust you with all that I am. Please take my heart and make it wholly yours, Jesus.

Day 39: Excuses
Read Today: Ephesians 4:17–32; Matthew 5:27–30

Questions for Reflection
1. Who are your teachers and professors when it comes to sex?
2. Do you enjoy the nudity and sex scenes you see in TV and movies? How do you justify viewing these images?
3. What are all of the areas you make excuses for? How do you sell yourself short of the design for purity God has for you?
4. What sacrifices do you need to make to fully obey Jesus' teaching to be sexually pure?

Prayer for the Day: Jesus, penetrate my heart with your grace. Transform me so that I long for your will over my will. Help me to trust you in all things, especially for my sexual purity and the sexual stimuli I put before me. I repent of the immoral teachers I've put before my eyes. The racy sex scenes and nude bodies I've allowed into my mind under the guise of enjoying good art or a good story. Give me the courage and humility not to make excuses anymore. Give me the courage and humility to take whatever steps are necessary to cut out all of the footholds Satan has built in my life in the area of sexual sin.

Day 40: Weightlifting

Read Today: Luke 22:19–20; John 15:1–11; Proverbs 27:17;
Hebrews 10:23–25; 3:12–13; 12:1–3; 1 Timothy 4:7–8

Questions for Reflection
1. Who can regularly meet with you to coach you in sexual purity and in your quiet time with Jesus?
2. Who can you coach?
3. What do your fans expect of you? Are you delivering it?
4. Are you in a healthy, gospel-centered church?
5. What next steps do you need to take to ensure that the growth you've experienced over these past forty days will not end when you close this book?
6. Who can you invite to read through this book with you over the next forty days?

Married Men Prayer for the Day: Lord, thank you for the coaches, teammates, and fans you've given me in my church and in my family. Give me the courage and self-discipline to build the relational bridges I need to have consistent spiritual and sexual purity in my life. Lord, I want to catch my kids and my wife in the trust fall. I want them to be able to trust me, knowing I'm there for them with my whole heart and mind. Thank you for your mighty, transforming power, Holy Spirit. Continue to make my heart more like yours, Jesus.

Single Men Prayer for the Day: Lord, thank you for the coaches, teammates, and fans you've given me in my church, in my family, and in my circles of influence. Give me the courage and self-discipline to build the relational bridges I need to have consistent spiritual and sexual purity in my life. Give me courage not to live isolated. Give me courage to be vulnerable and expose my shame to loving community. Remind me that you love me, Father. Thank you for your mighty, transforming power, Holy Spirit. Continue to make my heart more like yours, Jesus.

RESOURCES

Small Group Curriculum

Seven-Week Online Video Small Group Led by Noah Filipiak and the Beyond the Battle Team. Go through the *Beyond the Battle* small group curriculum with author Noah Filipiak by your side, diving deep into the concepts of the book while experiencing vulnerable community in this unique environment. Visit www.beyondthebattle.net for upcoming groups. Alumni of beyondthebattle.net online groups are invited to participate in a free weekly video call with Noah upon the completion of their seven-week group.

Free Video Small Group and Discussion Questions. You can also participate in your own in-person small group with friends or your men's church small group using Zondervan's free *Beyond the Battle* Video Small Group Curriculum. A QR code appears throughout the book—prior to chapter 1 and then after every two chapters, for a total of seven sessions. The website the QR code takes you to is www.beyondthebattle.net/videos. This one webpage includes all the resources you need to run your own small group, including instructions, discussion questions, and an orientation video for your first week.

Long Term Places to Find Vulnerable Community

Samson Society (www.samsonsociety.com). A Christian mutual-aid society that provides a platform to practice living in community (virtually). You can have a Silas (daily check-in) if you choose. These groups allow for someone who is ready to stop hiding, live in the light, and practice truth telling. There are anywhere from three to six video group meetings a day to choose from, and guys from around the world join to be vulnerable.

Pure Desire Ministries (www.puredesire.org). Online video group and counseling options structured for recovery and accountability. Content takes you deeper into the reasons why you started down the path of sexual sin to begin with, while providing structured accountability. It's a year-long group setting at an hour and a half per week. It's a safe place to be vulnerable with a small group of guys while you go through the Pure Desire curriculum. There is also one-on-one counseling available with licensed counselors.

Undone Redone (www.undoneredone.com). EMBARK Men's Recovery Intensive is a four-day deep dive into the issues that drive unwanted sexual behavior. You can join the Route1520 online community, as well as weekly offline and virtual sex addiction recovery groups. Life Beyond Betrayal online courses and community are available for women who have experienced betrayal trauma in their primary relationship. The Undone Redone Podcast hosted by Traylor and Melody Lovvorn features wisdom and insight from Christian thought-leaders on marriage, parenting, and health and wholeness.

BraveHearts University (www.braveheartsuniversity.com). Master's class on sexual addiction. Content is curated and organized into five-day themes. It takes around forty-five minutes each day to watch a video interview followed by three reflection questions. Membership also allows for a once-a-week live Zoom call with others on various topics with Michael Leahy.

Beyond the Battle (www.beyondthebattle.net). Alumni of the beyondthebattle.net online groups are invited into a free weekly video call with Noah and other alumni to review the truths of the book and for prayer, community, and accountability.

On Setting Up Your Daily Time with the Lord

Sacred Rhythms: Arranging Our Lives for Spiritual Transformation by **Ruth Haley Barton** (Downers Grove, IL: InterVarsity, 2006). If all you've ever known for quiet time with the Lord is cognitive Bible reading where you plow through the text, this book is a must-read for you. It will teach you how to get God's truth from your head into your heart, a must for your battle against the intimate lure of sexual sin.

On Discovering Who You Are in Jesus at a Soul Level

Strengthening the Soul of Your Leadership by **Ruth Haley Barton** (Downers Grove, IL: InterVarsity, 2008).
The Return of the Prodigal Son by **Henri Nouwen** (New York: Doubleday, 1992).

On Improving Your Sex Life with Your Wife

Sheet Music by **Dr. Kevin Leman** (Carol Stream, IL: Tyndale, 2003, 2008).

Online Resources

Screen Accountability for all of your online devices: www.CovenantEyes.com or download Covenant Eyes from your app store. Use promo code BEYOND to get your first thirty days free.
www.CovenantEyes.com/blog
www.vidangel.com. Filter out sex and nudity scenes from movies and TV shows. First month is free.
www.XXXChurch.com
www.noahfilipiak.com/BeyondBlog. All of Noah Filipiak's blog posts on sexual purity, marriage, and singleness.

On Masturbation

This topic was intentionally left out of this book but is written about at length in Noah Filipiak, "Is Masturbation a Sin?" blog post, October 23, 2020, www.noahfilipiak.com/is-masturbation-a-sin.

ACKNOWLEDGMENTS

A huge thank you to my wife, Jen, for persevering with me and this book. Thank you for walking with me through all the ups and downs of publishing and in loving me enough to let me invest so much of my time and energy into such a huge undertaking.

Thank you to all the great folks at Zondervan for this edition of the book, especially Ryan Pazdur for believing in me and in this message.

Thank you to Brian Phipps and Adam Barr for the extensive time they put into editing this manuscript. And thank you to Anne Cody, Jeremy Bouma, Zachary Bartels, and Sarah E. Filipiak for editing those early versions.

Thank you to Crossroads Church in Lansing, Michigan, for shining Jesus' light brightly and for walking in community with me while I wrote this book.

Thank you to all of my beyondthebattle.net online alumni guys. Thank you for putting flesh to this book. Thank you for your journeys, your vulnerability, and your love. Thank you for all you've done to help other men experience freedom.

Thank you to my mentors and my email accountability guys. Thank you for loving me and believing in me and modeling God's love to me.

Thank you to my parents, Jim and Stephanie, and their amazing forty-seven years (and counting!) of marriage. Thank you for this legacy.

And thank you to Pete, Chris, and Justin. I dedicated this book to you and I'll end my acknowledgements with you. Thank you for saying what God put on your heart to say. Without your words of prodding, this book never would have existed. That's pretty cool. I hope you can share in any fruit that God produces from it. Thank you.